CONFRONTING THE BODY

CONFRONTING THE BODY

The Politics of Physicality in Colonial and Post-Colonial India

Edited by
JAMES H MILLS
AND SATADRU SEN

Anthem Press is an imprint of
Wimbledon Publishing Company
PO Box 9779, London SW19 7QA

This edition first published by Wimbledon Publishing Company 2004

British Library Cataloguing in Publication Data
Data available

Library of Congress Cataloging in Publication Data
A catalog record has been applied for

ISBN 1 84331 032 5 (hbk)
ISBN 1 84331 033 3 (pbk)

1 3 5 7 9 10 8 6 4 2

CONTENTS

ACKNOWLEDGEMENTS

The editors are grateful for the role that a number of people have played in the completion of this volume. It grew out of the 'Representing the Body' Conference at Purdue University, Indiana, held on 24 February 2001, and was very much inspired by the papers and discussions at the event. As such thanks are due to Paul Brass, Cecilia Van Hollen, Indrani Chatterjee, Gwen Alphonso, Satish Kolluri, Mahua Sarkar, Aparajita Sagar, Virginia Van Dyke, and Julie Hughes, who attended the conference, and indeed to those contributors to this volume who were also present. Thanks are also due to the Purdue University for hosting this event, which was jointly supported by the Department of History, the Department of English, the Asian Studies Program and the Women's Studies Program. The financial assistance of Purdue University and of the University of Strathclyde is gratefully acknowledged. Finally, both editors would like to thank their wives, Rebecca and Silke, who have had to listen to the endless prattle of their husbands in the course of putting together this volume and, indeed, have to endure it at all other times.

NOTES ON CONTRIBUTORS

Joseph S Alter teaches in the Department of Anthropology, University of Pittsburgh. He has conducted research on Indian wrestling and physical culture, Ayurvedic medicine, sexuality and nationalism in contemporary India. Currently he is involved in a project investigating the scientific study of yoga and its medicalization in the context of Indian nationalism. His publications include *The Wrestler's Body* (University of California Press, 1992) and *Gandhi's Body. Sex, Diet, and the Politics of Nationalism* (University of Pennsylvania Press, 2000).

Paul Dimeo lectures in sports studies at the University of Stirling. He has conducted work on the sociology and history of sport in South Asian communities around the world and he organized the conference 'Football India: the Past, Present and Future' in 2000. His publications include the edited volume *Soccer in South Asia. Empire, Nation, Diaspora* (Frank Cass, 2001) and an edited collection of essays on sport for a special edition of the journal *Contemporary South Asia* (2001).

Satadru Sen is assistant professor of South Asian history at Washington University in St Louis. He is the author of *Disciplining Punishment: Colonialism and Convict Society in the Andaman Islands* (Oxford University Press, 2000), and *Migrant Races, Empire, Identity and KS Ranjitsinhji* (Manchester University Press, forthcoming).

James H Mills is Lecturer in Modern History at Strathclyde University, Glasgow. His work addresses the social history of medicine, drugs and sport in South Asia. He is the author of *Cannabis Britannica: Empire, Trade and Prohibition 1800–1928* (OUP, 2003), *Madness, Cunnabis and Colonialism. The 'Native-Only ' Lunatic Asylums of British India, 1857–1900* (Macmillan, 2000) and co-editor (with Paul Dimeo) of a number of collected studies of sport in South Asia.

Anand A Yang is Head of the Jackson School of International Studies at the University of Washington in Seattle. He is the author of *A Limited Raj; Agrarian*

Relations in Colonial India (University of California Press, 1989) and *Bazaar India. Markets, Society, and the Colonial State in Gangetic Bihar* (University of California Press, 1998). He has also compiled an edited volume, *Crime and Criminality in British India* (University of Arizona Press, 1985). He is currently working on a study of Indian convicts in Southeast Asia.

Deepali Dewan is Associate Curator of South Asian Civilizations at the Royal Ontario Museum, Toronto. Her research concerns the art schools that were established by British colonial officials in South Asia in the mid-nineteenth century. Her other research interests include post-colonialism, transnational identity and the visual cultures of South Asia and of the South Asian diaspora, and she contributed towards the publication of *No Place Like Home* (Walker Art Centre, 1997), which explored artistic responses to the concept of 'home' in the 1990s.

Nimmi Rangaswamy is Lecturer in Indian History at Bombay University and is on the editorial staff of the *Economic and Political Weekly*. Her research concerns the development of regional nationalism in South India.

Srimati Basu teaches anthropology and women's studies at DePauw University, Indiana. Her research interests are South Asian women and law, dowry and inheritance, feminist jurisprudence and theory and methodology, legal and development anthropology. She is the author of a number of scholarly articles and the monograph *She Comes to Take Her Rights: Indian Women, Property and Propriety (SUNY Press*, 1999).

Shoma Munshi is Assistant Director, Center for the Advanced Study of India, University of Pennsylvania. She is the editor of *Images of the 'Modern Woman' in Asia. Global Media, Local Meanings* (Curzon, 2001) and co-editor of *After September 11: Media and Public Debate in Asia* (Routledge-Curzon, forthcoming).

Sanjam Ahluwalia is Assistant Professor of Indian History and Women's Studies at Northern Arizona University. She has researched and written on questions of feminist theory, population issues and feminist legal practice, and her forthcoming publications include 'Rethinking Boundaries: Global and the Local in the History of Birth Control, An Indian Case Study', in *The Journal of Women's History*.

INTRODUCTION

James H Mills and Satadru Sen

Why do we say 'body'? It is where the fires are located
('Upanisad of the Embryo')[1]

Confronting the body

As this collection of essays was assembled, it became obvious that much of its significance would lie in its ability to address the gathering unease about the employment of 'the body' as an analytical tool in colonial and post-colonial studies. The popularity of the concept is based on the importance that has been attached in recent years to the work of Michel Foucault and of Edward Said.

Michel Foucault identified the body as central to the systems of organization, and 'discipline', employed in modern societies whereby docile and productive citizens were fashioned from otherwise impulsive and unruly individuals. The body was the focus, as it was the source both of the unruliness of desires and drives and of the productivity needed in the capitalist system. Bodies were cleaned up and prepared by the technologies of modern medicine, taught the correct way to function in schools, prisons and lunatic asylums and lined up for productive activity in the factories and armies of the nineteenth and twentieth centuries. In short, the body was central to the objectives and to the processes of modern societies.

Edward Said's work had as its focus the representation of the body, and more specifically the representation of the non-Western body, in the arts. His argument was that the body was a central trope of colonial discourses that constructed difference between the West and the non-West. This difference emphasized the superiority of the former and the inferiority of the latter and legitimated colonial rule through the logic that the superior necessarily dominates the inferior. Non-Western bodies were portrayed as weak, barbarous, unclean, diseased or infantile in comparison with the idealized bodies of the West, which were the opposite, that is strong, ordered, hygienic, healthy and mature.

As historians have engaged with the work of Foucault and of Said in a range of colonial contexts, the conviction has grown that the body was at the centre of justifications for colonialism, of the objectives of colonialism and of the processes associated with colonialism. In South Asia the bodies of the local population were imagined to be inferior by the British, who saw them either as weak and feminized or as brutal and martial.[2] The British examined the bodies of South Asians, convinced that, if watched closely enough, they would betray the weaknesses that lurked in each Indian. Criminality could be revealed, for example, by 'Mongolian features' among the Yanadis, caste or tribe could be discovered through careful measurement of skulls and dangerous habits could be exposed by attention to tell-tale scars or 'a peculiar leery look'.[3] These colonized bodies were subjected to the rigours of modern penal systems where they were watched and put to work.[4] They were vaccinated, dissected, drugged and carefully gendered by Western medical institutions.[5] They were drilled and disciplined in colonial factories, armies and schools.[6] The body was at the heart of the colonial encounter.

Not everyone, however, has been happy with this analysis. Concern with the recent emphasis on the body in colonial studies in general, and in South Asian studies in particular, has emerged from three inter-related sets of critiques. The first of these is the general observation that the focus on the body in late-twentieth-century social sciences is the result of a specifically Western intellectual crisis. Bryan Turner for example has argued that, since the Enlightenment, sociological theory has rested on assumptions about the duality of the mind and the body. In the nineteenth century the former was privileged as it was held to be the key to capitalism: the Marxist 'economic man' was primarily one who acted rationally within a framework modelled by Weber, Pareto and Parsons on economics and law. There was little room in these analyses for the implications of 'human embodiment'. However, as these writers have become less fashionable, their privileging of reason and mind over the body has been rejected, leaving the other side of the duality, the body, to dominate the field in the work of Nietzsche, Marcuse and Bourdieu.

Turner has also suggested that the recent popularity of the body as an analytical concept in the social sciences is related to wider beliefs in Western culture and processes in Western capitalism. As Western capitalism has come to rely less on the productive capacity of well-drilled bodies and more on the cultivation of consumption, the emphasis has changed from repressing whims and desires to encouraging them. Within the tangle of these whims and desires lay the modern consumer, and Western philosophical systems had always located these whims and desires in the vicissitudes of the body. Suddenly the liberation of the body's unpredictable demands, rather than their repression, was at the heart of capitalism and as such the body moved to the fore in Western cultures. Alongside this shift other Western developments, such as the feminist movement and the surge in life expectancy encouraged by medical interventions and lifestyle changes, focused politics on to the body. In short, it has been argued that the recent focus in the social sciences on the body is no isolated intellectual exercise but rather a manifestation in academia of wider social and cultural change in Western societies and economies.[7]

The second set of critiques emerges from the historical observation that the body was central to the tools of analysis used by the colonizers when viewing the communities they were working to subjugate. The belief that human cultural diversity was somehow explained by biological difference may have originated in the European development of the modern life sciences, but nowhere was it more fully employed as a weapon than in the colonies.

> Phenotypic variations, perceived often to be the causes of cultural diversity, were charted on the basis of objectifying, measuring and classifying the bodies of various peoples of colour whom white anthropologists and biologists encountered in their fieldwork in Africa, Asia and the Americas. Thus human cultural diversity was equated with biological difference.[8]

Taken together, these two sets of critiques of the body in recent social science should unsettle the investigator proposing to use the concept in analyses of non-Western societies. The first suggests that in adopting the body as an interpretive tool in South Asia the investigator is simply exporting a cultural product of late-twentieth-century Western society – the obsession with the body – to the non-West. The second implies that resorting to the concept aligns the investigator with the colonial anthropologist or biologist as, by choosing the body of the 'natives' as the correct means of understanding 'them', the investigator is simply replicating the power relations and tools of analysis of that time.

This possibility that present-day scholars of the body are implicated in the revival of a colonial practice and relationship becomes even more troubling when broader critiques of postmodernism in post-colonial studies are considered. As an analytical category, the body has been squarely identified with postmodern theorizing and, as such, it is not exempt from attacks on such approaches. It has been argued that the postmodern turn of recent academic discourse has pursued a 'methodological individualism' which has deliberately produced 'the depoliticising insulation of social from material domains' and a 'refusal of any kind of programmatic politics'. The most potent of these critiques is the argument that a focus on such modes of analysis as the body has resulted in a situation where:

> The true underclasses of the world are only permitted to present

themselves as victims of the particularistic kinds of . . . oppression which they share with preponderantly middle class American scholars and critics who would speak with or in their own voices. What such underclasses are denied is the ability to present themselves as classes: as victims of the universalistic, systemic and material deprivations of capitalism which clearly separate them off from their subaltern expositors.[9]

It seems that the body as an analytical tool may not simply reproduce the unequal relations between the West and the non-West of the colonial past but that it may be implicated in more recent strategies for denying the latter a collective voice and bargaining position. The focus on the body is accused of being one of the ways in which contemporary Western discourse asserts the dominance of its concerns while undermining attempts by others to claim power.

While aware of and informed by these critiques, this volume was compiled with the conviction that a wholesale rejection of the body as a way of analysing South Asia is mistaken. It is mistaken for the simple reason that the body was at the heart of systems of society, of metaphor and of identity in South Asia long before Europeans came to have an impact in the region, and certainly long before Western academics began to explore concepts of the corporal. In fact, a range of examples can be invoked to demonstrate the relevance of bodies in South Asian attempts to understand, structure and describe the world they inhabit. The organization of caste and rank provides important evidence as, despite all the diversity and contingencies, it has never-theless returned consistently to the 'body' as one of the key means of differen-tiation, as the manifestation and centre of 'purity' and 'untouchability'. The ways in which the body was fed, formed and carried, even the extent to which it was indulged sexually, were all key means of cultivating and demonstrating difference.[10]

Similarly, Indian societies have long placed the body at the heart of social organization in matters of gender. The body has been considered to be central to the definition of the possibilities of Indian females throughout history, and indeed it has been argued that 'in south Asia, biological reproductivity has been, in comparative context, a defining characteristic of female roles to an extreme degree'.[11] Females were carefully socialized to express correct femininity through control of their bodies, by observing the rules of *sharam*, or shyness, which meant 'a little girl soon learns to become modest about her decorum, the clothes she wears, her body movements, how she speaks'.[12] Specifically female bodily functions, such as menstruation and childbirth, were culturally constructed as 'polluting' and 'unclean' so that the body was represented as the site and source of female inferiority.[13] The body was also at the heart of relations between the sexes to the extent that 'texts like the Grhya Sūtras set out the rules about the exact movements of the body during intercourse, and also give the appropriate verses which a husband and wife should recite just before penetration of the vagina'.[14]

The body was not simply an object for the discursive processes of social organization and metaphor and a means of controlling individuals and relationships. It could provide a surface on which a whole world of messages was encoded and presented.

> Decorative tattooing among the indigenous tribal (adivasi) populations of the Indian subcontinent has existed for centuries. Nomadic communities tattooed themselves as a mark of identity, assuring their recognition as they wandered from place to place. Nineteenth century anthropologists detailed how tribal Gond women, for example, patterned their legs with a variety of symmetrical tattoos in indigo or gunpowder blue. Designs were said to include animals such as tigers, monkeys and birds, which had totemistic connotations. Banjara (traders) and Gadia Lohar (ironsmiths) in Rajasthan wore a particular design on the face. Marking the body was also said to be a sign of ritual status. Among the tribal Abors of Assam the presence of a tattoo was necessary to marry. The absence of tattooes on young Burmans' thighs was emasculating. Male Dhangars, an adivasi group from the Central Provinces branded, rather than tattooed, five marks on the lower arm with a hot iron as a sign of initiation to manhood.[15]

While the body has been used as a surface for artistic representation, its importance in South Asian cultures is also demonstrated by the fact that it has regularly been used to convey meanings in Indian artistic endeavours. While many in the West are familiar with the temple carvings at Khajuraho, few grasp their meaning. The complex arrangement of bodies, of partial bodily nudity and of sexual engagement is less a titillating depiction of the erotic and more the employment of a number of corporal codes that together articulate the many functions of the sculpture: 'magical defence, the concealment of a yantra, giving of delight to people; and over and above all others, embodying through sadhyā-bhāsā a subtle yogic-philosophic concept'.[16] This could only be possible in a culture that has such a long history of attaching a range of meanings to the body.

The body may have been important to colonial practices and it may preoccupy modern Western academics. But if South Asians have long used the body as an organizing concept and as a representational space in their societies and cultures, then it seems to be a legitimate and proper tool for examining and understanding those societies and cultures. This is not to suggest that the South Asian body is somehow an unique, different, unchanging, Other or Oriental. In fact it can be argued that the body can be used as a fruitful basis for comparison between societies and cultures. The ways in which South Asian communities have used their bodies to construct notions of rank, differ-ence and gender and the extent to which they have made them social surfaces resemble activities in other societies, and comparative study may cast light upon all these processes.[17]

This volume has a number of objectives in confronting the body. It seeks first and foremost to bring together a range of established and emerging schol-ars who have sought, in explicitly examining the body, to explore the ways in which it has been represented, repressed and used as a site of resistance in South Asia. In doing this they claim a space for South Asian bodies and reveal much about the intricate ways in which wider social and political processes have impacted on the region in the last two centuries. But the volume also confronts, and ultimately condones, the use of the body as an analytical tool. This is a challenge to those recent critiques of the body in the social sciences that have argued that it is simply a Western concept, the use of which repli-cates colonial power relations, reflects Western concerns and silences non-Western voices and experiences.

The body in colonial and post-colonial South Asia

The first three chapters in this volume, by Alter, Dimeo and Sen, all engage with the physicality of masculinity in India as manifested in the immersion of male bodies in activities that are usually subsumed under the awkward head-ings of 'sport' or 'play'. The creation and deployment of athletic bodies are an ubiquitous aspect of the larger project of nationhood. As Mrinalini Sinha and other scholars of colonial gender politics have observed, the body of the modern male – with its obsessive discipline, its peculiar knowledge and its cultivated capacity for violence – has been at the forefront of the British dis-course of imperialism in India; it has also been central to Indian fantasies of anti-colonial insurgency and statehood.[18] Yet relatively little attention has hitherto been paid to the processes by which athletic bodies have been produced in colonial and post-colonial India and to the precise meanings that these bodies have carried. Joseph Alter is one of the few scholars to have systematically examined these processes and to have focused specifically upon the production of bodies that seem to fall outside the colonial actors' obsession with modern masculinity. In a recent monograph Alter interrogated the notion that Gandhi's body was a living critique of modernity. He raised the possibility that the Mahatma's apparently eccentric notions of diet, sex, exer-cise and health were aligned with contemporary biopolitical experiments in

India and abroad which, while 'alternative', were not necessarily anti-modern.[19] In the present volume Alter examines the internal contortions of wrestling and yogic practice in India. He shows that the wrestler's discourse contains curious echoes of the colonial critique of the body of the 'baboo', while it seeks to create (or recreate) the 'pure' masculine body in an ideological setting that embraces the nation while rejecting other aspects of modernity. Manifesting the attempted reconciliation of restraining discipline and wildly excessive consumption, the wrestler's body that Alter presents is the opposite of Gandhian physicality, even as it reproduces the latter's hostility towards the body of the modern Indian, which is represented as consuming differently and practising other, inauthentic and inferior rituals of restraint.

Some of these other practices are taken up in the chapters by Dimeo and Sen. Like Alter, Dimeo analyses the uneasy relationship between 'traditional' athletic rituals and modern Indian identities and the attempt by Indian nationalists to construct a set of physical practices that are both modern and authentic and that can serve to empower local communities. Exploring the culture of Calcutta football, Dimeo discusses the shaping of social identity through the sharing between fans of physical experiences such as gastronomic deprivation and indulgence. Such rituals of communal identification are not, of course, unique to the Indian context; English football fans have been known to forego sex the night before their team plays an important match and, very sensibly, to wear the same clothes for the duration of a winning streak.[20] In the Indian context, however, Dimeo argues that these habits were crucial to renegotiating group identity in the aftermath of the migrations that came with Partition and also to confirming those identities at a time when they were challenged by the priorities of new generations of athletes and supporters.

While Dimeo and Alter both examine the post-colonial fallout of the colonial discourse of bodies and physical activity, Sen focuses more narrowly on the politics of physical education in the colonial school. His chapter explores two closely related processes. The first is the actual production of the 'improved' body within a particular site of colonial power. The second is the contest between British educators, Indian students, Indian parents and other interested observers over the meanings of exercise, drilled physiques and transplanted or re-imagined athletic rituals. Portraying physical education as an aggressive colonization of the student body and native society, Sen attempts to complicate the Indian response by distinguishing between the content and the context of this education. In his analysis of the modern Indian body, the site of production and display is as important as the product itself as each functions as a contested locus of power in the politics of colonialism.

Mills and Yang also inspect the relationship between bodies and institutions, but in the contexts of medicine and punishment, respectively, rather than

sport and play. Both these chapters are located firmly within the historiography of utilitarian institutions in British India,[21] and they extend this
scholarship by re-examining the institutionalized body as a site of power and
resistance. Disagreeing sharply with those who have depicted colonial psychiatry as minimally interventionist,[22] Mills focuses attention upon the physical
coercion that was practised within the colonial lunatic asylum: the force-
feedings, the tea 'injections' (which are, quite literally, the reverse of the tea
rejection that Alter describes in his post-colonial wrestlers) and the chemical/
surgical manipulation of patients' bodies. Arguing that the asylum sought not
only to produce healthy minds but also to root those minds in strong, orderly
and productive bodies, Mills portrays psychiatric medicine as a physical confrontation between doctors, patients and the local community over the bodily
experience of labour, domination and shame that has colonial origins but also
a post-colonial history.

Anand Yang, who pioneered the post-Foucauldian historiography of
Indian crime and punishment,[23] uses his chapter to show how the body of the
convict could constitute the limits of the power of the incarcerating colonial
state. His discussion of the 'lotah emeutes' fleshes out what might be described
as the body politics of the prison ward. This was made up of attempts by
both British and Indian elites to supervise or transform rituals of defecation,
association, child-rearing, sexual intercourse and, most commonly of all,
rites surrounding the preparation and consumption of food. None of these
attempts went unopposed, both because the convicts – like the lunatics and
the schoolchildren mentioned elsewhere in this volume – had their own ideas
of acceptable physical conduct and because they contested the notion that the
habits of the body were legitimate targets for corrective institutions. Thus the
body of the inmate could function not only as a representation of civiliza-
tion/barbarism and its racial content but also as a fluctuating boundary
within colonialism, where the acceptable limits of British authority, native
autonomy and the modernizing project could be manifested and fought over.

The pieces by Deepali Dewan and Nimmi Rangaswamy examine the political uses of representations of the body. Dewan's chapter, like Sen's, is an
analysis of colonial pedagogy. However, whereas Sen looks at the British
manipulation of flesh-and-blood native bodies, Dewan proceeds from the
assumption that actual bodies are inherently difficult to colonize and control
with anything nearing efficiency. Accordingly, her essay describes how graphic
representations of the native craftsman at work came not only to express
British anxieties about industrialization and the loss of the 'traditional arts' in
the imperial metropole but also the desire to render orderly what was troublesome in the colony. Implicit in her discussion is an essential ambivalence
within the British encounter with the Indian craftsman. On the one hand,

representing the craftsman as an orderly worker reflected the reforming drive of Macaulayan colonialism and was not dissimilar from reforming projects simultaneously underway in the prisons and asylums. Like Soviet graphics of heroic and happy workers and American drawings of Rosie the Riveter, the body of the native craftsman in colonial iconography could represent the transforming heroism of a state project. On the other hand, the 'native craftsman represented' also manifested a pure, pre-colonial native self, rescued and maintained through British intervention, which acted as an embodied survival of the Romantic vision in the age of Liberal Utilitarian reform[24] and indeed as a curious counterpart of the 'pure' post-colonial wrestler, retrieved from the physical, cultural and moral accretions of contact with the impure and the inauthentic.

Rangaswamy's chapter also analyses the search for national revival through embodied purity. The physically strong, hyper-masculine and 'pure' Dravidian heroes at the centre of her discussion appear to be ideologically aligned with multiple and separate strands of Indian nationalism from the late nineteenth and early twentieth centuries: the aggressively modern physicality of revolutionary terrorism and Mohun Bagan football; the remorselessly introspective and experimental attitude towards the body exemplified by Gandhi; and, of course, the cultural defensiveness shown by rural wrestlers who perceived themselves to be surrounded by effete decadence and embodied immorality. Nevertheless, Rangaswamy's human 'bulls' are a breed apart. While they approach Gandhi in their masochism, their explicit glorification of violent self-sacrifice is more closely aligned with the sentimentalized self-destruction of Gallipoli, the kamikaze pilot and the suicide bomber. In their unabashed refusal to divest the heroic body of its emotional baggage, the Tamil *thondans* are far removed from the stoic model of self-discipline that marks the elite athletic-military hero in contemporary Britain and India, but not so remote from the overtly emotional, anti-rational hero of German Romanticism and Volkisch fantasy. This distance reflects the role of class in shaping the stoic body of the Victorian hero and his colonial cousins. Just as the assertion of the stoic model was a statement of class privilege, the assertion of raw emotion in physical courage constitutes the reversal of a moral value and, as such, the subversion of a political hierarchy.

The final three chapters of this volume extend the study of the politicized body to Indian women. Continuing the exploration of represented physicalities, Shoma Munshi and Srimati Basu confront the body of the new Indian woman in the middle-class culture of the post-1980s economy. Basu explores the dilemma confronting the women's magazine at a time when modernity, as interpreted through consumer culture, calls for a certain acceptance of the female body as a self-contained and autonomous sexual entity. At the same

time she shows that the peculiar anxieties and ambivalence towards globalization in the context of a decolonizing society impose the constraints of cultural
authenticity and moral superiority. Thus the modern Indian woman is
allowed to be sexual in terms of the rituals of consumption that surround her
body, but this sexuality is necessarily limited by the rival discourses of motherhood, marriage and heterosexuality.

The consumption of the body is even more central to Munshi's analysis.
Linking the new urban, middle-class, female body to changes in the Indian
marketplace, she describes the transformation of how this body is shaped,
how it moves and how it is assessed. This is, on the one hand, a study of the
Indian Cosmo Girl who goes to the gym, diets and buys the right cosmetics
and whose mother has taken to power-walking in Lodi Gardens. It portends
the imminent demise of what one observer (who must remain unnamed)
described as the '*bhadramahila* walk': the placid waddle of the talcum-
powdered matron out for her evening stroll. On the other hand, it is a study of
the techniques by which new, overtly sexual female bodies are contained
within discourses of 'Indian culture' and mobilized as symbols of nationalist
self-assertion and participation in the transnational world. After Yukta
Mookhey won the Miss World competition in the autumn of 1999, the *Times
of India* crowed that the country had become a 'beauty superpower'. In a
sense, Indian beauty pageant contestants are also warrior-bodies and athlete-
bodies, representing the nation in the world of nations in ways that are not
fundamentally dissimilar from those of soldiers and cricketers. All are highly
disciplined, inherently narcissistic, and shaped by the demands of transnational
encounters, but they are also culturally authenticated and charged with that
mixture of envy, assertiveness and exhilaration that Liah Greenfeld calls
ressentiment.[25] Like the athletic bodies that were created by colonial schools and
the imperial experience of an earlier era, the body of the 'new' Indian woman
is susceptible to cosmopolitanism and multiple citizenship, and this alluring
diffusion of allegiance cannot always be controlled. This is why the 'Hindu
Right' is ambivalent, but not uniformly hostile, towards the cult of the beauty
pageant, much as earlier generations of Indian nationalists were unsure about
'brown' men who played 'white' sports.

Sanjam Ahluwalia's paper, which concludes this volume, demonstrates
how – in a society emerging from colonialism – the body of the female citizen
is a powerful instrument of modern patriarchal fantasy and simultaneously a
source of anxiety that must be controlled and contained. This study was
chosen to close the anthology as it brings together so many of the themes
explored by the other authors. The middle-class men who debated the
objectives and appropriate uses of birth control saw female bodies as thoroughly modern engines through which a strong, healthy, internationally

competitive and racially correct population might be produced. Such a population would not only overcome an existing set of political and moral problems that could be perceived in the bodies of Indian women and their offspring (British rule, assertive Muslims and low-caste activists, the proliferating poor) but also ensure a social hierarchy that was 'healthy' in multiple senses of the word. However, as Ahluwalia points out, those advocates were unwilling to tolerate the female body in which the disconnection between sex and reproduction had generated other kinds of social/sexual opportunities and political demands. The imperatives of racial improvement, national liberation and international competition did not, in this case, coincide with the imperative of gendered order in Indian society. Under the circumstances, the sexual body of the female had to be disciplined, rendered reproductive and heterosexual, and subjected to the supervision of husband, medical specialist and nation.

Taken together then, the essays in this volume identify the political dynamics of colonialism and post-colonial state formation and the cultural contests generated by globalization at the end of the twentieth century. Using their case studies they demonstrate that the modernizing impulses of metropolitan Europe were modified both by the imperative of producing colonial subject-bodies that were fundamentally different from European citizen-bodies, and by the agendas and methods of resistance in South Asia. They depict a set of relationships between body, society, nation and globe that are marked by the 'dominance without hegemony' of the old imperialism and by the diffuse and contested politics of more recent arrangements in which dominance and hegemony are often both ghostly and uncertain.

The idea for this volume came from the conference 'Representing the Body in Colonial and Post-Colonial South Asia', which was held at Purdue University, Indiana, in February 2001. This is not a 'conference book' in a strict sense, as not all the chapters are based on papers that were presented at Purdue and not all the papers presented at Purdue found their way into the book. The partial correlation between 'event' and 'record' reflects the different realities of conferences and edited volumes and the fact that some scholars whose work was ideal for the event were unable to attend the conference but were able to contribute to the book. More importantly, it reflects a reconceptualization of the objectives at Purdue. The conference was focused quite narrowly on the role of the body in colonial and nationalist projects in South Asia, but discussions ranged far more broadly and began to disturb the neat lines between authentic, colonial, nationalist, post-colonial, diasporic, globalized and so on. The editors of the volume therefore sought to construct a volume that reflected the spirit of these discussions and extended them, convinced that if the body was indeed where the fires are located, it would be interesting to see just what would combust in a blaze.

Bibliography

Alavi, S, 1995, *The Sepoys and the Company: Tradition and Transition in Northern India 1770–1830*, Delhi, Oxford University Press.

Alter, J, 2000, *Gandhi's Body: Sex, Diet, and the Politics of Nationalism*, Philadelphia, University of Pennsylvania Press.

Anderson, C, 2000a, *Convicts in the Indian Ocean: Transportation from South Asia to Mauritius, 1815–1853*, Basingstoke, Macmillan.

Anderson, C, 2000b, 'Godna: Inscribing Indian convicts in the nineteenth century', in J Caplan (ed.), *Written on the Body: The Tattoo in European and American History*, London, Reaktion.

Appadurai, A, 1996, 'Playing with Modernity: The Decolonization of Indian Cricket', in C A Breckenridge (ed.), *Consuming Modernity: Public Culture in Contemporary India*, Minneapolis, University of Minnesota Press.

Arnold, D, 1993, *Colonizing the Body: State Medicine and Epidemic Disease in Nineteenth Century India*, London, University of California Press.

Arnold, D, 2000, *Science, Technology and Medicine in Colonial India*, Cambridge, Cambridge University Press.

Bates, C, 1997, 'Race, Caste and Tribe in Central India: The early origins of Indian Anthropometry', in P Robb (ed.), *The Concept of Race in South Asia*, Delhi, Oxford University Press.

Bayly, S, 1999, *The New Cambridge History of India: Caste, Society and Politics in India from the Eighteenth Century to the Modern Age*, Cambridge, Cambridge University Press.

Beteille, A, 1991, *Society and Politics in India: Essays in a Comparative Perspective*, London, Athlone Press.

Butalia, U, 1998, *The Other Side of Silence*, Delhi, Penguin.

Caplan, J (ed.), 2000, *Written on the Body: The Tattoo in European and American History*, London, Reaktion.

Caplan, L, 1997, 'Martial Gurkhas: The persistence of a British military discourse on "race"', in P Robb (ed.), *The Concept of Race in South Asia*, Delhi, Oxford University Press.

Chowdhury-Sengupta, I, 1997, 'The effeminate and the masculine: nationalism and the concept of race in colonial Bengal', in P Robb (ed.), *The Concept of Race in South Asia*, Delhi, Oxford University Press.

Clark, A (ed.), 1993, *Gender and Political Economy: Explorations of South Asian Systems*, Delhi, Oxford University Press.

Das, V, 1985, 'Paradigms of Body Symbolism: An analysis of selected themes in Hindu culture', in R Burghart and A Cantile (eds), *Indian Religion*, London, Curzon Press.

Desai, D, 2000, 'Art and Eroticism: Going beyond the erotic at Khajurho', in B Goswamy (ed.), *Indian Art: Forms, Concerns and Development in Historical Perspective*, New Delhi, Munshiram Manoharlal.

Ernst, W, 1991, *Mad Tales from the Raj: The European Insane in British India*, London, Routledge.

Foucault, M, 1973, *The Birth of the Clinic: An Archaeology of Medical Perception*, New York, Vintage Books.

Foucault, M, 1989, *Madness and Civilization: a History of Insanity in the Age of Reason*, London, Routledge.

Greenfield, Liah, 1992, *Nationalism: Five Roads to Modernity*, Cambridge, MA, Harvard University Press.

de Haan, A, 1993, 'Migrant Labour in Calcutta Jute Mills: Class, instability and control', in P Robb (ed.), *Dalit Movements and the Meanings of Labour in India*, Delhi, Oxford University Press.

Harrison, M, 1994, *Public Health in British India: Anglo-Indian Preventive Medicine 1859–1914*, Cambridge, Cambridge University Press.

Holmstrom, M, 1984, *Industry and Inequality: The Social Anthropology of Indian Labour*, Cambridge, Cambridge University Press.

Jeffery, R, and Jeffery, P, 1993, 'A Woman Belongs to Her Husband: Female autonomy, women's work and childbearing in Bijnor', in A Clark (ed.), *Gender and Political Economy: Explorations of South Asian Systems*, Delhi, Oxford University Press.

Mangan, J, 2001, 'Soccer as Moral Training: Missionary Intentions and Imperial Legacies', in P Dimeo and J Mills (eds), *Soccer in South Asia*, London, Frank Cass.

Metcalf, T, 1995, *Ideologies of the Raj*, Cambridge, Cambridge University Press.

Mills, J, 1999, 'Re-Forming the Other: treatment regimes in the lunatic asylums of British India, 1857–1880', *The Indian Economic and Social History Review*, 4.

Mills, J, 2000, *Madness, Cannabis and Colonialism: The 'Native-Only' Lunatic Asylums of British India 1857–1900*, Basingstoke, Macmillan.

O'Hanlon, R, and Washbrook, D, 1992, 'After Orientalism: Culture, Criticism and Politics in the Third World', *Comparative Studies in Society and History*, 34.

Omissi, D, 1994, *The Sepoy and the Raj: the Indian Army, 1860–1940*, Basingstoke, Macmillan.

Rosen, S, 1996, *Societies and Military Power: India and its Armies*, London, Cornell University Press.

Said, E, 1986, 'Orientalism Reconsidered', in Francis Barker *et al.* (eds), *Literature, Politics and Theory*, London, Methuen.

Said, E, 1989, 'Representing the colonized: anthropology's interlocutors', *Critical Inquiry*, 15.

Sen, S, 2000, *Disciplining Punishment: Colonialism and Convict Society in the Andaman Islands*, Delhi, Oxford University Press.

Sharma, M, and Vanjani, U, 1993, 'Engendering Reproduction: The political economy of reproductive activities in a Rajasthan village', in A Clark (ed.), *Gender and Political Economy: Explorations of South Asian Systems*, Delhi, Oxford University Press.

Sinha, M, 1995, *Colonial Masculinity: The 'Manly Englishman' and the 'Effeminate Bengali' in the Nineteenth Century*, Manchester, Manchester University Press.

Terry, J, and Urla, J (eds), 1995, *Deviant Bodies: Critical Perspectives on Difference in Science and Popular Culture*, Bloomington, Indiana University Press.

Tolen, R, 1995, 'Colonizing and Transforming the Criminal Tribesman: The Salvation Army in British India', in J Terry and J Urla (eds), *Deviant Bodies: Critical Perspectives on Difference in Science and Popular Culture*, Bloomington, Indiana University Press.

Turner, B, 1991, 'Recent Developments in the Theory of the Body', in M Featherstone, M Hepworth and B Turner (eds), *The Body: Social Process and Cultural Theory*, London, Sage.

'Upanisad of the Embryo', 1988 (trans. L Kapani), in M Feher (ed.), *Fragments for a History of the Human Body*, part 3, New York, Urzone.

Yang, A, 1985, *Crime and Criminality in British India*, Tucson, University of Arizona Press.

Yang, A, 1995, 'The Voice of Colonial Discipline and Punishment: Knowledge, Power and the Penological Discourse in Early Nineteenth Century India', *Indo-British Review*, 21/2, pp. 62–71.

Notes

1. 'Upanisad of the Embryo', 1988 (trans. L Kapani).
2. See Caplan 1997, pp. 261, 270–72; Chowdhury-Sengupta 1997, pp. 283–303.
3. Tolen 1995, p. 87; Bates 1997, pp. 231–41; Mills 2000, p. 55.
4. Sen 2000; Anderson 2000a; Arnold 1993.
5. Mills 1999; Harrison 1994, pp. 202–226; Arnold 1993, pp. 61–116, 200–239; Arnold 2000, pp. 71–5.
6. De Haan 1993, pp. 203–209; Holmstrom 1984, pp. 26–75; Alavi 1995, pp. 264–91; Omissi 1994, pp. 93–4; Rosen 1996, pp. 175–80; Mangan 2001, pp. 41–57.
7. Turner 1991, pp. 1–36.
8. Terry and Urla 1995, p. 8.
9. O'Hanlon and Washbrook 1992, pp. 141–67.

10. Bayly 1999, pp. 51–2.
11. Clark 1993, p. 11.
12. Sharma and Vanjani 1993, p. 35.
13. Jeffery and Jeffery 1993.
14. Das 1985, p. 199.
15. Anderson 2000b, p. 102.
16. Deasia 2000.
17. Beteille 1991; Butalia 1998; Caplan 2000.
18. Sinha 1995; Appadurai 1996.
19. Alter 2000.
20. *Times of India*, 28 May 2002.
21. Arnold 1993; Harrison 1994; Mills 2000; Sen 2000; Yang 1995.
22. For example Ernst 1991.
23. See Yang 1985.
24. Metcalf 1995.
25. Greenfeld 1992.

1

Body, Text, Nation: Writing the Physically Fit Body in Post-Colonial India

Joseph S Alter

Indeed I wonder whether, before one poses the question of ideology, it wouldn't be more materialist to study first the question of the body and the effects of power on it. Because what troubles me with these analyses which prioritize ideology is that there is always presupposed a human subject on the lines of the model provided by classical philosophy, endowed with consciousness which power is then thought to seize on.[1]

You notice that the metaphor of surface begins to break down. The metaphor of surface becomes the surface of metaphor; the relation among signifiers, posited as a material historical relation, nevertheless continues to be haunted by the deferred ontology that is its point of origin. What has been suppressed is the alterity that will erupt as nature and death – the alterity of the Real.[2]

There will be in this [expressive] view of the world, a day in the indefinite future when word and object will be perfectly articulated in the OM, when event and description will be perfectly attuned. But herein lies the danger: in the seduction, the hope, the illusion that someday there will be a perfect closure.[3]

Introduction: bodies and bodies of knowledge

In most parts of the world, but certainly in modern India, there is a great deal of concern among various groups with the relationship between health, identity and the moral integrity of both the nation as a whole and the citizenry who constitute that whole through individual embodied acts and collective social action. Often body discipline is regarded as both the means and the ends of nationalism. Based on ethnographic research conducted among wrestlers in North India who advocate the embodiment of nationalism and among a yoga society with a similar nationalistic agenda, this chapter is concerned with popular publications in which communities that define themselves in terms of physical fitness and physiological health seek to 'write the body' into popular consciousness.

The nationalism associated with wrestling, known as *Bharatiya kushti* or *Pahalwani*, takes shape in the context of gymnasiums where young men gather to engage in a complex regimen of physical fitness training. Each gymnasium is a social world in itself, but there is an important sense in which the institutional structure of gymnasiums collectively defines an 'imagined community' of men intent on building their bodies so as to rebuild the nation. Although wrestling is a 'popular' sport, as a way of life it is thought to have been marginalized by modernity. Relatively speaking, there are not many wrestlers in India, and popular publications are in part designed to counteract this trend by inspiring young men to join gymnasiums and embody a wrestling lifestyle.

Yoga in India has a long association with nationalism.[4] The particular form with which I am concerned is a yoga society, the Bharatiya Yog Sansthan (BYS), that advocates the public performance of secularized mass-drill yoga as a regimen of fitness designed to counteract the harmful effects of modernity on public health. The BYS is unique inasfar as it is explicitly nationalistic. It is a registered society, based in Delhi but extending into a number of other North Indian cities, and it has an official, dues-paying membership of several thousand. Its publications are meant to define the relationship among yoga, social reform, physiological health and national fitness.

Of particular interest to this chapter are the two magazines *Bharatiya Kushti* (Indian Wrestling) and *Yog Manjari* (Yoga in Bloom). In the age of the World Wide Web, *Bharatiya Kushti* and *Yog Manjari* are decidedly anachronistic in their continued format as ink-on-paper publications distributed by mail. The former, measuring 20 by 15 centimetres, contains some black-and-white photographs and is typically about 50 pages in length. The latter measures 28 by 18 centimetres, with colour photographs on the front and back pages, and is typically 35 pages in length. *Bharatiya Kushti* is published by Ratan Patodi, who founded Bharatiya Kushti Prakashan (The Indian Wrestling Press) explicitly to define Indian wrestling as a nationalistic way of life and to communicate ideas about this way of life to wrestlers and would-be wrestlers. *Yog Manjari* is the organ of the BYS and is designed to communicate the ideals associated with a nationalist way of life defined in terms of yoga practice. In many ways the two magazines are quite similar as regards topics and structure. Nevertheless they are different in important ways that are germane to the key issue under discussion here. The community of wrestlers and would-be wrestlers constituted through the medium of *Bharatiya Kushti* do not belong to an organization as such. They are simply imagined, by themselves and by those who subscribe to their views, to be out there as a potent and powerful force. The BYS, on the other hand, is an organization similar to the Rashtriya Swayamsevak Samaj or Boy Scouts, where membership is paramount and the social performance of community through meetings, administrative structure, rank hierarchy of membership and parades is a significant part of what counts as nationalistic. In other words, while both are concerned with embodied reform, *Yog Manjari* addresses itself to a body of members and *Bharatiya Kushti* addresses itself to 'everyone' but to no institutionalized body as such. In any case, the key problematic in these magazines has to do with the way in which ideas that take shape as words, sentences and whole texts relate to the materiality of the body as meaningful and powerful in itself and the problematic presumption of the body's 'unmediated' relationship to nationalism.

In many respects nationalism is a form of ideology. As recent scholarship has shown, however, thinking analytically about nationalism as simply ideological is problematic since nationalism involves social acts rooted in the materialism of geography, land and other physical phenomena such as the body. To focus on ideology directs analytical attention to the structured coherence of beliefs, however fantastic and utopian these ideas may be, and away from the materialist and mimetic contingencies of historical development.

Because the body is a tangible material thing that reveals, and is implicated in, the artifactuality of ideas, it is useful to theorize nationalism in terms of the body. In this regard the body is not 'read' as a text. It provides a medium through which to undertake a genealogy of the present as a condition of contingent – as opposed to coherent – meaning. The body gives form to meaning even as that meaning is produced as the consequence of the body's imbrication in the mimetic effects of history. The body thus stands in a peculiar relationship to ideas in general and to ideology in particular. In Daniel's terminology, the body fills that space, both logical and material, wherein there is the seductive illusion of hope that event and description are the same. In Susan Stewart's terms, the body is the ghost of deferred ontology that haunts the play of signifiers; and in nationalism the play of signifiers can take on epic, rhetorical significance.

In my previous work I have looked at the way in which Foucault's notion of body discipline provides a means with which to analyse the cultural politics of nationalism.[5] Foucault's theorizing is often referred to as discursive. This is somewhat misleading, since it is designed to deconstruct the rational continuity of canonical discursive knowledge by locating 'the history of ideas' in places other than texts, for example in bodies. A theory of body discipline produces a pervasive tension in the construction of knowledge, a tension wherein the history of ideas manifest in bodies is subject to representation in written, textual forms that are not embodied. Although problematic, since the body can be 'read' in various ways and reading is not subsumed by the mechanics of discipline, the distinction between text and body is useful. In some sense embodied practice resists the textualization of knowledge and all that it signifies in terms of the production of logical, rational, structured and ultimately published bodies of knowledge.

As Benedict Anderson's work makes clear, writing in particular and print capitalism in general are closely linked to, and constitutive of, post-colonial nationalism.[6] Imagined communities are imagined through the medium of writing. However closely linked to the text-based constitution of imagined communities, nationalism is clearly not simply a knowledge system. It involves bodies, embodied acts, and both commonplace and elaborate forms of social practice. Moreover, some forms of nationalism are so deeply invested in body discipline that writing about the body creates both logical and visceral dissonance in the production of an embodied community engaged in practice.

To understand this it is necessary to answer two interrelated questions. Firstly, there is the question of how nationalists write the disciplined body so as to imagine community. Secondly, there is the issue of how it is possible to translate a sense of imagined community back into context-specific practice, which is where the nationalist body must take 'literal' shape, without losing touch with the figurative, often utopian idea of nationalist sentiments manifest in a decontextualized, transcendent sense of imagined community. Another way of putting this is to question the relationship between rhetoric as a discursive form of practice and embodiment as an act of self-discipline, and ask how the regimes of truth and power that are specific to each are reconciled. How does this reconciliation produce a specific form of nationalist politics?

To address these questions, a body of literature has been selected that is explicitly nationalistic and, significantly, is also concerned with the disciplinary reform of bodies to produce conditions of health that reflect identity. Although this is not the place to pursue such an assertion, this literature probably represents a much broader, cross-cultural genre, which deserves critical analytic attention. This genre is concerned with the representation of disciplined bodies and might be called the political prose of physiology. Within this genre would fall, for example, many eugenicist tracts of the early twentieth century, literature on aesthetic surgery in Weimar Germany, books on nature cure in early-nineteenth-century Europe, and the extensive popular literature on nineteenth-century Muscular Christianity in the USA.

The cases of wrestling and yoga reflect broad patterns of nationalist thought that have developed over the course of the twentieth century as well as unique features associated with a kind of nationalism which is ambiguously linked to the standard features of linguistic, ethnic and religious identity and which is ambivalent about the distinction between modernity and tradition that is often made in nationalist discourse.[7] The literature in question is self-consciously nationalist and programmatically political, albeit in a cultural mode. *Yog Manjari* and *Bharatiya Kushti* are special-interest magazines where the clear articulation of ideology matters and where those who are counted as the community are those who subscribe to the magazines, even though the imagined community extends well beyond delimited membership and subscription rosters.

Clearly there are other kinds of texts that can be nationalist. Perhaps most significant, in the context of this discussion, are those books that are so thoroughly fetishized as to have a virtual life of their own: the Koran, the Bible, the Gita, the Ramacharitmanas and the Guru Granth Sahib, to name but a few. These texts take form and have specific, although by no means singular, meaning through the medium of print capitalism. They are, however, a step beyond the field of rhetoric and ideology in the sense that for believers they are the truth unto themselves as things, rather than simply representations of the truth in other arenas. Thus, to a degree, these kinds of texts break down – in the sense of obfuscating – the kind of tension between text and body that characterizes those kinds of nationalism that are not subsumed under the mantle of religious faith and holy books. Viewed from the other side, religion is not inherently nationalistic and so the textuality of holy books must be rendered nationalistic, which is not at all the case with the programmatic texts under investigation here.

Reading the wrestler's written body: articulating somatic nationalism

> In this modern age we have reached a point of progress and development in which strength has no value. Blind, lame and men with crippled limbs who have not even the strength to flip a switch, affect the stance of warriors even as they engage in their own self destruction.[8]

Wrestling in India is much more than a sport insofar as its social significance is not delimited by the terms of competition and contest.[9] It also has a long history that extends well beyond the nationalist concerns of modern wrestlers. In contemporary practice, wrestling as a way of life is not subsumed by nationalism. Just as there are non-nationalistic forms of religious faith, so there are apolitical expressions of wrestling. Nevertheless, wrestling in contemporary urban India is clearly nationalistic insofar as many wrestlers are principally concerned with the way in which their bodies engage with modernity in order to reform India and rebuild national character in terms of hypermasculinity. It is important to note that wrestling is self-consciously marginal, pitted against the kind of commercialized elitism and high-profile, patriotic nationalism that is manifest in international cricket, field hockey and athletics.[10] This is not necessarily to say that wrestling is categorically subaltern in terms of social location and cultural form.[11] However it does tend to be regarded as a kind of traditional rural sport linked to an ethos of rustic simplicity.

The nationalist project of wrestling, if it can even be referred to as a project, is not in the least structured. There is no concern with governmentality in the sense of organized political action. The body is the nation and the nation is the body in a direct, one-to-one equation. Significantly, incremental recruitment of young men into the wrestling 'community' is thought to establish a nation of wrestlers. Nationalism in this context is embodied as both individual and collective biomoral strength. In this sense it is an extreme example of cultural politics wherein culture is understood as an interpretive, unbounded system of meaning. What anchors this cultural politics is meaning rooted in physiology rather than in the structure of social practice.

Social practice is manifest in the arena of the gymnasium, which is most certainly an institution in the good, old-fashioned, sociological sense of the term. Indeed, gymnasiums are thoroughly embroiled in local politics. But this kind of politics is not thought to provide an institutionalized structure for the politics of nationalism. Historically, many modern gymnasiums were established in the context of the Indian nationalist struggle, but here again the concern was less with building a network of organized resistance than with body-building of a particular kind as an end in itself. There is, as one might guess, a high degree of disconnection between local political action and embodied nationalist vision. However, in an important sense the social form of collective gymnasium life, rallying in support of a municipal candidate for election or inviting neighbourhood notables to a festival, is regarded as political and thereby somewhat tainted rather than as meta-political in the sense that nationalism is imagined to be. Gymnasium affiliation can relate directly to a local community identity and examples include Yadav dairy farmers, Brahmin priests, recently urbanized peasants, Muslim weavers, unionized labour and college students. However these designations, along with the associations of class, caste and occupation, are relatively unimportant in the context of a way of life that is geared towards personal transformation on the one hand and national reform on the other. In more general terms, therefore, the body is to nationalism in the context of wrestling what rhetoric is to ideology in the context of the nation–state, and it is this level of material-ized abstraction that I concerned with.

In practice, wrestling is a form of extreme self-discipline, perhaps more so than other sports which require rigorous training. To be a good wrestler, and thereby a good person, one must abide by a strict regimen that is all-encompassing and forms a way of life. Wrestlers involve themselves in train-ing on a daily basis, but there are several key features in this that are better understood outside the framework of the day-to-day regimen.

Probably the single most important aspect of a wrestler's encompassing identity is celibacy. Semen is the source of his power and the locus of his moral character. In many ways the whole regimen of wrestling is geared towards the production and protection of semen, and this finds expression in many of the explicitly symbolic features of gymnasium life. Hanuman, the patron deity of most gymnasiums, is powerful by virtue of his celibacy and absolute selflessness. He is often depicted as a powerful deity with human and simian features holding a mace on one shoulder. The festival of Nag Panchami, when snakes are ritually given milk to drink, is also the occasion when gymnasiums are repainted and when fresh earth is mixed into the wrestling pit in a symbolic act invoking fertility and the symbolism of self-contained sexual power that is emblematic of the ritual complex as a whole.

The concern with celibacy and the embodiment of semen means that wrestling is a self-consciously masculine activity. It is predicated on the abstract demonization of female sexuality on the one hand and the glorification of nurturant fertility on the other. On account of the importance of semen, as a sexual fluid, to the strength and growth of the body in which it is produced, themes of masculine conquest and power based on the trope of sex as a kinetic act do not factor into the regimen as a whole. In fact, kinetic sexuality is highly problematic precisely because it is so clearly linked to sensuality and desire. It is on this front that celibacy is thought to be linked to modernity, since modernity – epitomized by popular cinema, government corruption and changes in diet and fashion – is thought to be a condition of pervasive lust, self-interest and greed. Wrestling is a kind of structured response to the way in which modernity threatens to undermine a particular construction of embodied Indian masculinity.

A second key feature of wrestling as a way of life is the guru/*chela* (disciple) relationship. Every wrestler must have a guru or master teacher and in principle, if not in fact, must submit completely to his authority. Here again Hanuman is the idealized model in terms of his relationship to Lord Ram, hero of the *Ramayana* epic. On the level of daily practice, which is where the guru/*chela* relationship produces a particular kind of embodied power, the wrestler must do nothing on his own initiative. He must, as a common saying expresses it, 'not so much as urinate' without being told to do so. The guru/*chela* relationship is important for a number of reasons, but one of the most significant features is that it is a relationship of intense personal intimacy based on rigid hierarchy and absolute power. The guru is, quite literally, greater than God while – apart from his guru – a *chela* has nothing and is nothing. What this means, significantly, is that the wrestler as *chela* is regarded as a blank slate. His body and his character can be moulded and inscribed to the extent to which he submits to the authority of his guru. As will be argued, this is an important configuration precisely because of the way it allows for writing – and rhetoric about the body in general – to become part of the disciplinary project as a whole. If a wrestler must, in fact, 'not so much as urinate' until told to do so by his guru, then the act of speaking about urination, and by extension about every detail involved in the regimen, is almost more important than the act itself. It is this relationship between speaking and writing on the one hand and embodied acts on the other that is of importance to this chapter.

Beyond celibacy and the guru/*chela* relationship, wrestling involves daily practice and the performance of precise embodied acts, many of which are seemingly mundane but nevertheless of great importance. Defecation, bathing, teeth-brushing, tongue-scraping, eating and sleeping must each be done with conscious concern and in accordance with the guru's instructions. In many ways the whole spectrum of these relatively mundane activities is configured in relation to the central regimen of physical training. For approximately three hours in the early morning wrestlers spar with one another in terms of what is referred to as the exercise of *jor*. *Jor* is thought to produce *shakti*, which is regarded as a condition of metaphysical hyper-fitness. Apart from *jor*, which is an embodied act designed to transform the very nature of the body, the second important feature of metaphysical training is *vyayam*. *Vyayam* is usually performed in the late afternoon and involves the performance of two types of exercise. The first is *dands*, a kind of jackknifing push-up, and the second is *bethaks*, a kind of jumping deep-knee bend. *Vyayam* and *jor* are only possible if a wrestler consumes a specific diet of milk, *ghee* [melted butter] and almonds. The health value of this diet is meaningful within the framework of Ayurvedic medical discourse, where it is associated with humoral balance. It also has a fairly explicit symbolic structure insofar as all three items are associated with fertility in general and semen in particular.

In this way wrestling is a form of embodied practice that may be thought of as combining highly ritualized forms of symbolic expression on the one hand and highly abstracted, or abstractable, forms of body discipline on the other. That is to say, it must be understood as a richly textured system of meaning unto itself, as this 'system of meaning' is situated within a field of power that is located in both the minutiae of embodied practice and the meta-politics of nationalism, as nationalism is an engagement with the problem of Indian modernity.

The magazine *Bharatiya Kushti* was founded in 1963 by Ratan Patodi, a journalist and editor of one of Indor's Hindi newspapers. The expressed purpose of the magazine is to popularize and promote Indian wrestling as a sport and as a form of physical self-development for men. Beyond promoting health, wrestling is presented in the magazine as distinctly Indian. The magazine represents wrestling as the antithesis of everything foreign, but in particular those 'foreign' and modern things that corrupt the body: soft drinks, tea, vegetable oil, hair tonics, synthetic clothes, cricket, hockey and football, excessive reading, office work and above all else films, videos and television. Wrestling, which requires self-control, emotional stability and the balanced transubstantiation of food into semen, entails a discourse against the immodest, sensual consumerism of modernity. It is represented as indexing the glory of ancient Indian civilization. Although clearly oriented towards what might be called the 'Hindu' features of wrestling, there is no sense in which *Bharatiya Kushti* is militantly pro-Hindu. It is unselfconsciously biased, but not prejudiced. The contemporary demise of wrestling, which is a pervasive theme in articles and editorials, is blamed on the corrupting influence of modernity at large, rather than on any group or institution in particular, even as wrestling is held up as the last defence against these corrupting influences.

The magazine is published on a quarterly basis. Most issues contain an editorial by Patodi, a collection of five or six articles by 'contributing editors' and a very short section on 'letters to the editor and other communications'. Besides these, larger sections include 'wrestling news', 'biographical sketches', 'poetry', 'diet', 'hygiene', 'moves and their application', 'technical tips from experts' and 'exercise'. Although the magazine has always included articles and notes from a range of contributors, a small cadre of men have contributed far more than others. These are Shanti Prakash Atreya and Govardandas Malhotra of Banaras (Varanasi), Bhushan Dwivedi of Delhi, Kamala Prasad Singh of Patna and Ramchandar Kesriya of Ratlam.

Clearly it would be possible to do a sociological study of the magazine based on an analysis of discrete quantifiable data: the number of articles containing explicitly nationalist statements in each issue; the number of urban versus rural subscribers broken down in terms of occupation, level of education and religious affiliation; the number of articles devoted to the subject of celibacy in each year of publication; the number of biographical sketches of Muslim wrestlers measured against an annual index of communal violence. This would, if delineated and carefully defined, produce valuable and interesting information. However, beyond noting that the magazine addresses itself to peasants and urban intellectuals alike, that it has a circulation of over 1,000 and is available at the modest annual subscription rate of 75 rupees (US$1.50), I will not concern myself with trying to delineate the sociology of content or the social profile of subscribers. Its concern is simply with the way in which Patodi and the cadre of contributing editors write about the body, and how 'writing the body' is very different from body discipline, even though one is thought to be a direct and unambiguous representation of the other.

The mutation of ideology and biology is framed in *Bharatiya Kushti* by a pervasive tone of anger and frustration, on the one hand, and impassioned, visceral nostalgia on the other.

> Today independent India is blinded by its freedom. Wrestling, which once made India strong beyond compare . . . is now practiced by only five or ten people. There are only a few villages which have akharas and one can count on one's fingers the number of city akharas . . . There was a time when every village had an akhara . . . This sport, which costs nothing, has made India great in terms of strength and fitness . . . Not until every man in India has spent ten or twelve years in the earth of an akhara can we hope to regain our national strength.
>
> These days the strength of society, not only in the villages, but everywhere, is being spent on intoxicants of all kinds. Our energy should be spent building strength and wisdom. In this way we can prevent the wastage of our national health. The health of the nation will increase. The character of the nation will grow.[12]

Akharas (gymnasiums) are the localized context upon which the nationalist vision is focused. As such, they are regarded as environments within which the disciplinary work of self-development takes place. The simple sentence 'There was a time when every village had an akhara' and the idea that every village and urban neighbourhood should have one are linked directly to the disciplinary work that will improve national health, wisdom and character. Significantly, however, the scope of the nationalist ideal only takes shape in the abstract vision made possible by textual representation and not in the localized, singular, spatialized place of a particular, named gymnasium, even though that place is where every man is directed to spend ten to twelve years 'detoxifying'. This disjunction between representational rhetoric and materialized, spatialized form is not problematic, given that *akharas* are a means to achieve body discipline rather than an end product in and of themselves. In this sense, talking about or writing about them simply serves to underscore their importance.

But when rhetoric turns more directly to the body itself, things get more complicated. This is because the body itself, rather than that written about, the idealized body, is where nationalism is materialized and thereby made meaningful. Consider several examples:

> The earth will make you great. The Indian wrestler puts on his g-string and wrestling shorts and enters this earth. Upon doing so his body takes on a radiant aura. Can the office clerk, effete proclivities, flabby physique, white clothes and all, decked out in the finest cloth milled in Bombay and Ahmedabad compare with this half-naked wrestler's radiant magnificence? Never! Absolutely not!.[13]

> Brothers! It is time for us to renounce our poisonous desires and follow the path of brahmacharya with a pure heart. We must make our bodies, fit, strong and radiant. We must set our minds on the rules and attitudes which will ensure that our bodies will be healthy, beautiful, taut and invigorated.[14]

> A brahmachari is righteous. He is not a slave to his senses. He takes no pleasure or satisfaction in worldly things. He has complete control over his thoughts and stands firm on the limits he has set for himself. He stands as huge as a mountain: firm and grand. His seriousness reflects the depth of the ocean. He is a beacon of light and therefore brilliant and resolute. Like a lighthouse he prevents the ship of life from wrecking itself on the rocks of desire. The brahmachari does not break his vow. His life is pure and untainted. His roots run deep and he does not fall like a stone from a mountain. No: he is an immovable granite ridge.[15]

Clearly these are embellished rhetorical statements which struggle to express the inexpressible. They struggle because, in some sense, the body must stand for itself. To represent it otherwise, no matter how glowing and radiant (not to say purple) the prose, is to displace meaning and, significantly, to displace the 'material, physical, corporal . . . exercise of power'[16] vested in the body through the mechanics of self-discipline. This has the effect of transforming the disciplined body into a 'human subject' which, even though it might seem to be the point of the whole exercise, privileges an ideological configuration of power wherein the metabolic body is discursively dematerialized and becomes both metaphoric and represented metaphorically. As the epigraph taken from Susan Stewart's literary work indicates, this is not a situation unique to wrestling by any means. But given that the wrestler must embody nationalism and that embodiment entails disciplinary regimentation and the 'investment of power in the body', textual representations of the body tend to divest the body of power while appearing to do exactly the opposite. Moreover, rhetorical representations of the idealized body impinge on the disciplinary project insofar as the mode of self-discipline engages with the idealized image and ends up, invariably, producing real bodies that fall short by trying to be much more than they can possibly be.

It is important to note the extent to which many informants would talk about the need to do thousands of *dands* and thousands of *bethaks*, and eat and drink huge volumes of milk and *ghee*. In practice, very few – if any – ever did more than several hundred *dands* and *bethaks* or drank more than a litre of milk per day with perhaps 100 grams of *ghee* mixed in. This is still an accomplishment, and integral to the investment of power in the body and the production of somatic nationalism, but the gap between discourse and practice undermines the kind of disciplinary rigour that is integral to biopower. This gap is produced, in large part, by a rhetoric of excess that finds expression in published life histories.[17] These life histories are surreal in that, in some respects, they are believable and comprehensible as embodied history rather than as disembodied myth and yet, in other respects, they are simply unbelievable. For example Baldev Chobe's regimen of self-discipline is described by Govardandas Malhotra as follows:

> Everyday at the age of 29 Baldev Chobe would do two thousand *bethaks*, run five miles and wrestle with twenty other wrestlers in the morning. In the evening he would do two thousand *dands*. He would regularly eat half a liter of *ghi*, half a kilo of almonds and drink five liters of milk . . .[18]

This is almost, but not quite, believable. While the physical demands entailed are unlikely to have been met, the economics involved in securing such large amounts to be consumed put the story even further into doubt. Indeed, it is in this 'shadow of doubt' that the massively muscular 'body of one color' slips from disciplined and delineated self-control into a nervous obsession with excess in pursuit of an ideal that is always just out of reach.

> Chandan Pahalwan, who engaged in vigorous contests with many of the country's best known wrestlers, would daily do five thousand *dands*, three thousand five hundred *bethaks*, run eight miles, dig the pit four times with a heavy spade and then spar with between thirty and thirty-five other wrestlers. He was a pure vegetarian and daily ate 3/4 of a liter of ghi, 1½ kilograms of almonds, and drank seven liters

of milk along with grape and orange juice. In addition to butter, cream and condensed milk he would eat potions made of gold, silver and ground-up pearls.[19]

The following article comes closest to linking somatic nationalism with the nationalism of the Indian National Congress. Dr Shanti Prakash Atreya uses the language of excess to write the wrestler's body into political history as he makes the claim that Bhagwandas, a prominent intellectual in the Freedom Struggle, 'daily did 5000 *bethaks*, 2500 *dands* and drank a lota full of *ghi*' and asserts that Madan Mohan Malaviya, leader of the Hindu Mahasabha and founder of Banaras Hindu University, 'daily did 2000 *bethaks* and 1000 *dands*'. Indeed, he goes on to claim that 'Tilak, Gokhale, Lajpat Rai and all other Freedom Fighters were strong and robust'.[20]

The simple but important point to be made here is that, in some sense, somatic nationalism cannot be written accurately and that when it is represented it becomes ideological, and thereby powerful, but vested with a very different kind of power than that vested in real bodies subject to a disciplinary regimen. The ideologization of what is inherently, or at least primarily, somatic transforms disciplined bodies into human subjects 'endowed with consciousness that power is thought to seize on'.[21] As Foucault indicates, an ideological frame of reference restricts power to a particular kind of effect. If this specific problem is related to the more general question of 'imagined communities', it shows that imagined communities are ideological constructs even though what is imagined through the medium of writing is – as is the case with the body in this example – essentially material. But more significant than this, the ideological nature of the imagined community transforms the means into the end. Here 'imagination' – the possibility that Bhagwandas could do 5000 *bethaks* – rather than 'community' is privileged and prioritized in the discourse of nationalism. Thus the project encoded in *Bharatiya Kushti* as it seeks to textually represent and define the embodied project of somatic nationalism is deeply contradictory, in the sense that it tries to locate what is embodied and what is ideological in the same conceptual space. In writing about why and how to produce a nation of wrestlers concerned with physical self-development, Patodi and his cadre of contributing editors construct fantastic images of bodies. Ironically, these bodies are impossibly strong and therefore inherently imagined and idealized human subjects. The practice of a disciplinary project of regimented self-control is subverted by textualized life history.

Yoga: writing and the transformation of body discipline into community identity

Yoga is no longer new and unfamiliar to the ordinary person. Rampant modern progress and development has made people's bodies decrepit, and has unsettled their minds. A troubled and disoriented mind causes the brain to become disconnected from the centers of consciousness, and it is the boon of consciousness that keeps humanity on track. In this chaotic environment where poison is pervasive and strife commonplace, the practice of yoga is a like a beacon of hope for rejuvenation and the recovery of humanity. Through the establishment of free, public centers for yoga training and practice, the Bharatiya Yog Sansthan introduces people to the systematic practice of *asana, pranayam* and *dhyana*. Slowly, with regular practice, the full beauty of yoga becomes visible. Vigilant of his responsibility to society and living a disciplined life, the practitioner of yoga will automatically come to embody moral principles and rules of self-purification in all areas of life. Gradually, in addition to becoming strong, his resolute practice and regimen of self-discipline will make of him an exemplary figure.[22]

The Bharatiya Yog Sansthan (BYS) was founded in 1967 by a group of men who were sympathetic to the broader agenda of Rashtriya Swayamsevak Sangh (RSS), a militant Hindu nationalist organization that had been established in the early part of the twentieth century. However, a number of the founders of the BYS felt that the RSS was, in some respects, inherently violent, exclusively ethnocentric and fanatical. In founding the BYS they sought to establish a kind of nationalism based on the 'universalist' principles of yoga. Yoga was thought to be spiritual, but not narrowly religious, and inherently humanitarian by virtue of being based on principles of non-violence, truthfulness, personal purity and strict self-discipline. The following general statement of purpose is published on the back of many of the organization's numerous books and pamphlets:

The Bharatiya Yog Sansthan believes that Yoga is for all. It is a discipline which possesses the potentials of revolutionizing the whole world and curing all ills. It is the only discipline today which can give right direction to [the] human mind besides keeping the body fit. It can thus become a vehicle of mental and spiritual transformation of society. It can be a savior of mankind because it replaces hatred, exploitation and violence with love, fraternity and peace.

The relationship between mind and consciousness on the one hand and the body and fitness on the other is a pervasive theme, as is the expansive universalist rhetoric that extends nationalism into the transnational domain of the 'whole world'.[23] Nevertheless, the BYS clearly thinks of itself as championing the cause of 'Indian national culture' as this culture is defined with reference to the *Bhagvad Gita* and other religious texts. Albeit suffused with the sentiments of incipient Hindu nationalism, the rhetoric of the BYS is not religious. It is focused on the disciplined body.

Although based on what might seem to be an ideological position, as an organization the BYS takes shape, quite literally, only in embodied practice. The founders of the organization believed that the practice of physical postures and breathing exercises, along with embodied forms of meditation, would provide the means by which individuals who were sick would be able to restore themselves to health. 'Sick' in this case could mean ill in a specific sense or suffering the more general malaise of modernity.

To promote national recovery from the manifold problems of dystopic modernity, including westernization and rampant materialism, the founders of the BYS established a unique regimen of practice. The founding group met in a public park in Delhi and taught themselves yoga. They would meet on a regular basis every morning at dawn; they laid out carpets in symmetrical rows and performed a sequence of postures, breathing exercises and adapted 'yoga calisthenics' for approximately one hour. The founding regimen was based on the principle that yoga is simple and straightforward, even though its effects are profound. The original group adopted a missionary attitude towards their project and invited anyone interested to join them. Doing yoga in public was crucial to the project as a whole, since a group of middle-aged men performing apparently difficult, contortionist-like exercises attracted attention. Thereby, it was hoped, the organization would win converts. Of course the original members also told friends, relatives and colleagues and encouraged them to participate. The performances of the small group of founding members therefore emphasized the simplicity of yoga practice, its social aspects and its ability to completely transform the individual sense of self. Significantly the regimen of daily practice, although clearly an adapted form of modern calisthenic yoga,[24] is exclusively physiological in the sense that the group does not meet to discuss, debate and exchange ideas about yoga philosophy or, for that matter, anything else. They meet to practise and thereby promote their own and one another's health.

A key idea in the transformation of a group of friends meeting to practise yoga and the founding of the BYS as a nationalist organization based on practice was the founding principle of geometric growth and social expansion. As the original group attracted new members, it split in two. The original group remained in place to attract more new members, grow and fission again, just as the new branch group moved to a different park to attract new members, grow and ultimately fission. In this way the simple, if fantastically utopian, idea was to expand through geometric growth, ultimately establishing small groups of yoga practitioners in every public park of every town and city throughout the country, thus locating the antidote to the sickness of modernity in the embodied enlightened practice of every man, woman and child. Based on estimates drawn from the organization's self-perception there are currently over 300 units of the BYS throughout the country, with a clear concentration in Delhi and other urban centres in the north. However, given the very nature of the decentralized, de-institutionalized project as a temporarily configured growing entity that only takes shape for an hour every morning, it is virtually impossible to know how many people have 'joined'. It is interesting to note that urban parks in and of themselves are designed to counteract the 'unnatural' effects of an urban lifestyle. For example the so-called playground movement associated with the era of health reform in the USA put into practice an agenda of healthy recreation that is comparable, in many ways, to the BYS project.

It was not until 1977, ten years after the foundation of the group, that *Yog Manjari* began to be published as a quarterly journal. At about the same time an administrative hierarchy of president, vice-president and general secretary was established, along with the associated bureaucratic apparatus of an institution. This gave a new kind of permanent shape and form to the organization, even though local, informal, self-motivated, embodied group practice remains the ideal. *Yog Manjari* provides a textualized, and thereby mutated, representation of this ideal. Among other things the journal provides an accounting of geometric growth, claiming that 'in the last two decades [before 1987] over 200,000 have benefited from the daily free training classes'.[25] According to the same source the journal has a circulation of 5,000 with over 1,000 life members. Beyond participation in the morning training sessions, which are free and open to the public and therefore inclusive rather than exclusive, membership includes subscription to the journal and notification about specialized training camps and field trips, which are organized on a regular basis. Although these training camps introduce a slightly different kind of practice into the performance of yoga, including lectures given by experts and renowned adepts, almost all involve the performance of mass-drill yoga exercises. These are often on a massive scale with several hundred participants. Thus the ideal, even though expanded, is still conceived of as embodied social action. Among the most powerful images in *Yog Manjari* are the pictures of these masses of people lined up in drill formation performing synchronized yogic postures.[26] In being cropped so that the number of participants can be imagined going on indefinitely beyond the frame, these images are as precisely imprecise as is the organization's use of really fictive numbers.

As might be expected, *Yog Manjari* contains articles on yoga practice. It also includes letters to the editor and a section on news about the organization, both in terms of growth and expanding programme activities. The following is a representative sample of articles taken from back issues of the journal: 'The Regimen of Practice and Daily Life', 'The Shashank Posture', 'How I Changed My Life By Yoga', 'Breathing Exercises and the Element Air', 'Immunity From Horrible Diseases', 'The Yoga and The Scientist', 'Backaches', 'The Bhujangasan and Makarasana Postures', 'Important Insights on the Practice of Concentration', 'Overcoming Diabetes with Yoga: A Personal Account'. By far the majority of articles are devoted to health issues, although the editorial in each issue tends to be more explicitly concerned with social reform and cultural revival as directed towards the broader nationalist goal. Thus the mundane concern with health, better body function and embodied yoga technique is framed by an explicitly nationalist discourse. As Prakash Lal, the current president, explained in an interview:

> [Y]oga can bring about a change in the life of society, the life of every person. It can bring about a priceless transformation in what a person is like, what his place in society is, his purpose in life, and in the energy which animates him and makes the world turn. This is what yoga can do. And if people understand these things, then they will no longer encounter any problems. Nothing in the whole world will get in their way and everything will exist in peace and harmony – this is our Indian culture.

Bharatiya Kushti is a textual space where the wrestler's body is transformed, through the mimesis of rhetorical and embodied excess, into a powerful – and powerfully restricted – mutation of ideology and biology. *Yog Manjari*, however, is primarily concerned with a kind of endless refinement and elaboration that is designed to produce and reproduce, in writing, a perfect embodied modern citizen. It is concerned with that which is precisely left out in the discourse of wrestling, society and the embodied form of community life. The critical problem in the textual representation of yoga is to keep self and society linked one to another, as that link is effected through collective embodied practice, and also to prevent the legitimate concern with mundane health, backaches, indigestion and hypertension from trivializing the project as a whole. Trivialization is never a problem in the discourse of wrestling, which is, to invoke Daniel's epigraphic terminology at the start of this essay, enabled by the very seductive hope that word and object are perfectly articulated.

Most of what is published in *Yog Manjari* is technical in nature and designed to instruct and inform. It is, in essence, an educational tool designed to translate knowledge produced through embodied practice back into embodied practice, a fact perhaps best exemplified by detailed descriptions of different *asana* techniques that are published and republished in issue after issue. These descriptions reproduce the disciplinary mechanics of practice and allow for the terms of physical self-discipline to be circulated in the community at large. Significantly, however, this community constituted through embodied practice, which is otherwise simply out there on the expanding horizon of geometric growth, takes textual shape in a form that brings self, body and nation together in the written word. Consider several examples from various issues. A letter from four young women reads as follows:

> We are students in the final year of our college education. Every day we go and practice yoga together from 5:15 to 6:15 at Picnic Hut park where the Bharatiya Yog Sansthan has established a training class. In this way we make are [*sic*] bodies light, and make ourselves healthy. By practicing breathing exercises we have made or [*sic*] digestion strong and regular. We are now in the habit of waking early. Yoga has given us good health.[27]

Standard reports on the organization's activities always include a specification of dates, locations and numbers which, although commonplace and not noteworthy in themselves, bracket the specific embodied activities in a particular kind of textualized sociality.

> From 6 to 9:30 am on October 20th 1991 at Ratan Devi Arya Girls College, Krishna Nagar, there was a demonstration class for the performance of *shankh prakshalan* [a purificatory procedure in which the digestive system is 'flushed out' with water]. One hundred and thirty-five men and women participated. The program was supervised by Jawaharlal Mehra and Netharam Sharma. It is conducted regularly every six months.[28]

In every issue there is a standardized report charting the park-by-park expansion of the organization as a collective body. Many of these reports, such as those focused on special events concerning *shankh prakshalan*, nature cure, *surya namaskar* and *pranayam,* link together the physical bodies of members with the idea of the organization as an expanding community.

> On November 23 1986 in Krishna Nagar park, vice president Satyapalji gave a lecture demonstration on yogic massage to a

gathering of 80 members from the three adjacent units of the Bharatiya Yog Sansthan. After the demonstration there were practice sessions. The lesson included information about massage in the winter, rubbing massage, the difference between water and oil massage as well as the specific effect of different kinds of massage on various parts of the body.[29]

Underlaying the organization's attempt to maintain the direct, visceral link between embodied yoga practice and the community as a nationalist body, there is a curious ambivalence in *Yog Manjari* about the relative importance of the body in itself. In terms of content there is no question but that the journal is concerned, almost exclusively, with physiological health. For example an issue picked at random from a collection of 40 contains articles on how yoga can be used to prevent and cure diabetes, guidelines for a safe and healthy pregnancy, instructions on how to stop hiccups, a recipe for mixed salad, a collection of natural home remedies and an essay on how the human body is like a temple wherein health is likened to ritual purity.[30] Strikingly, another issue, also picked at random, contains an editorial with the following commonly expressed statement by the editorial board. After pointing out that *Yog Manjari* has published a series of special issues, starting with one on the treatment of diseases, the editors write in an issue devoted to yoga posture exercises:

> We have no doubt that this special issue will have wide appeal. However we hasten to caution our members that they not simply use yoga to ward off disease. Yoga is not physical exercise, it is a mode of self-discipline. Yoga does not only purify the body and make it fit and healthy. By making the mind peaceful and focused it leads one toward consciousness and final transcendence.[31]

The ambivalence reflected in the contradiction of saying that yoga is not physical exercise, in a special issue devoted to yoga as physical exercise, reflects the inherent tension between embodied practice and the project of textual reproduction. Invoked in practice and writing, the body as significant in itself must be invoked and suppressed. The tension manifest in this is – to make reference once again to Susan Stewart's insights – a function of the way in which an ontology of the body haunts the play of signifiers related to it as the always deferred alterity of the Real.[32]

Conclusion: a materialist reading of the 'written' body

Ironically, Foucault's historical perspective on disciplined bodies necessarily entails a direct, representational understanding of language and writing. This carries over into his own writing, where the body is analysed as though it can be understood through, but apart from, language and textual representation. This post-structuralist irony notwithstanding, he is right in pointing out that it is necessary to go straight to the body, so to speak, and not 'prioritize ideology' in seeking to understand configurations of power. The problem, however, is how to get straight to the body without running up against the fact that writing is reproduction rather than production and therefore incipiently ideological. Ideology sets an arbitrary limit of meaning around what is to be included as significant, relevant or important in an analysis and thereby obscures the contingency of power and the power of contingent effect. But Foucault, in pointing out that 'there is nothing more material, physical, corporal than the exercise of power' and in then asking '[w]hat mode of investment of the body is necessary and adequate for the functioning of a capitalist society such as ours [or theirs]?',[33] does not take into account the power of language to usurp the body and define for it a function informed by ideology rather than by power at large.

The problem of writing about disciplined bodies is that the act of writing displaces the effects of power on the body with the powerful imperative to understand – with greater clarity, refinement and textured nuance – what bodies mean. Nationalism, at least of a particular kind, is configured through biopower and a mechanics of self-discipline that is concerned with regimentation for the sake of regimentation. It is consequently ambivalent if not completely hostile to meaning. There are traces of this in both wrestling and yoga in the performance of hundreds, if not thousands, of *dands* and *bethaks* and the neatly configured carpets of BYS members doing mass-drill postures. These traces are real and clearly visible to the ethnographer. But, however much a *dand* or an *asana* may function to discipline the body, the performance of one or the other is inherently done with reference to the discursive representation of each act as such, and so mass drill and 'thousands' of *dands* take on meaning insofar as they function to connect body and text. This becomes particularly clear under those circumstances where communities preoccupied with body discipline take on the task of imagining themselves on a scale larger than the singular event and try to construct an ideology to go with that image. This is where the insights of literary criticism become directly relevant. At the moment that the body is represented, both the body and its representation displace one another endlessly. As with printed and published accounts of violence, 'writing the body' is a problematic exercise in which laterality is both concrete and illusively ephemeral. In different but clearly related ways this is the focus of both Susan Stewart's analysis of 'contained representation' in various literary genres and E Valentine Daniel's endeavour to 'write the violence' of ethnic conflict in Sri Lanka.[34]

Most would agree that the 'literature' on yoga and wrestling considered in this essay is of a rather different kind than the 'high' literature stretching from the Gothic to the postmodern that was examined by Stewart, just as the 'bodies' in question are not implicated in anything like the violence analysed by Daniel. Nor are the problems attendant in writing the wrestler's body nearly as serious, in both a political and a moral sense, as the problems in Sri Lanka. Yet what is going on is analogous, the key difference being in the domain of regimented discipline and the connection of discipline to imagined community by means of writing. It is here that the process of 'imagining discipline' confounds Foucault's logic, for the written body dematerializes the Real body and one is left, like it or not, with ideology into which the body is squeezed rather than with a physically fit body invested with power. That is, one is left with ideology into which the body is placed, but only and always until wrestling practice and yoga classes begin again, day after day, on a regular basis and the body as such is directly disciplined. Writing is, therefore, not primarily a system of regimentation, control and surveillance focused on the body invested with power. Rather, it functions to extract the body from a configuration of modular biopower and establishes what can be analytically understood as a mimetic mutation of biology and ideology, in which national-ism is both the real and the imagined by-product of the reflection, refraction and duplicating one-for-the-other replacement/displacement of body and text.

Bibliography

Alter, J, 1992, *The Wrestler's Body: Identity and Ideology in North India*, Berkeley and Los Angeles, University of California Press.

Alter, J, 1993, 'The Body of One Color: Indian Wrestling, The Indian State, and Utopian Somatics', *Cultural Anthropology*, 8, pp. 49–72.

Alter, J, 1995, 'The Celibate Wrestler: Sexual Chaos, Embodied Balance, and Competitive Politics in North India', *Contributions to Indian Sociology*, 29, 1–2, pp. 109–131.

Alter, J, 1997, 'A Therapy to Live By: Public Health, the Self and Nationalism in the Practice of a North Indian Yoga Society', *Medical Anthropology*, 17, pp 309–325.

Alter, J, 2000, *Gandhi's Body: Sex, Diet, and the Politics of Nationalism*, Philadelphia, University of Pennsylvania Press.

Alter, J (forthcoming), 'Nervous Masculinity: Consumption and the Production of Embodied Gender in Indian Wrestling', in D Mines and S Lamb (eds), *Everyday Life in South Asia*, Bloomington, Indiana University Press.

Anderson, B, 1991, *Imagined Communities: Reflections on the Origin and Spread of Nationalism*, London, Verso.

Atreya, S, 1973, 'Saccha Pahalwan Devta Hota Hai', *Bharatiya Kushti*, 10, pp. 7–9, 21–4.

Atreya, S, 1996, 'Bharat Me Sharirik Shiksa', *Bharatiya Kushti*, 31, 12, p53

Chatterjee, P, 1993, *The Nation and Its Fragments: Colonial and Postcolonial Histories*, Princeton, Princeton University Press.

Daniel, E, 1996, *Charred Lullabies: Chapters in and Anthropography of Violence*, Princeton, Princeton University Press.

Garg, T, 1986, 'Shashank Asana', *Yog Manjari*, 9, 2, p 13.

Foucault, M, 1980, *Power/Knowledge: Selected Interviews and Other Writings, 1972–1977*, New York, Pantheon Books.

See Guha, R, 1982 'On some aspects of the historiography of colonial India' in R. Guna (ed.), *Subaltern Studies I*, Delhi, Oxford University Press.

Gupta, R, n.d., *Mallyudha, Athwa Akhara Gyan*, Delhi, Dehati Pustak Bhandar.

Malhotra, G, 1989, 'Brajwasi Baldev Chobe', *Bharatiya Kushti*, 26, p. 4.

Malhotra, G, 1990, 'Chandan Pahalwan', *Bharatiya Kushti*, 28, p. 1.

Manchanda, S K, and Keswani, N H, 1983, 'The Yoga and the Scientist', *Yog Manjari*, 5, 4, pp. 15–23.

Mehra, J, 1987, 'Sansthan Ki Gatiwidhiyan', *Yog Manjari*, 9, 4, pp. 22–6.

Nandy, A, 1983, *The Intimate Enemy: Loss and Recovery of Self Under Colonialism*, Delhi, Oxford University Press.

Nandy, A, 1995, *The Savage Freud and Other Essays on Possible and Retrievable Selves*, Princeton, Princeton University Press.

Pal, Y, 1991, 'Saqmpadakiya' in *Yog Manjari* 14, 2 p.1.

Prakash, G, 1999, *Another Reason: Science and the Imagination in Modern India*, Princeton, Princeton University Press.

Rameshwaranand, S, 1978, 'Pranayama Aur Vayu Bhagyan', *Yog Manjari*, 3, p. 27.

Rathi, R, 1994, 'Sadhana Aur Vyavahar', *Yog Manjari*, 17/ 1, pp. 25.

Saraswati, G, and Jain, P, 1988, 'Yog Dwara Madhumeha Par Vijay', *Yog Manjari*, 11/ 3, p. 11.

Sardana, N, 1988, 'How I Changed My Life By Yoga', *Yog Manjari*, 10/ 4, pp. 31–2.

Sharma, R, 1986, 'Do Vishisht Asana: Bhujangasana Aur Makarasana', *Yog Manjari*, 9/1, pp. 33–5.

Singh, S P, 1985, 'Vyayam Vidya Awen Parivritit Svarup', in *Smarika Pratham Jila Jori Gada Pratiyogita*, eds. Jila Khelkud Protsahan, pp 19 –20.

Stewart, S, 1994, *Crimes of Writing: Problems in the Containment of Representation*, Durham and London, Duke University Press.

Notes

1. Foucault 1980, p. 58.
2. Stewart 1994, p. 274.
3. Daniel 1996, p. 128.
4. See Alter, forthcoming.
5. Alter 1992, 1993, 1995, 2000.
6. Anderson 1991.
7. See Chatterjee 1993; Nandy 1983 1995; Prakash 1999.
8. Singh 1985, p. 19.
9. Alter 1992.
10. Alter 2000.
11. Guha 1982.
12. Atreya 1973, pp. 21–4.
13. *Bharatiya Kushti*, 11 (1973), pp. 1–3.
14. Gupta n.d., pp. 3–4.
15. *Bharatiya Kushti*, 9 (1972), pp. 7–9.
16. Foucault 1980, pp. 57–8.
17. Alter 2000, pp. 113–45.
18. Malhotra 1989, p. 47.
19. Malhotra 1990, p. 101.
20. Atreya 1996, p. 53.
21. Foucault 1980, p. 58.
22. *Yog Manjari*, 14 (1991)
23. See Alter 1997
24. See Alter 2000.
25. *Yog Manjari*, 10 (1987), p. 1.
26. Alter 1997.
27. *Yog Manjari*, 15 (1992), p. 3.
28. *Yog Manjari*, 14 (1991).
29. *Yog Manjari*, 10 (1987), p. 1.
30. *Yog Manjari*, 13 (1991).
31. *Yog Manjari*, 9 (1986), p. 1.
32. Stewart 1994, p. 274.
33. Foucault 1980, pp. 57–8.
34. Daniel 1996, p. 128.

2

'A Parcel of Dummies'?
Sport and the Body in Indian History

PAUL DIMEO

Introduction: the body in history

Douglas Booth recently criticized historians of sport for 'losing sight of the body' and generally ignoring it 'as a locus of scholarly interest'. He advocated that ideas of the body ought to be more thoroughly applied to analyses of what he calls that 'most popular of all embodied pursuits, namely sports'.[1] For all the vigour of his accusation, a more generous assessment might be that the body is always implied in sports histories, if not always articulated. However, to bring the body to the foreground of analyses requires a reconsideration of how the functions, actions, movements and styles of bodies in specific times and spaces are socially relevant.

On the one hand the body is sensed, experienced and lived in, rather than explicitly presented as a site for textual construction. As such, Bryan Turner has argued that bodies remain notoriously 'difficult to define, identify and isolate'.[2] Body image, mannerisms, styles, movements and cultures appear 'natural' and their practices are rarely recorded for the benefit of future historians. On the other hand the body is a 'conspicuous marker of identity and meaning'[3] that conveys messages of social class, gender, race and status. It can be a focus for repression and resistance. It is political, cultural and social.

Sport is particularly relevant to analyses of the body as it is, in Andrew Blake's words, 'first and foremost about the body . . . the culture of sports controls and directs bodily movement, as well as the shape of the body'.[4] Modern sports are especially important as they have been implicated in a culture 'marked by the quest for physiognomical and physical regimes of embodiment that are based on the assumption that the surface and interior of the body are amenable to reconstruction or re-incorporation'.[5]

Taking the focus of sport and the region of South Asia, scholars have produced some fine work focusing on the relationship of the body in sporting practice there. For instance, Joseph Alter has analysed North Indian wrestling as an embodied pursuit, as an 'elaborate way of life involving general prescriptions of physical culture, diet, health, ethics and morality'.[6] Philip Zarrilli takes a similar approach to the Keralan martial art, *kalarippayattu*, outlining the symbiosis of martiality and spirituality in this bodily discipline.[7] These important studies will be discussed more thoroughly in the course of this essay, but for the moment their relevance is that they flag up one of the themes worthy of attention when discussing the body in South Asian culture: that of indigenous practices that formalize local systems through embodied disciplines, symbols, styles and rituals.

The contrasting perspective provided by Tony Mangan's work on the planting of the English public-school 'games ethic' in foreign soils is that of colonial sport.[8] This acted both as a means for the self-disciplining of colonial elites and for the transformation of the colonized 'other'. It is clear from Mangan's case studies that sport played several complex and often contradictory roles: that of fostering respect for the colonial culture; that of incorporating local elites within the colonial order; that of ensuring distance from indigenous peoples; and that of displaying colonial superiority in a physical sense (even though this very display signalled insecurity and anxiety). Prominent colonialists in Victorian India such as the Viceroy, Lord Curzon, and Bengal's Lieutenant-Governor Sir George Campbell firmly believed in sports as a means of developing character, morality and a sense of discipline combined with fair play that provided training for war, for life and for the building of civilized societies. These ideas were implemented through pedagogical games played in schools and in religious settings; they sought to change Indian physical culture and to bring it under colonial control and discipline. However, despite the many confident assertions from colonial pedagogues, there were ambiguities and ambivalences within Indian physical culture during the Raj period that complicate the picture. This paper focuses on the colonial relationship: on the ways in which traditional games, rituals and sports were discouraged and the Indian body was constructed in specific and negative ways. However, local traditions of physical culture remained, while the sports of the colonialists were incorporated into Indian society in various ways that were not always consistent with the original intentions. The sporting body thus became a site for political engagement.

The rest of this chapter will address sport as a bodily practice that is about discipline: the discipline of rules, of space and of culture. The body within this analysis is socially constructed and sociologically significant. It moves within defined criteria, its styles accord with specific paradigms, the institutions that are built up around particular body-sport practices are political, and the social practices that are aligned with them imply both distinction and differentiation. Consequently, the sporting body becomes the 'epistemological starting point'[9] for a social analysis that focuses upon how bodies are experienced and presented in ways that impact upon broader currents of social, cultural, political and environmental change.

To achieve this the chapter will draw on three overlapping perspectives. The first comes from Henning Eichberg. It is best summarized by the editors of a collection of his essays, John Bale and Chris Philo, who argue that Eichberg's paradigm

> . . . concentrates on the body in conjunction with historical change and cultural variability, seeking to understand the threads that run in every direction possible between situated bodies (the bodies of given peoples in given times and places going about their business, travel, dances, games and sports) and the broader formations (social systems, cultural practices, political organisations) that encompass what people do, think and even feel in these historically and geographically specific situations.[10]

As such, the focus is not simply on sport but rather on how certain body cultures are 'written into specific constellations of sports' and are consequently 'viewed as integral to the overarching processes and transformations of a given period and region'.[11] This notion of temporal change in body cultures aligned with social conditions is supported in Michael Anthony Budd's succinct comment that every age has its characteristic body politics.[12]

The interconnection between the body as practice and the body as social is central to developing an understanding of what the body has come to mean in Indian society through the playing and watching of sports. The second conceptual framework is set out by Philip Zarilli when he identifies four interactive arenas for the practice of *kalarippayattu*: the literal arenas of practice; the social arenas of practice; the arenas of cultural production such as media representations; and the arena of experience and self-formation 'where embodied practice helps shape a self'.[13] In other words, the embodiment of sport works on a number of levels, from the mind–body level to public forms of representation, organization and politics.

The third source of ideas is Michel Foucault,[14] who has argued powerfully that the body is neither natural nor autonomous and that the structures of power in society can be read on the body. In other words, the body is not just the irrelevant surface of the more important psyche but the source and focus of disciplinary mechanisms of power.

One of the principal means by which discipline proceeds is the spatial distribution of individuals in certain ways: through separation from others, through the hierarchies of position and rank, or through the allocation of preferred spaces according to status.[15] Not only can the construction of space allow for surveillance, it can develop self-discipline through an awareness of being regulated. Individuals also come to behave in specific ways according to the spaces they inhabit, as these spaces can have their own cultures.

A second means of discipline is through the regulation, supervision and control of activities, which might also entail a process of segmented learning in a training or pedagogical sense.[16] While this latter point may seem more relevant for playing sports, both types of discipline can equally be applied to watching sports. Spectators learn how to behave through the very specific rituals and practices that are part of the process of watching, supporting, encouraging, celebrating or suffering. For instance, in Calcutta the supporters of the teams East Bengal and Mohun Bagan choose a different type of food to consume after matches. The *hilsa* is part of the winning meal of the Mohun Bagan fans, while their rivals prefer the *chingri* (prawn), although both rarely eat at the same time as the fans of the losing team traditionally go to bed on an empty stomach. Such disciplines establish identity as a bodily experience.

However, realizing how discipline works does not diminish the role of agency. Apart from anything else, players often engage with their game only partially, incompletely or in creative ways: 'Between each discourse of power and the (potential) exercise of that power there exists what might be called a "field of possibilities"; the possibility that particular discursive constructions of power will actually be exercised on the body in space and time'.[17]

It is important then also to consider the agency of the players caught up in sports, as their own agendas and agency often produce a 'field of possibilities' that ensures that the impact of power is often radically different from that envisioned in discourse.

Colonial discourses and the Indian body

One of the most obviously important ways in which the body has taken on social symbolism and practices related to discourses and disciplines of power in Indian history is through its place in colonialism. The body was the focus of specific representations which, when put into practice, changed the ways in which bodies were regulated, managed and controlled in ordered spaces and which also opened up new forms of agency, leading not just to resistance but to the reformulation of body cultures through less oppositional or confrontational motifs. Central to these processes were colonial negations of the Indian body and the consequent responses from local communities.

Even by the early nineteenth century, colonial observers such as Abbé Dubois had begun the process of separating the Indian 'races' according to their supposed body cultures:

> The courage of a people depends on climate. In the northern parts of the kingdom, firmer fibres produce a proportionate degree of resolution: in the southern parts all is sensibility . . . southward of Lahore we find throughout India a race of men whose make, physiognomy and muscular strength, convey ideas of effeminacy.[18]

This commentary was written in 1817 for a British readership and portrayed India as a region of distinct races and contrasting environments whose people were physically inferior to their colonial rulers.

Beliefs in the influence of the environment fostered the idea that northern 'races' were hardier, more industrious, more courageous and more moral, thanks to the difficult terrain and cold weather. For instance Sir J J H Gordon, a senior officer in the British Army, insisted that Punjabi Sikhs were 'a fine martial race' whose traits were 'steadfast loyalty, dogged tenacity, and dauntless courage',[19] a consequence of 'climate, occupation and the northern strain of their character'.[20] Southern 'races' had, it was claimed, become soft, lazy, weak and diseased in the subtropical heat. As Thomas Babington Macaulay, a member of the Governor-General's Supreme Council, opined in the 1830s, 'The physical organisation of the Bengalee is feeble even to effeminacy. He lives in a constant vapour bath. His pursuits are sedentary, his limbs delicate, his movements languid'.[21]

This attitude towards Bengalis did not dissipate, and events such as the 1857 Mutiny were interpreted though the lens of racial prejudice to reinforce further the stereotypes of inferiority. Despite the fact that it was made up of upper-caste sepoys from western Bihar and the United Provinces, rather than soldiers from Bengal itself, the role of the Bengal Army in the Mutiny provided further 'proof' of the local character: '. . . after the Mutiny of the Bengal Army, effeminacy and cowardice were epithets commonly ascribed to the Bengali character, whilst Sikh regiments loyal to the British were correspondingly lauded for their martial spirit'.[22]

However, 'race' was not the only lens through which the Indian body was observed. There was clearly a gender theme. The accusation of 'effeminacy' was generally assumed to be a criticism; also, women were entirely absent from these representations of bodies. When the colonized body was being assessed against the colonialist body, it was presumed that both were male and both should have 'masculine qualities'. Caste was also an issue. In late-nineteenth-century Kashmir, the fervent English colonialist Cecil Earle

Tyndale-Biscoe set out to 'grind grit into Kashmir' through sports. The targets for this exercise in disciplinary power were the Brahmin boys under his tutelage at the Church Missionary Society School.[23] Tyndale-Biscoe considered their body culture to be too decorous and delicate, and criticized their view that physical strength and muscularity were associated with manual labour and thus with the lower castes. The schoolmaster undertook a series of initiatives to persuade his pupils of the virtues of sport, health and exercise and their link to moral worth. He changed their clothing so that their traditional long robes would not interfere with football, cricket, rowing and swimming and thus radically asserted colonial visions of what the body should ideally be wearing. He threatened them with beatings if they did not play football with the leather ball they considered unholy (the first boy to kick the ball was considered defiled and so was not allowed back into his family home). He raised the school fees for any boy who could not swim and forced boys to join the fire service and life-saving corps. This was, in essence, discourse put into practice: the belief in the inherent effeminacy of the Hindu upper castes combined with a commitment to the ideals of Muscular Christianity.

However, Bengalis in particular bore the brunt of colonial prejudice. By the end of the century, writers in popular newspapers published for English readers in India could openly construct the Bengali body as effeminate. For instance, the journalist G W Steevens wrote in 1899:

> By his legs you shall know the Bengali. The leg of a free man is straight or a little bandy, so that he can stand on it solidly . . . The Bengali's leg is either skin and bones; the same size all the way down, with knocking knobs for knees, or else it is very fat and globular, also turning in at the knees, with round thighs like a woman's. The Bengali's leg is the leg of a slave.[24]

In the same year, an article published in the *Indian Planters' Gazette and Sporting News* made the claim that the youth of Calcutta were often reproached as effeminate and unsporting and 'are popularly supposed to be able to do nothing'. The blame for this was laid squarely with their 'grave and revered seniors' who 'put their veto on their boys taking part in any sport into which any of the slightest danger can creep'. Football and steeplechasing had apparently been banned by these Indian 'seniors' and, in the opinion of the newspaper, 'it seems a bit rough on the boys to prevent them from putting in their spare time at something which is likely to make men of them'. All of this was taken with the utmost sincerity as having lasting consequences: 'This stopping of every manly sport by *burra sahebs* will in time turn the rising generation into little better than a parcel of dummies'.[25]

It is apparent that there was a curious contradiction within colonial representations and practices (enforced or encouraged) of the body. There was a project to 'effeminize' the Bengali body and to make the 'northern' body 'martial': yet both ideas were based on the presumed physical and moral superiority of the European body. However, this negation produced two colonial responses. The first was to set out means by which the Indian body could be 'improved'. The second was to separate the 'pure' white body from the 'polluted' Indian body. In other words, it was suggested that Indians should engage in the physical culture systems of the British, such as modern team sports, and that they should give up traditional and indigenous pastimes. But they were kept at a 'safe' distance, either through direct exclusion from playing the sport (in the case of golf, rowing and horse racing) or through the construction of racially bounded teams to play against each other (in the case of cricket, hockey and football). In conceptual terms this meant the Indian body was seen to benefit from the types of discipline the British tended to impose upon themselves in such projects as Muscular Christianity. However, it also partially reveals a fear of the unknown and of Indian agency and a strong desire that the types of disciplines engaged in by Indians should be understood and controlled by the colonial power. The reason for this, Armstrong and Bates point out, is that indigenous physical cultures undermined the assumptions of colonialism:

> More than the martiality which they express, however, the importance of traditional sports lies in the possibilities they offer for cultural and national assertion: the development of the inner, private space . . . as a basis for opposition to colonial imperialism . . . The importance of games such as *kabbadi* lay in their claims to longevity. This permitted an insistence that despite being conquered and ruled by others, the cause of this was treachery and not any lack of vigour or virility, as claimed by colonial commentators.[26]

Therefore, anxiety as much as self-confidence underpinned British attempts to discipline the Indian body. However, their strategies were not entirely successful as indigenous body cultures remained to represent pre-colonial identities, rejections of colonial cultures, and responses to accusations of effeminacy.

Martial body cultures

Joseph Alter's history of *Bharatiya kushti*, or Indian wrestling, in North India shows it to be a fusion of Hindu sporting traditions dating back to the eleventh century and Persian martial skills introduced by the Mughal armies of the sixteenth century. The importance of the sport through the twentieth century lay in its longevity and in its provision of an arena for Indians to challenge, ignore and reinterpret the rules of social and moral engagement or, as Alter concludes, 'wrestling only contingently reaffirms pervasive cultural themes such as rank and status; more significantly, it opens up the stage for a protean, maverick revision of these themes'.[27]

Alter's work shows that the wrestler's body is at the centre of a wider social system revolving around *akharas* (gymnasiums). For the individual, the commitment to the rigours of the wrestler's life signals a personal search for the answers to the philosophical questions, 'who am I, and what am I put on this earth for?'. The answers to these questions come from physical discipline and from the subjection of the body to challenging regimes. This was made explicit by K P Singh, one of the most prolific writers on Indian wrestling, who insisted that:

> When you seek to develop your character, develop it in such a way that it becomes a treasure trove of magnetic power. Do not expect that the riches of life will fall at your feet. You must search for the true meaning of life. Whether through enterprise or through the rigid practice of *vyayam* [exercise], the goal is to plant the seed of human magnetism in this flesh and bone body. When milk is boiled cream develops and when gold is fired it shines.[28]

Alter's study of the Indian game of *kabaddi*[29] offers a contrasting example to that of wrestling. Both have been used as sites for the construction of ideological myths about 'Indian-ness', but the history of each sport highlights the different versions of 'Indian-ness' that various nationalist groups have used indigenous games to construct. Wrestling, based on individual commitment and development, Indian spiritual exercises and an 'Indian' diet was used to represent 'anti-modern' Indian-ness. This was a version of India manufactured by proponents who rejected modernity and saw India as quintessentially non-modern. *Kabaddi* could also be presented as authentically Indian, but at the same time it had many of the aspects of 'modern' sports, especially in its focus on team discipline and coordination. It therefore appealed to such groups as the Rashtriya Swayamsevak Sangh (RSS), the Hindu extremist political organization, which was eager to promote a version of Indian-ness that emphasized modernity and mobilization.[30] The different histories of the two games in the twentieth century – wrestling remains obscure, while *kabbadi* has been exhibited at the Olympics – reflect their selection as emblems of two very different ideological articulations of India's national essence.

The RSS has brought the body into the sphere of politics in a more powerful and explicit way by integrating sports and games into its disciplinary regimes. As explained by Armstrong and Bates:

> The Hindu nationalist RSS . . . went as far as the Nazi party in Germany in its espousal of physical training as a means to strengthen and revive the nation. Since its foundation in 1925, mass uniform displays of gymnastics were, and still are to this day, a characteristic feature at RSS rallies, along with a variety of displays in unarmed or lathi-wielding combat.[31]

They go on to argue however that, at the level of local branches of the society, games of pursuit with names such as 'strengthening the nation' are taught to young male recruits of school age in order to inculcate the notion that play, physical fitness and patriotism are intimately related. At the same time older children and teenagers play such games as kho-kho (which allegedly used to be played on chariots in ancient times) along with kabbadi, known as chedugudu or hu-tu-tu in southern parts of India, hadudu (among men) and chu-kit-kit (women) in eastern India. The game is meant to develop self-defence, in addition to responses to attack and reflexes of counter-attack, and is seen by some even as a form of training for armed combat in crowd situations.

Kalarippayattu is also an important and interesting body culture, notably for its development of spirituality alongside physical strength, flexibility, response and martiality. Emerging from Keralan and Tamil martial traditions, kalarippayattu was popularized in its modern form in the 1920s by C V Narayanan Nayar and his teacher Kottakkal Karnaran Gurukkal and belonged to 'the wave of rediscovery of the traditional arts throughout south India which characterized the growing reaction against colonial rule'.[32] It is practised at the kalari, which is a centre for training and healing and a temple 'where the guardian deity was either a form of the goddess or Siva/Sakti in combination'.[33] In fact, the religious tradition may have deeper roots, as many practitioners believe that it was the sage Parasurama who founded both the art and the first kalari, as well as Kerala itself, in the eleventh century. Although there are a variety of styles of practices, the central and common activities link martiality, healing and spirituality and include preliminary exercises that combine with full-body massage and application of oils to prepare for advanced practice and fighting; combat with wooden weapons such as sticks; techniques of empty hand fighting; special breathing and meditation exercises; knowledge of the body's vital spots, which practitioners learn to attack and defend; medical treatments for injuries and disease; and the rituals of combat and practice.[34]

The experience of the body in kalarippayattu begins with a challenge to the body–mind dualism, leading to the preferred term 'bodymind'. Through daily practice the practitioner eventually attains the proper 'body expression' (*deham bhavam*) and advanced students are said to 'flow like a river', meaning they have achieved an immersed state of embodiment that is conveyed through their 'serpentine, graceful, yet powerfully grounded movements'.[35] In fact, the ideal state of accomplishment is, like Indra, thousand-eyed, in which 'the body becomes all eyes' (*meyyu kannakuka*). This is, Zarrilli explains, 'an optimal state of awareness and readiness, often compared to the intuitive, instinctual state of an animal in its natural environment where it is ready to respond to any stimuli in that environment'.[36] In spite of this isolated state of immersion, *kalarippayattu* clearly has political implications. Its twentieth-century revival was linked to anti-colonialism, while in the early 1980s Hindu and Muslim students were putting it into practice in communal violence against the other community. The development of 'self', so crucial to martial arts, is socially contingent, depending as it does on the uses to which the practice is put. This implies that the same bodily activity can have different implications for individuals connected to social and political circumstances.

Nevertheless, *kalarippayattu*, *kabaddi* and *Bharatiya kushti* are all evidence of the tradition and continuity of Indian martial traditions that challenge colonial accusations of effeminacy. There are other examples, such as that of the late-nineteenth-century Indian revivalist and nationalist Swami Vivekananda, who preached that '*jiva* is Shiva': that every being is a part of God; that Indians should have muscles of iron and nerves of steel; and that they should 'awake, arise and stop not till the goal is reached'.[37] He was also famous for suggesting that the youth of India could become closer to heaven through football than through the *Gita*, and he practised wrestling himself after being taught by Kshetra Guha.[38] His encouragement of physical culture was based on the idea that national regeneration required physical strength. Especially in Bengal, such claims were directly linked to colonial stereotyping and Indians responded directly to British slurs upon their manhood. John Rosselli has shown that the Bengali elites 'sought in physical culture and martial arts redress for what they experienced in humiliation'.[39]

Religious and cultural revivalist leaders who promoted sport drew upon a longer history of sports being linked with religion. Physical perfection has been promoted by some religious leaders as an integral part of Hinduism and one of the means to fully realize one's Self, being defined as the body-way or *dehvada*. In this way, salvation (*nirvana*) was to be gained through physical perfection or *kaya sadhana* and achieved through perfect understanding of the body and its functions. The key to the popular exercise of *hatha yoga* is strength, stamina and control of the body functions with the aim of achieving a fusion of meditation and physical movement: the 'eight-fold method' encompassing techniques associated with breathing control or *pranayama*, body posture or *asanas* and withdrawal of the senses or *pratyahara*.[40] This historical basis informed the revival of traditional martial pursuits in India that drew sports and spirituality together in highly disciplined body cultures. While the colonial rulers rightly feared the continuity of such practices, many Indian communities developed them as a riposte to colonial negations of their physical capabilities. They became one means of proving that the practitioners had the moral and physical strength necessary for political independence. At the same time, the sports of the colonialists were being used, first as a vehicle for nationalism and then integrated into local cultures in diverse and fascinating ways that gave the sporting body new meanings.

Colonial sports and the body

Ashis Nandy locates ideas of the body as central to understanding the passion found in India for that most colonial of sports, cricket. The British assumed team sports to be 'manly' in the traditional Victorian sense and cricket was no exception. However, Nandy revises this point, suggesting that the British unknowingly had 'a rather classical Brahminic concept' of masculinity in mind:

> The good cricketer was masculine because he had control over his impulsive self and symbolized the superiority of form over substance, mind over body, culture over nature. Above all, cricket was masculine because it symbolized serenity in the face of the vagaries of fate and it incorporated the feminine within the game's version of the masculine.[41]

This is an interesting line of argument, even if it does echo colonial stereotypes of Indian effeminacy. Cricket took on a host of subtle meanings in India, as the Victorian ideal of the gentleman–amateur player was consistently undermined by the social divisions of the game, the profiteering of professional cricketers and the emphasis placed on functional performance over rituals and form. The game thus allowed Indians to 'assess their colonial rulers by western values reflected in the official philosophy of cricket'.[42] The everyday reality of cricket was contrasted with the ideals of Christianity and British civilization that were embedded in the morality tale spun around the game by the colonial elite. Inevitably, the rulers were 'found wanting':

> The assessment assumed that cricket was not the whole of Englishness but was the moral underside of English life which the

English at the turn of the century, even with much of the world at their feet, found difficult to live down. The assessment thus antici- pated the nationalist and particularly Gandhian critiques of the British which judged the everyday Christianity of the British in India with reference to philosophical Christianity.[43]

The cricketing body has come to mean something different in the modern age, where commerce and technology provide the catalyst for a more aggres- sive masculinity, the triumph of substance over style, the physical over the mental. Throughout the twentieth century a key motif for cricket culture in India was that of purity and defilement. Cricket was popular among Brahmins because there was no bodily contact, which meant the game could be played without risk of defilement through contact with lower castes. On the rare occasion that a player emerged from such lower castes as the Untouchables, the game might be played without risk of direct bodily contact, but after the game the physical barriers were hastily re-erected and rigidly enforced. Ramachandra Guha illustrates this with the example of the Untouchable Palwankar Baloo, a member of the Chamaar caste (a community of leather- workers) who learned to play the game as a servant at the British club in Poona. He ended up playing for the Deccan Gymkhana as their leading bowler. Despite his obvious skill, Baloo remained an outcast off the field: 'The Brahmins played with Baloo on the cricket field but would not dine with him off it. In fact, during the game's ritual "tea interval" he was made to stand outside the pavilion, at a distance from his team-mates, and served tea in a disposable cup'.[44]

In the post-colonial period cricket has become less about purity and more about 'bodily competition and virile nationalism'[45] and it has become one of the chief means by which Indian males experience such important aspects of their identities as 'maleness' and 'Indian-ness'. The sport rose to prominence after Independence as a means of expressing national identity to both the former colonizer and the wider world on the back of several key overseas victories in the 1970s. Its success is also linked to the class structure of Indian sports in the sense that cricket is preferred by those classes at the centre of economic, social and geographic power. While football could have become India's national sport after Independence, and certainly had a larger follow- ing through all the layers of Indian society, it has never emerged as a focus of national expression owing to a consistent lack of success at that level.

However, football does have a huge domestic presence, most notably at the economic, social and geographic periphery. For example, over 120,000 attend some matches in Kolkata between the traditional rivals East Bengal and Mohun Bagan. The earliest known victory for an Indian team over the

British colonialists was in 1911 and was celebrated in corporal terms that responded directly to colonial stereotyping:

> It fills every Indian with joy to learn of the victory of the Mohun Bagan team over English soldiers in the Challenge Shield competition. It fills every Indian with joy and pride to know that rice-eating, malaria-ridden, barefooted Bengalis have got the better of beef-eating, Herculean, booted John Bull in the peculiarly English sport. Never before was there witnessed such universal demonstration of joy, men and women alike sharing it and demonstrating it by showering of flowers, embraces, shouts, whoops, screams and even dances.[46]

The body played a different role in football compared with cricket.[47] A physical contact sport with fewer restrictions on spatial movements and more diversity in body styles, football's appeal spread across all communities and classes. However, as with cricket, teams came to represent distinct communities. During the early twentieth century, Indian teams shared a sense of antagonism towards British civilian and military sides. By the 1930s and 1940s the main rivalry which shaped football and which the game in turn helped to shape was that of religious communalism, as largely Hindu teams battled against the supremacy established by the Mohammedan Sporting Club. After Independence, the migration of around two million Hindus from East Bengal into Calcutta forged the ongoing rivalry between two largely Hindu clubs, Mohun Bagan and East Bengal.

In this rivalry, the chief body motif has been that of sacrifice. As noted earlier, supporters of the losing side starve themselves to suffer along with their team. However, sacrifice was taken to an altogether more extreme level in 1975, when a teenage Mohun Bagan supporter killed himself to bring good luck to his team (East Bengal had won the Calcutta League six times between 1970 and 1975.) Another aspect of sacrifice is the violence that has surrounded games between these rivals since Independence: an expression not just of football passion but of deeply felt social antagonisms dating back to the era of immigration. Throughout the 1950s, 1960s and 1970s, matches were regularly abandoned as a result of crowd violence and the conclusion of games often brought attacks on opposing clubhouses, players and officials.

In August 1980, this all reached a tragic denouement in Calcutta's Eden Gardens Stadium when rioting between rival supporters and the belated intervention from the police caused a stampede which left 16 fans dead and more than 100 injured. The body was the site of suffering once more: 'One heard sickening tales of people jumping from the [upper-tier] terraces to avoid mob fury and of bodies literally bursting under foot'.[48] The response to this tragedy was not the abandonment of football, as many critics called for at the time, but instead a fresh collectiveness based on the annual Football Lovers' Day held in August in memory of those who died. This is a blood donor camp, where the motif of bodily sacrifice is given an altered set of meanings: individuals give their own blood to help preserve future lives.

Football has had a different history to cricket: more physically rambunctious on the field, while its spectator culture has been expressive, at times violent and at times tragic. Cricket offers national victories, is professionally organized and is patronized by the elite and middle classes, although at the club and local level the game generates little interest among fans. For football fans, knowledge of international failings is a source of embarrassment and many locate themselves within the global game by supporting South American and European nations at such competitions as the World Cup. The sport is the game of the margins in India, populated by poor Bengalis, Goans and Muslims, and plays up localized rivalries to produce passionate support. These colonial sports have been taken into Indian sporting cultures in different ways, and the playing and watching of them tie into diverse memories, desires, fantasies and identities. They have shaped bodies into something new, making cultural and political statements through physical disciplines. Yet the legacy of colonial stereotyping remains as Indians agonize over and debate the reasons for sporting success and failure. In 1993, the Indian Football Association claimed there to be a 'genetic imperfection of Indian footballers concerning physical fitness'.[49] More recently, in a newspaper article entitled 'Football isn't in our blood', C Mitra argued:

> . . . since 1911, Indian football has rarely enjoyed a moment of glory. I believe football is too swift a game for our temperament or stamina. Indians excel when some intellectual input is required in an activity. Also, we are a ritualistic people and take time to warm up to something. That's why cricket fits into our psyche with such ease.[50]

The implications of 1911 for Indian corporeality may well have been celebrated at the time, but today it is the internal divisions of their society that occupy supporters of Indian football clubs. The feeling is strong that Indians do not have the physique for the game at the international level, as they do for cricket. Notions of the body continue to be inextricably tied to somatic practices, to the social arenas of physical activity and to ideologies of identity.

Conclusion

The history of the body and sport in India is rich and complex, and this paper has focused on colonial agendas and local responses. It has argued that by negating the body, British colonialists wanted to control it, to regulate it and to enforce disciplinary power while anxiously reasserting both superiority and distance. The response from Indians was to undermine the colonial stereotype from within through the revival of traditional martial pursuits and through the use of colonial sports for political resistance. Such processes brought specific body cultures into Indian society and these have been readjusted in post-colonial circumstances to reflect the internal fragmentation of India, so that bodies have been reformulated and have changing meanings contingent with changing times. There are many strands to this history, including explicit right-wing nationalism, traditional and spiritual disciplines, the continuity of colonial sports and their reinterpretation, the continuity of colonial stereo-types and their internalization. This is a multifaceted history which precludes easy conclusions but which demands that attention is given to the workings of power and the workings of agency, to that 'field of possibilities' in which the visions of the hegemonic are disrupted, the motivations of the powerful can be questioned and the supposedly powerless subjects make their choices.

The historian must also avoid making essentialized judgements about body practices, communities and politics. Structures are open to agency and to numerous strategies of engagement. It is important to remember that individuals can immerse themselves in their sport, or they may pick and choose more selectively how and when to become involved. Also, individuals can move between sports and skills, practising a traditional martial art one day and playing golf the next. Therefore different body cultures might impact upon selfhood in a more transient way, so that each forms only a moment in the construction of self and fails to become a totalizing lifestyle experience. In considering how individuals and communities have enjoyed and used physical cultures, this paper has pointed the way towards some aspects of the social history of the Indian body that are formulated and expressed through sport. In doing so, it places both the body and sports at the heart of the analysis: two themes that have all too often been overlooked in the history of South Asian cultures.

Bibliography

Alter, J, 1992, *The Wrestler's Body: Identity and Ideology in North India*, Berkeley, University of California Press.

Alter, J, 2000, 'Kabaddi, a national sport of India: the internationalism of nationalism and the foreignness of Indianness', in N Dyck (ed.), *Games, Sports and Cultures*, Oxford, Berg.

Appadurai, A, 1996, 'Playing With Modernity: The Decolonization of Indian Cricket', in C A Breckenridge (ed.), *Consuming Modernity: Public Culture in Contemporary India*, Minneapolis, University of Minnesota Press.

Armstrong, G, and Bates, C, 2001, 'Reflections on sport in South Asia', in P Dimeo and J Mills (eds), *Sport in South Asia*, special issue of *Contemporary South Asia*, 10/2 (July), pp. 191–205.

Bale, J, and Cronin, M (eds), 2002, *Sport and Postcolonialism*, Oxford, Berg.

Blake, A, 1996, *Body Language: the Meaning of Modern Sport*, London, Lawrence & Wishart.

Booth, D, 2001a, 'Sporting Bodies: Evidence from the Beach', paper presented to the North American Society for Sports History Conference, University of Western Ontario.

Booth, D, 2001b, *Australian Beach Cultures: the History of Sun, Sand and Surf*, London, Frank Cass.

Budd, M A, 1997, *The Sculpture Machine: Physical Culture and Body Politics in the Age of Empire*, New York, New York University Press.

Chowdury-Sengupta, I, 1995, 'The Effeminate and the Masculine: Nationalism and the Concept of Race in Colonial Bengal', in P Robb (ed.), *The Concept of Race in South Asia*, Oxford, Oxford University Press.

Dimeo, P, and Mills, J (eds), 2001a, *Soccer in South Asia: Empire, Nation, Diaspora*, London, Frank Cass.

Dimeo, P, and Mills, J (eds), 2001b, *Sport in South Asia*, special issue of *Contemporary South Asia*, 10/2 (July).

Dubois, Abbé, 1817, *Description of the Character, Manners, and the Customs of the People of India; and of their Institutions, Religions and Civil*, London, Longman, Hurst, Rees, Orme and Browne.

Eichberg, H (ed. J Bale and C Philo), 1998, *Body Cultures: Essays on Sport, Space and Identity*, London and New York, Routledge.

Foucault, M, 1973, *The Birth of the Clinic: an Archaeology of Medical Perception*, New York, Vintage Books.

Foucault, M, 1989, *Madness and Civilization: a History of Insanity in the Age of Reason*, London, Routledge.

Gordon, Sir J J H, 1904, *The Sikhs*, Edinburgh and London, William Blackwood & Sons.

Guha, R, 1998, 'Cricket and Politics in Colonial India', *Past and Present*, 161.

Hancock, P, Hughes, B, Jagger, E, *et al.*, 2000, *The Body, Culture and Society: an Introduction*, Buckingham and Philadelphia, Open University Press.

Harrison, M, 1999, *Climates and Constitutions: Health, Race, Environment and British Imperialism in India, 1600–1850*, Oxford and Delhi, Oxford University Press.

Indian Football Association, 1993, *Role, Achievements of the Indian Football Association (W.B.) in the Promotion and Development of the Game of Football in India*, IFA, West Bengal.

Mangan, J A, 2000, *The Games Ethic and Imperialism: Aspects of the Diffusion of an Ideal*, London, Frank Cass.

Mangan, J A, 2001, 'Soccer as Moral Training: Missionary Intentions and Imperial Legacies', in P Dimeo and J Mills (eds), *Soccer in South Asia: Empire, Nation, Diaspora*, London, Frank Cass.

McDonald, I, 1999, 'Physiological Patriots? The politics of physical nationalism and Hindu nationalism in India', *International Review for the Sociology of Sport*, 34, pp. 343–58

McHoul, A, and Grace, W, 1998, *A Foucault Primer: Discourse, Power and the Subject*, London, University College London.

Mitra, C, 2002, 'Football isn't in our blood', *The Pioneer* (27 June 2002) (http://www.dailypioneer.com/archives1/FORAY.ASP?fdnam=jun2702 &CAT=1).

Montague, F C, 1903, *Critical and Historical Essays: Contributed to the Edinburgh Review by Lord Macauley*, vol. III, London, Methuen & Co.

Nandy, A, 2000, *The Tao of Cricket: on Games of Destiny and the Destiny of Games*, New Delhi, Oxford University Press.

Nandy, M, 1990, 'Sports in Calcutta', in S Chaudhuri (ed.), *Calcutta: The Living City*, vol. II: *The Present and Future*, Calcutta, Oxford University Press.

Rosselli, J, 1980, 'The self-image effeteness: physical education nationalism in nineteenth century Bengal', *Past and Present*, 86, pp. 121–48.

Sinha, M, 1995, *Colonial Masculinity: The 'Manly Englishman' and the 'Effeminate Bengali' in the Nineteenth Century*, Manchester, Manchester University Press.

Turner, B, 1994, 'Theoretical Developments in the Sociology of the Body', *Australian Cultural History*, 13.

Zarrilli, P, 1998, *When the Body Becomes All Eyes: Paradigms, Discourses and Practices of Power in Kalarippayattu, a South Indian Martial Art*, New Delhi, Oxford University Press.

Notes

1. Booth 2001a.
2. Turner 1994, pp. 21–2.
3. Booth 2001a.
4. Blake 1996, pp. 23–4; see also Bale and Cronin 2002.
5. Hancock, Hughes, Jagger *et al.* 2000, p. 3.
6. Alter 1992, p. 5.
7. Zarrilli 1998.
8. Mangan 2000.
9. Eichberg 1998, p. 118.
10. Ibid., pp. 11–12.
11. Ibid., p. 12.
12. Budd 1997.
13. Zarrilli 1998, p. 9.
14. Foucault 1973, 1989.
15. See McHoul and Grace 1998, p. 68.
16. Ibid., p. 69.
17. Ibid., p. 8.
18. Dubois 1817, p. 201.
19. Gordon 1904, p. 3.
20. Ibid., p. 225.
21. Cited in Montague 1903, p. 80; see also Sinha 1995 and Harrison 1999.
22. Armstrong and Bates 2001, p. 194.
23. Mangan 2001.
24. Cited in Chowdury-Sengupta 1995, p. 298.
25. *Indian Planters' Gazette and Sporting News* (8 July 1899).
26. Armstrong and Bates 2001, pp. 194–5.
27. Alter 1992, p. 6.
28. Cited in Alter 1992, p. 258.
29. See Alter 2000.
30. See also McDonald 1999.
31. Armstrong and Bates 2001, p. 194.
32. Zarrilli 1998, p. 51.
33. Ibid., p. 26.
34. Ibid.
35. Ibid., p. 19.
36. Ibid.
37. Armstrong and Bates 2001, p. 194.
38. Nandy 1990, p. 328.

39. Rosselli 1980, p. 121.
40. See Armstrong and Bates 2001, p. 193.
41. Nandy 2000, p. xx.
42. Ibid., p. 7.
43. Ibid.
44. Guha 1998, p. 170.
45. Appadurai 1996, p. 25.
46. *Nayak* (30 July 1911).
47. For further discussion on the past and present of football in South Asia, see Dimeo and Mills 2001a and 2001b.
48. *Amrita Bazar Patrika* (20 August 1980).
49. Indian Football Association 1993, p. 1.
50. Mitra 2001, *Pioneer* (27 June 2002).

3

Schools, Athletes and Confrontation: The Student Body in Colonial India

SATADRU SEN

Introduction

In the decades following the war of 1857, the first boarding schools of the colonial era began to emerge in India: Rajkumar College in 1870, Aligarh College in 1875, the Ramkrishna Mission and the Imperial Cadet Corps at the turn of the century. Within the apparent diversity of these developments lurk some interesting commonalities. In each of these institutions, an extraordinary amount of attention was paid to the physical bodies of the inmates, who were young Indian males. In each case, strenuous efforts were made by the British and by elite Indians to hammer those bodies into something they were supposedly not: strong yet obedient, energetic yet docile, individual yet orderly, playful yet useful. What we see in colonial India at this period is a highly developed and intensely politicized pedagogy of the body. It was not always successful. The new educational processes met with resistance at every step of the way: in their objectives, in their methods and in their outcomes. Even when this education 'worked', the problem of the undisciplined native body was far from resolved. The newly educated bodies threatened to subvert the racial and gendered categories under which imperial society was organized. Moreover, physical education and corporal punishment combined to create disciplined young men who might serve either the colonial order or the emerging counter-order of a nationalist shadow-state.

The idea that schools exist in order to generate 'docile bodies' is, of course, not new.[1] Foucault's rather simplistic original picture of discipline has been complicated quite effectively by studies that take into account the overwhelming evidence of successful resistance and constant compromises in a variety of institutional contexts, both metropolitan and colonial. Donzelot has looked at the French reformatory school, Mills and Ernst have unlocked the colonial lunatic asylum, and the nineteenth-century prison has been quite thoroughly re-examined in Britain as well as in India.[2] The colonial Indian school, however, has largely escaped this analytical onslaught. Those scholars who have studied educational institutions – David Lelyveld in the case of Aligarh, Nita Kumar in Benares, Barbara Metcalf with the Deoband *madrasa*[3] – have for the most part focused on locating these institutions within the political and intellectual geography of colonial India. They have paid relatively little attention to what might be described as the politics of internalized discipline as manifested in the external appearance and behaviour of the student body. The rise of a culture of physical exercise in late-nineteenth-century India, including the *akhara* 'movement', has been noted by those who study the origins of Indian nationalism and in recent works in South Asian sports history.[4] These scholars, however, have not tried to locate their studies within a particular institutional culture which imposes its own priorities and constraints upon the content of education. The objective of this essay then is to establish some connections between two contested sites in the empire: the school on the one hand and the body of the student on the other.

Sport, drill and discipline

In 1891, a college newspaper in Cambridge ran the following essay, entitled 'The Sporting Man':

> Sporting, if one wished to define it, would seem to be a culture of the body to the neglect of the soul. And the Sporting man is one who makes mistakes in his spelling, even of ordinary ones. If he goes in for a scrutiny, he will receive only one mark for arithmetic. He will wear a large and brilliant tie, and presume upon it; and he is partial to a thick light jacket, with a band round the middle. Instead of grumbling at the authorities, he will, for the most part, ignore them. He will rise late in the morning and drink soda. It is just like him also to take things out of the store-room at unseasonable times, and eat them. And walking in the corridors he will warble. In his conversation he will mention nothing but horses, footballs, and rowing boats; but if a philosophical question is started he will look frightened, and after a short interval take his departure. And he will drink his wine in rather large quantities, and drive nails into his shoes. If he wants to arouse an acquaintance he will shout to him from the street, using two notes, like the cuckoo. For those who read he will show a fine contempt. And meeting a friend he will say, 'I have just had my hair cut,' or 'I got drunk last night.' He will smoke infinite tobacco, and all the while he will think to himself, 'What a fine fellow I am.' Having come

in the rooms of others he will make hay, even in winter. And having
much more to say about him, I willingly refrain.[5]

Written by an undergraduate at Trinity College, 'The Sporting Man' suggests
that the triumph of the Rugby ethos over older anxieties about the over-
exercised body was complicated and internally fractured along the lines of
class even within the cloisters of elite education.[6] Far from being a uniform
homage to Tom Brown's youth, the discourse of athletic education in late-
Victorian England was a cacophony of discord between middle-class patience
and aristocratic 'dash', between would-be amateurs and future professionals,
between top-ranked schools and their less highly regarded counterparts,
between the established elites and the upwardly mobile. It was not that the
horsey elites and the middle class played different sports at school or differed
substantially in their opinions of the value of a physical education. Rather, the
places they occupied in English society and their attitudes towards each other
determined how each group approached the project of educating the body,
and indeed how they viewed the approaches of their competitors. When this
educational project was transplanted to colonial India in the 1870s, some of
the discord became muted because the problem of negotiating athletic values
across the lines of class was supplanted, very substantially, by the possibly
greater challenge of negotiating with Indian elites across the lines of race and
across the broader political relationships of a colonial empire. There were two
basic problems. One was that the values of an athletic education were so
closely tied to the English 'Self' – and to the British imperial project – that
imparting this knowledge to Indians was fraught with existential dilemmas.
The other was the fact that elite Indians, and this includes both the students
and their parents, were themselves ambivalent about the content and the
context of this education.

   The objectives of physical education in colonial India were only superficially
similar to those that applied in Britain. In both places much emphasis was
placed on developing 'character', i.e. emotional and physical self-control, an
almost paradoxical balance of self-assertion and self-sacrifice, and subordina-
tion in the face of authority,[7] by making organized sport central to the school
curriculum. However, the character that was shaped on the playing fields of
Eton was also closely tied to British nationalism and imperialism. It was tied
to an exclusive racial identity that was both self-evident and permanently
imperilled. Threats to this identity existed at home, where there were Irishmen
and other immigrants to contend with, and to an even greater extent in the
colonies, where the privileges of Englishness were under attack from restless
natives. As such, the character that Indians might learn by playing cricket and
football could not be exactly the same as that which English schoolboys were

taught, unless the political structure of the empire was radically altered to give coloured boys the identity and the privileges of whiteness.

Superficially, colonial academies such as the Imperial Service Corps (ICC) attempted to do just that. By training young Indian aristocrats to accept the king's commissions in the Indian Army, the ICC would seem to exemplify Cannadine's hypothesis of an empire in which class solidarity trumped racial exclusion.[8] Up to a point that is indeed how Lord Curzon, the creator of the ICC, envisioned the institution that he called his 'dear child'.[9] Yet the draft rules for the ICC stated that the cadets were to be given 'such a general education that, whilst in course of time they may be able to take their places in the Imperial Army as British Officers, they may never lose their character and bearing as Indian Gentlemen'.[10] No British school in India tried to make Indian boys English, mentally or physically, and when that seemed imminent (usually in the case of Indian boys educated in England) colonial educators and administrators inevitably warned that 'denationalization' would be disastrous for the boys, for India and for the Empire alike.[11]

It should be noted that even with its limited goals, the ICC was a failure, as the all-white officer corps of the colonial army stubbornly resisted the Viceroy's plans for aristocratic bonding across the lines of race. The fiasco did considerable damage to Curzon's own career. Curzon was in some ways exceptional in his vision of education and empire: an intelligent Tory building strategic alliances against the tide of middle-class meritocracy, white and black, by teaching aristocrats some of the merits of the middle class. Much more typical of the colonial educator–administrator was Lord Harris, Governor of Bombay in the 1890s. Rejecting the idea that English educational models could be recreated in India, Harris said in a speech at Rajkumar College:

An attempt has been made to introduce the public school system in its entirety here and elsewhere in India, but you must not think you have got a close imitation of it. I do not think it would be possible in India to produce a counterpart of it, for I am not at all sure that it is suited to Oriental customs, habits of thoughts, and habits of mind and body. The English public school gives no advantages to birth or wealth; the son of the poorest and humblest squire may, and aye often does, far excel in the estimation of his school fellows whether from moral, intellectual or physical qualities, the son of the highest and the wealthiest. English public schools are model republics where the prizes are gained by his own prowess not by favour, and where each member has to regulate his behavior to suit the convenience of the general body, not of himself, and where the mode of life, luxurious though it may be, as compared with the mode of not many

decades back, is still Spartan as compared with the mode of educational institutions in this country meant to be of the same character.
Pray do not misunderstand me: I am not finding fault that these
Indian institutions are not exactly the same as the English public
schools. I acknowledge that every allowance should be made for
climate, racial and customary differences. Still it is impossible to
make an exact copy of it.[12]

In other words neither English schools nor English bodies could be reproduced with native material. Yet Harris is remembered in India not for his
opposition to recreating Eton in the tropics but for his aggressive promotion
of school cricket in Bombay against the opposition and indifference of those
Anglo-Indians who thought the game unsuited politically, physically and
temperamentally to coloured boys.[13] Harris and such colonial educators as
Henry Siddons (at Aligarh) promoted school sports in India because they
believed that although playing English sports would not make Indian boys
English, it would nevertheless teach them something that was uniquely
valuable in the colonial–Indian setting.

This 'something' was a model of male subject-hood that was distinct from
the contemporary English ideal of citizenship. References to creating 'manly'
spirits and bodies saturate the writings of colonial educators who set out to
describe what they were doing. Baden-Powell, for example, described the task
of colonial education as 'that great work of developing the bodies, the character and the souls of an otherwise feeble people'.[14] The work of the Church
Missionary Society's school in Srinagar (henceforth referred to simply as
the CMS) was, in the words of the principal, CE Tyndale-Biscoe, 'putting
backbone into jellyfish'. This ideal of the manly student did not include the
commitment to political self-rule that distinguished nineteenth-century English
masculinity from the languid despotism of the Turk. Rather, it was closer to
what Mrinalini Sinha has called 'colonial masculinity',[15] that is, a gendered
identity based on a conviction that the status quo of Indian masculinity was
fundamentally deficient in strength, courage and self-control.[16] The colonial
masculinity that British educators sought to create did not include active political participation. Rather, its highest political values were based on recognizing and accepting one's place in the imperial order. A manly boy, in this
context, was loyal to his team, his school, his regiment, his social compart-
ment and, above all, to the British Empire. All of this implied that he was not
to go about making unseemly demands for political rights for which, he had
been told, he was racially unsuited. Heather Streets has pointed out that after
1857, loyalty without political demands was central to the construction of
masculinity in colonial India.[17] Accordingly, the creation of such loyal/male
bodies, which Ashis Nandy has characterized as childlike (but not childish) in

their innocence, dependence and love for the colonizer,[18] was a basic objective of those educational institutions in India that were directly or indirectly under British supervision. These included not only Rajkumar College and the ICC, but also Aligarh and the CMS.

These latter were, on the surface, very different schools. The CMS was a lay missionary institution that worked with the children of the middling elite in a princely state. When the school began in 1880, the students were drawn overwhelmingly from the Pandit (Kashmiri Brahmin) community.[19] It was not until the turn of the century that Muslims were represented in appreciable numbers. The ICC, on the other hand, was based in British India (in Meerut and Dehra Dun). The cadets were drawn from the elites of the princely states and Muslims eventually outnumbered Hindus, although there is no evidence that this statistical imbalance was intentional.[20] Rajkumar College, like the ICC, was created for the sons of princely families and existed to train a new generation of Indian princes in loyalty to the empire and in some of the physical, social and intellectual habits of elite Englishmen. Aligarh differed from all the others in the fact that it was controlled by an Indian board of trustees to which the English staff was nominally subordinate. Its students, headed for careers in the modern professions and the colonial bureaucracy, came mostly from *ashraf* families, who occupied a very different social position in India than either the Pandits or the princes.[21]

The academic curricula varied considerably although each was marked by a variant of what G Vishwanathan has described as the colonizing function of English-language education.[22] The ICC, being a military academy, trained students in the skills of the modern army officer (which included immersion in the lives of Napoleon, Washington and Plutarch), as well as relatively practical training in surveying, riding and sharp salutes. Aligarh College came closest to approximating the English public school, with its emphasis on linguistic studies and the classics, its debating tradition and its disdain for anything that might be construed as useful. Rajkumar College fell somewhere in between. The CMS was much more humble in its academic and professional ambitions for its graduates than were any of the others, aiming to impart basic literacy in English, some training in mathematics, history and geography and vocational instruction for the less than scholarly. The CMS was also a day school, while the other three were residential institutions where the students were removed from the direct supervision of their parents.

What these schools shared was a very similar set of goals for the physical habits of their students. Sport was central to education at each place, although the specific sports varied. The ICC and Rajkumar College emphasized polo and cricket. When they were not fencing or drilling on horseback, boys at Rajkumar College were required to exert themselves in the gymnasium.[23]

Cricket was the major sport at Aligarh, while the directors of the CMS favoured boating, swimming, boxing and football. The CMS and Rajkumar College both mythologized incidents in which the cricket field became the site of physical clashes against hostile outsiders and had to be literally claimed for the school and civilization.[24]

It must be asked what specifically was new about this education. First, while athletic pursuits such as wrestling and polo had a pre-colonial pedigree in India, the idea of teams with fixed identities and stable memberships was entirely new when cricket, football and polo teams began to appear in India in the second half of the nineteenth century. Even polo, with its characteristic rules, dress and vocabulary, was essentially reinvented in the late nineteenth century as a colonial sport. It became a ritual that would allow British administrators, military officers and the princes, all raised on the nineteenth-century British historian Tod's vision of the Rajput past, to share a field and a fantasy. Second, while colonial educators borrowed and continued pre-existing athletic–military traditions such as horsemanship and sword-fighting, especially in 'martial' schools like the ICC and Rajkumar College, they dramatically altered the manner in which these activities were conducted. Riding a horse or wielding a sword with a flourish was no longer enough, as the student/athlete/warrior now had to be able to ride in formation, to drill with precision and to observe elaborate new sets of rules that defined the exercise. What mattered now, as much as the ability to control a horse, was the ability to control one's own body, to be punctual, to function as a predictable part of a well-ordered machine. The importance given to sport and to physical exercise at colonial schools was thus a self-conscious cultural innovation that had to be pushed in the face of indifference and even resistance on the part of the students and their families. In this sense, the promotion of sport in the school and the subjection of the students' bodies to physical exercise was an act of subjugation that extended British authority into uncharted new territory.

The CMS and the Pandit body

Of the four schools in this analysis, nowhere was an athletic education pushed so stridently as at the CMS. To some extent, this was because the students who attended the school seemed to demand the most work on the part of educators. The missionaries who ran the school took it as an item of faith that Kashmiris were a peculiarly effeminate people whose spirit had been crushed by repeated invasions and further attenuated by the Pax Britannica. The Pandit boys, especially, were seen as excessively studious and disinterested in games, and it was thought that this was an attitude encouraged by parents who apparently saw sports as a waste of time that was better spent memorizing lessons. Kashmiri effeminacy, like the Bengali variety, was also seditious and manifested itself bodily in what Tyndale-Biscoe called 'the Pandit eye': a silent stare of insubordination and contempt.[25] The Pandit eye was taken very seriously at the CMS and was subject to punishment when detected. There were few overt disciplinary problems, in the sense that the boys were considered too effete and cowardly to be rowdy. Nevertheless the bodies were undisciplined in other ways: the students did not come together in neat, orderly groups, they did not come together on time and sometimes they did not come at all. Undesirable sexual behaviour, from early marriage and fatherhood to homosexuality and a taste for pornography, was a chronic problem. The boys were physically dirty and even their clothes were disorderly: Kashmiri *pherans* were regarded by the teachers as antithetical to cleanliness and rapid movement, and turbans and clogs were considered laughable. Facial jewelry was regarded as both a source of infection and a mark of effeminacy.

To combat these assorted problems, the missionaries engaged in a series of battles which they described in terms of a simple five-point formula: (i) compulsory Christian teaching; (ii) compulsory fees; (iii) corporal punishment for misbehaviour; (iv) compulsory swimming; and (v) compulsory games.[26] None of these was easy to apply. The Church Missionary Society leadership in India was eager to make conversions,[27] but the missionaries in Srinagar were a pragmatic lot and preferred to save heathen souls by working on their bodies. Even then, laying hands upon the student had the potential to wreck a school in colonial India. Corporal punishment was an explosive issue early on at Aligarh where, Lelyveld has noted, only Syed Ahmed Khan, in his role as surrogate father in a surrogate home, could strike the students.[28] Baden-Powell felt compelled to preface the narrative of the CMS with an apology about the 'rather severe' measures used by the missionaries.[29] Unlike Aligarh, however, the CMS was not constrained by an Indian board of trustees or a proprietorial Indian founder. As such, the missionaries were able to manipulate the students' bodies with greater, though not perfect, impunity. In Tyndale-Biscoe's account of the school these manipulations became a series of titanic struggles between heroic teachers and wily students, each culminating in victory for the former. Boys with an apparent reluctance to be touched by dogs or Englishmen were literally dragged into communal tubs and scrubbed with dog-soap by the Muslim porter. This washed away dirt, skin disease, caste pride and anti-English snobbery simultaneously. Other students were tied with ropes and dipped in the river. This cleaning-up was then presented as a process of gender repair because the dirtiness of the students was interpreted as a sign of moral indiscipline. Tyndale-Biscoe wrote:

> . . . not only were they dirty in fact and clean in imagination, but
> they were utterly unmanly, while at the same time they thought of

themselves superior to all creatures. They had lost their self-respect, and one way to put that into them again was to make them clean instead of filthy, and smart instead of slipshod.[30]

The campaign to change the dressing habits of the CMS students evidently began with the missionaries asking (themselves), 'What can you expect of a people whose national costume is a night-gown?'.[31] The answer being self-evident, the boys were coaxed into new clothes that were not quite English-style uniforms but accoutrements that Bernard Cohn would have recognized as signposts of the wearer's relocation in the colonial universe.[32] *Pherans*, clogs and Kashmiri turbans gave way to trousers, boots and turbans of the Rajput variety, and facial jewelry was discarded. The mechanism of this transformation was itself highly physical as the boys were forced to endure a series of games which made their old 'costumes' awkward, embarrassing or painful. Boxing eliminated nose rings, gymnastics shamed the wearers of the *pheran* (who shared the Scottish suspicion of underwear) and football was hard to play with clogs on your feet.

The deployment of athletic activity to bring about a change of clothes was neither coincidental nor insignificant. The relationship between sport and dress has a rich history in colonial India, and the struggles at the CMS are a good example of how this relationship could carry ideas that had no inherent connection either to sport or to sartorial aesthetics. For instance, the flowing clothes of early Parsi cricketers generated amusement and derision in equal measures among English observers, who saw it as a reflection of Indian unfit-ness for cricket and self-government alike.[33] In England in the 1890s, reports that Indians played cricket in bare feet were greeted with astonishment and interpreted as evidence of a freakish insensitivity to pain.[34] Conversely, in the recent film *Lagaan*, the loincloths and tunics (and bare feet) of the peasant cricketers who defeat the English team become uniforms of an authentic Indian identity and represent a triumphant rejection of the Englishness of the sport. The victory of the Mohun Bagan footballers over the East Yorkshire Regiment in 1911 is a landmark event in the popular mythology of Indian nationalism, and any retelling of that story would be incomplete if it were not mentioned that the Indians were barefoot while the Yorkshiremen wore boots.[35] In 1891 the Yorkshire regiment had been humiliated – this time at cricket – by another group of barefooted Indians, to the general astonishment of English sportswriters.[36] Thus, the clothes worn on the playing field became the source of meaning in explaining who had won, or who had been defeated, in the sporting battles of the colonial wars. Gazing proudly upon his students in 1930, Tyndale-Biscoe had no doubts about what he saw. He was able to describe a successful colonization: 'So here we have the boy as he is today. A real boy who we hope will grow into a true man. The badges of degradation are gone and the signs of self-respect are taking their place'.[37]

Thus, the pattern that emerges from the manipulations of the student body at the CMS is that athletics served an instrumental purpose, bringing about a visible change in the physical habits of the student, which in turn reflected a deeper moral transformation. Team sports taught group loyalty, 'which is terribly lacking in Kashmir'.[38] The teachers helped this process along by encouraging the boys to compete for prizes that were awarded not to the individual athlete but to the class he represented. Boxing taught the boys not only to overcome their irrational aversion to leather (football was helpful here as well) but also to overcome their horror of blood. In fact, boxing was promoted quite explicitly as a way for students to settle their quarrels without crying to the school authorities, which would have been womanly, and without becoming visibly angry, which would have been equally unmanly because it reflected a failure of self-control. The intimate relationship between physical appearance and moral content was evident not only in the missionaries' view of the boys' clothes and their cleanliness but also in their perception of flesh-and-blood bodies. Kashmiri boys were myopic and much too delicate, Tyndale-Biscoe observed, and this delicacy reflected a horror of muscles because muscles signified physical labour in a culture that prized book-learning and clerical occupations. Thus, building muscles through athletic activity was not only the development of a new aesthetic of the male body but also the creation of a new attitude towards work and workers, and implicitly a critique of the subversive potential of intellectuals in a colonial environment. 'Through athletics', Tyndale-Biscoe wrote, 'we hope to raise up useful citizens instead of first-class blood-suckers'.[39]

Yet the promotion of sport, the instrument of those other changes, was the most difficult of the various battles that the missionaries fought over the bodies of the boys in their charge. Some sports came easier than others. So, for example, Tyndale-Biscoe observed that cricket met with relatively little resistance in Srinagar because the boys had seen Europeans playing the game and associated it with social prestige. Cricket was not, however, universally welcomed by boys who were forced to play it at various colonial schools. In spite of the eventual popularity of the game at Aligarh, compulsory cricket there nearly died an early death because of the students' indifference and their reluctance to pay a special fee.[40] At the ICC a cadet named Amar Singh made no secret of his intense dislike for the sport.[41] Lloyd and Susanne Rudolph, who have been working on Amar Singh's diary, have suggested that Amar Singh's Rajput background made him dislike any sport that did not involve riding a horse. The connection between Rajput identity and dislike of

cricket is best taken with a pinch of salt. M K Gandhi, who was certainly not a
Rajput but who is another favourite of the Rudolphs, was also a reluctant
schoolboy cricketer,[42] while Amar Singh's Rajput contemporary Ranjitsinhji
became one of the most celebrated cricketers of his generation. It seems then
that where compulsory sports are unpopular, it may be the compulsion of the
body – rather than the particular sport itself – that is the major factor in the
students' response.

To a great extent this compulsion explains the violent opposition that was
generated by the missionaries' efforts to introduce the CMS boys to football,
boxing and aquatic sports.[43] Nobody moved when the students were first
herded on to the field and ordered to chase after a football. It was only when
the principal brought in men armed with staffs and threatened to beat the
reluctant athletes that the game began. Tyndale-Biscoe's description of the
episode, like much of his narrative of the CMS, is rendered unreliable by his
overall triumphalism and must be read with caution and against the grain.
Nevertheless, it reveals a physical drama that included the spectacular disrup-
tion of clothing norms: 'Not only did they kick the unholy leather, but with
hands and claws they fought each other to get near it. *Pugarees* flew out like
pennants, clogs and shoes shot into the air. Football had started in Kashmir'.[44]

That was not the end of the struggle between students and the missionaries.
In an athletic variation on machine-breaking in the early factory, the boys
used pins to puncture the football. It would appear that Tyndale-Biscoe exaggerated his students' fondness for cricket as well. In the effete tradition of the
seditious petition, some boys at the school went over the principal's head and
wrote a letter of complaint to the CMS headquarters in London, expressing
their resentment of the athletic regime and its enforcers:

> We, the inhabitants – Hindus and Muhamadans of Kashmir – want
> this, that if Mr. Biscoe is allowed to remain in Kashmir as a Principal
> of the school, not a single boy will attend it, and the Society will have
> to close it for good. Therefore, please, sir, transfer Mr. Biscoe for
> he is exceedingly a bad man, illiterate, deceitful, ill-mannered, un-
> cultured, cunning, and a man too fond of cricket.[45]

The possibility that the school might be boycotted was quite real. It indicates
that the politics of compulsory sports extended beyond the school to the community of parents, neighbours, caste-fellows and casual onlookers. When the
missionaries made it mandatory that the boys learn to swim, parents threatened to withdraw their sons from the school, and a great deal of persuasion
and pressure had to be applied before they were dissuaded. Multiple and
seemingly incompatible discourses could supply ammunition for families

determined to fight the missionaries' claims on the bodies of their children. Some parents brought forth medical certificates as well as statements from astrologers 'proving' that their sons would die if they entered the water.[46] The introduction of rowing as a sport triggered an instant crisis. To the missionaries, rowing carried the self-evident moral virtues of disciplined teamwork (quite literally, the ability to 'pull together') and physical exertion while at the same time generating edifying visions of boat races at Oxford and Cambridge. The general public in Srinagar, however, tended to associate the activity with low-status boatmen who ferried people and cargo across the lakes and rivers of the region. The English master who conducted the first demonstration was greeted with cries of 'Coolie Sahib, Coolie Sahib', and when the first boatload of students was persuaded to row themselves down the river, the banks and bridges of the Jhelum were lined by a jeering and thoroughly entertained crowd. The rowers drew their shawls over their faces to avoid recognition and disgrace.[47]

A more effective challenge came in 1901 when more than 300 students and many of the Indian staff quit the CMS in protest against the school's efforts to involve the students in a different manipulation of bodies, purity and pollution. The focus here was sanitation work and corpse removal during a typhoid epidemic. The missionaries believed that Annie Besant had instigated this particular rebellion in order to lure the boys to her rival school, but clearly, even if the Theosophists had been involved, they found a receptive audience in the parents and staff. It is worth noting that the physical rituals of epidemic medicine and the rituals of the athletic regime were closely linked at the CMS, where sporting events became more frequent during outbreaks of cholera and typhoid. For example, student boatmen were instructed to row up and down the river singing and shouting in public displays of cheer and defiance. Betraying a vision of sport that is reminiscent of the ironic/defiant 'football assaults' of the Great War,[48] Tyndale-Biscoe wrote: 'our boys died like others, but their places in the boats were filled each day by others'.[49]

What is evident from this narrative is that in spite of the hostility of parents, students, Theosophists and germs, the missionaries were able to find enough students to man the boats. After the desertions of 1901, which left the CMS with barely half a dozen students, the school eventually recovered. Clearly, resistance was neither uniform nor all-pervasive.

Contesting and claiming the Indian sporting body

The limited and contextual nature of resistance is shown by the fact that Indians often voiced their support for the goals of colonial educators of the Indian body. Echoing the CMS missionaries' antipathy towards jewelry, a

Rajkumar College graduate named Nasrullah Khan wrote approvingly about similar efforts underway at his old school:

> In this country, people not only consider jewelry as an ornament to female beauty, as people in other countries do, but they also regard it as necessary for men of high rank to adorn themselves with them. One can well understand and appreciate the view that jewelry gives an added charm to female beauty. But it seems most ludicrous to think that ornaments, as for instance, earrings, bracelets, and anklets, make a man more attractive, or enhance his personal charms. On the contrary, they merely make him look effeminate and ridiculous.[50]

Nasrullah Khan's is the voice of the recent convert to colonial pedagogy. There can be little doubt that he had wide support. The British discourse of Indian effeminacy generated an obsessive search on the part of Indian males for properly masculine bodies, and this search led them to the gymnasium, the wrestling *akhara*, the playing field and the military recruitment office.[51] But this obsession needs to be placed alongside the anxiety about 'English' sports in colonial schools, for it was not just Kashmiri parents who complained that their sons were wasting time that was better spent on books. Critics of Aligarh cricket made the same point, and many college principals were themselves not convinced that running around with a bat and a ball was worth any serious investment of time and money.[52] The hesitation is most palpable in journals with Indian editors and readerships. In 1896, the apogee of Vivekananda's career as the missionary of physical nationalism, the *Bankura Darpan* noted that cricket and football had been introduced in local boys' schools 'as forms of exercise' and expressed doubts as to whether 'these forms of play are suited to native boys'.[53] A few days later a more prestigious Bengali paper, the *Bangabasi*, declared that it was not at all opposed to the principle of educating the body. In fact, the editors implied, such education was desperately needed in the colonial era. They wrote:

> In days gone by, the people of this country were not so effeminate as they have become. In every village, there were gymnasiums in which wrestling, fencing with *lathis* and other athletic exercises were regularly performed, and the youth of the village took a lively interest in them. Strong and stalwart young men were not then a rarity in the Bengali villages. The people were not so helpless as they are now, and they could successfully defend themselves against dacoits. The Musalman Government, moreover, was not ingenious enough to invent an Arms Act, and people could keep and use shields and

swords, guns and spears without taking out passes for them. Nowadays, however, the people have been disarmed, and have become helpless and effeminate. They have become fond of service, and they detest manly sports and exercises. Having given up all manly sports and exercises, they have now to depend entirely upon the police for the protection of their property and the honor of their women. English education has not civilized us; it has made us puppets and tools in the hands of others.[54]

This apparent self-loathing, which John Rosselli and Tanika Sarkar have identified as the language of a class asserting its hegemonistic aspirations in colonial society, was not a peculiarly Bengali neurosis, as almost identical sentiments had been expressed by the Bombay paper *Jagadhitechchhu* earlier that year.[55] Echoing these newspaper articles with uncanny precision is the voice of Nasrullah Khan:

The Rajkumars are not usually so fond of physical training as could be wished. In too many cases they simply drive about and consequently do not get sufficient exercise. In some principalities, however, as for instance in Rajputana, every Kumar from his childhood is taught like his ancestors some soldierly exercise, such as gymnastics, fencing, riding and archery. But in almost all other cases the Kumars spend their time in idle talk. What a contrast there is in this respect, at all events between a Rajkumar of past times and of these days? In former days every Rajputra, whether Hindu or Mahommedan, was from his youth initiated into the art of fencing, tilting, wrestling and similar manly sports; but nowadays such exercises are seldom encouraged and so are becoming obsolete. In olden times it was a part of the education, not only those who participated in wars and battles, to be instructed in such manly exercises, but of other Kumars also. It was on expertness in these accomplishments that every Rajputra prided himself.[56]

Nasrullah Khan went on to describe the typical soldier in contemporary Kathiawar as a coward and an opium user, dressed in an uniform that gave the impression of 'a scarecrow set to frighten the birds away'. Like the *Bangabasi*, he saw British rule as a precipitator of this decline in Indian physical culture although, like Tyndale-Biscoe, he believed that the damage was an accidental consequence of imperial pacification.[57] He supported education regimes such as that of Rajkumar College because he saw them as reparative rather than damaging. Some Indians, he noted, needed this education more urgently than others. Specifically, he identified the junior members of princely families as pathologically idle and as a consequence physically weak and morally depraved, given over to opium and cannabis. These habits not only marked them physically, making them appear 'seedy' and 'brutalized' (a description of the cannabis user that was apparently borrowed from the colonial lunatic asylum), but also rendered them politically unfit and socially useless.[58]

How do we reconcile the desire for physical 'revival' with the suspicion of the physical training promoted in colonial schools such as Rajkumar College and the CMS? Part of the answer lies in Reno, Nevada, where on 4 July 1910 the black heavyweight boxer Jack Johnson defeated his white opponent Jim Jeffries. The Jackson–Jeffries fight was a major event in America, not least because Johnson's victory was followed by race riots in several cities, in which fair numbers of people were injured and killed. The event was closely followed by the native press in India. These journalists understood exactly what was at stake, as they knew that Jeffries had declared that his mission was to defend the 'athletic superiority of the white race'. The British government, together with the South African authorities, tried to censor photographs of Johnson's victory, and Winston Churchill's mild criticism of the government on this issue was welcomed by Indian observers.[59] In an era when physical confrontations between Indians and whites were an everyday reality in the streets and railway carriages of the Raj, the political significance of Johnson's victory, the mob violence and the British discomfiture was ripe for appropriation by the native press. The *Gujarati* wrote: 'The Johnson–Jeffries fight conclusively proves that the Western nations have not yet advanced from their uncivilized condition and that they still delight in barbarity'. Elaborating upon this theme, the *Indian Spectator* asked:

> What did the riots mean? They meant that the Americans not only claimed superiority to the Negroes in every respect, even in physical strength, but they could not brook the idea of an individual Negro developing larger and tougher muscles than an American known for his strength. Jealousy in mere physical strength argues the depth of barbarism.[60]

There are, it would seem, two things going on here. One is that for Indians, as for colonial educators, the athlete's body could function as a measure, a mirror and a writing-pad of civilization/barbarism. Just as it was apparent to the CMS missionaries that Indians were morally inferior because they had no muscles or rules of disciplined physical conduct, it was clear to Indians that white athletes, governments and societies did not always conduct themselves according to the rules. The barbarism of the enemy thus lay in the rules as well as in their violation: in the raw physical violence of the boxing match as well as in the inability of white Americans to accept the outcome of the match. The same formula for barbarism is found in the film *Lagaan,* where it is the English who try to 'fix' the cricket match and physically assault one of the Indian players, and where cricket itself is depicted as a collection of bizarre, arbitrary and silly customs. It is only the black/Indian victory that redeems the game, and this is the redemption that comes with ownership. By then, of course, the game has been transformed almost beyond recognition, not only because the wrong colour has won but also because the right to make the rules has been usurped by the winners.

The other significance of the Indian reaction to a boxing match in Nevada is that the physical confrontation inherent in athletic activities re-enacted those other clashes of bodies against bodies in colonial India and in Jim Crow America. The everyday rituals of defeat and humiliation could be reworked and replayed in such prominent victories as Johnson's triumph and the Mohun Bagan victory of 1911, or in the sly pleasure of tripping up the English policeman during a football match (described ruefully by George Orwell in *Shooting an Elephant*). Here, you could quite literally attack the body of the colonizer or feel yourself subjected to attack. In either case, it would be an experience of what Appadurai has called 'the erotics of nationalism'[61] – the physical pleasure of a political conflict.

Like the missionaries at the CMS, Indians who experienced or commented on the colonial school wanted to create useful bodies that would be capable of modern, disciplined activities both inside and outside the boxing ring and foot-ball field. Nasrullah Khan wanted the junior princes to go to the gymnasium, not so that they could be great gymnasts but so that they might become bureaucrats and barristers (he himself became one of the latter). Under the circumstances, the battles over athletic programmes did not really reflect any fundamental difference of opinion about the value of the disciplined body. They reflected a contest over the site of the education, the body of the individual student as well as the school, and a reaction against the political identity of the educator.

These battles over student bodies and athletic programmes reflected an awareness on both sides that physical education was, among other things, the inculcation of loyalty. A body that swam, wore boots or removed corpses against the wishes of the parent literally demonstrated a particular loyalty in the politics of colonialism, just as a body that refused to do these things demonstrated the opposite choice. Just as one set of decisions infuriated the CMS missionaries, so the other set infuriated the parents. The same question applied in the evaluation of useful bodies: to whom, or rather, to which side in colonial society would the bodies be useful? It is quite clear that editorial opinion in the native press saw the answer as central to its judgement of the products of athletic education. When Ranjitsinhji, who began his cricket education at Rajkumar College, became the ruler of Nawanagar in 1907, the native press almost universally welcomed him and made specific references to his education, declaring that a great sportsman could only be a great ruler.[62] Within two years the newspapers had reversed their opinions and had decided that the true allegiance of the cricketer–prince lay with England and his English friends rather than with his 'own' people. Ranjitsinhji was now held responsible for doing nothing to help the people of Nawanagar and his cricketing background came to be seen as a mark of moral failure and political unfitness.[63] It was not that Indian opinion about cricket had suddenly changed. It was that the cricketer, the useful body, had shown himself to be useful to the wrong side.

Similarly, when the *Bankura Darpan* and the *Bangabasi* grumbled about cricket and waxed nostalgic about 'lost' indigenous athletic tradition, they did not articulate any genuine anxiety that cricket bats were not as Indian as *lathis* or that Indian boys were more comfortable in the *akhara* than on the football field. Nor did they express 'self-respect as well as self-indulgence', as Mangan has suggested in his analysis of resistance at the CMS.[64] What they voiced, rather, was a perception that the football field, the cricket field and the boxing ring were located in an alien geography: the British-controlled school, the whites-only club or, for that matter, colonial society itself. The *akhara*, in contrast, was not usually attached to schools such as the CMS or Rajkumar College, which frequently drew the ire of the native press. ('If inability to join in English games makes an Indian unfit to mix in English society, it is better for Indian princes to avoid such society altogether', the *Sahachar* editorialized about Rajkumar College in 1896.) The football fields of the Ramkrishna Mission and Mohun Bagan, and even the cricket fields of Aligarh, drew less opposition than the boating events of the CMS because the former were not directly under British control. They were in a sense 'liberated' arenas, like the boxing ring in Reno and the cricket field in *Lagaan*, which could function as metaphors of the reconquered nation. There the sport, the athlete and the stadium had all been reclaimed by the legitimate owners and redirected towards legitimate political purposes.

Conclusion

To return very briefly to the satire of 'The Sporting Man' in *The Trident*, it would seem that the writer of the essay did not attack sport at all. The English middle class was then so deeply immersed in the culture of athleticism that a blanket critique of the value of sport on a university campus would have been ludicrous. Nevertheless, the Victorian era was also a time when the middle class in England aggressively colonized sports such as cricket and football, imposing its own values upon these games.[65] There was room for conflict on the playing field between discernible groups in English society, and the physical person of the athlete could serve as a page on which these groups inscribed their criticisms of one another. Similarly, the playground in colonial India was occasionally a battlefield, not only between conflicting views of the native body but also between conflicting claims on the body of the young Indian male.

The first set of conflicts had to do with the moral meanings that were attached to the bodies of the students in all manifestations: in their dress, their cleanliness, their musculature, their movements, their stillness, their sounds and their silences. In this confrontation, there seems evidence of a fairly rapid, albeit incomplete victory on the part of colonial educators in the sense that the elite Indians who attended the schools came to accept most of the moral meanings of physical appearance and behaviour. The boys learned to wear boots and boxing gloves and turbans of the right kind, to accept the importance of punctuality and precise drill, and to obey the umpire in silence even when the umpire was wrong. They learned to swim and play football, they learned to remove corpses in times of cholera, and they learned that these were noble, manly and modern activities that set them apart from, and above, those who did not do these things.

The second set of conflicts had to do with who owned these activities, the educated bodies, and the theatre in which these bodies played. It is a mistake, at this stage, to speak of 'English' or 'Indian' bodily habits. The ownership of the sports and the bodies was continuously contested and what determined ownership at any given moment was the combination of victory and venue. When Johnson defeated Jeffries, boxing was an Indian sport, and football was Indian in Calcutta in 1911. When cricket was played at the ICC and under compulsion it was an alien activity. The objective of those who criticized colonial sports was not to banish the new discipline; rather it was to assert ownership, or at least a measure of control, over a resource that was at least as useful to nationalist fantasies as it was to the colonialist.

What emerged from these conflicts is a set of cultural artifacts that was quite new. Lord Harris was right when he argued (to Nasrullah Khan's great annoyance) that the English public school and its primary product, the public school boy, could not be reproduced in India. This is not to agree with Harris, who was convinced that Indian bodies and climates were fundamentally different from their English counterparts. It is because the conflicts over interpretation and ownership necessarily altered the product that resulted from the manipulation of the body. This is where we see what might be interpreted as the triumph of the unruly student over the rules of the teacher. Cricket and football as they are played and imagined in India and Pakistan today are very different sports from what British educators tried to teach their students. At least some of the venues have been liberated, the body language has changed and the 'Pandit eye' has returned. There is now a great reluctance to obey the umpire automatically, especially when the umpire is perceived as a white man favouring white athletes. The modern Indian cricket fan is not always the product of elite schools where C L R James' puritanical 'public school code' might have taken hold.[66] He, and increasingly she, is often a product of the less prestigious schools, a recent migrant to the city, an immigrant in Indian colonies such as Sharjah and Toronto, or an 'export–import' businessman who has gatecrashed the clubhouse in the era of economic liberalization without bothering to learn the rules of the well-behaved. These are not so much the products of the CMS missionaries or other educators of the colonial period. Rather, they are the children of the peasant cricketers of *Lagaan*, imagining and celebrating their mythological ancestors.

Bibliography

Alter, J, 1992, *The Wrestler's Body : Identity and Ideology in North India*, Berkeley, University of California Press.

Appadurai, A, 1996, 'Playing With Modernity', in C Breckenridge (ed.), *Consuming Modernity*, Delhi, Oxford University Press.

Cannadine, D, 2001, *Ornamentalism: How The British Saw Their Empire*, Oxford, Oxford University Press.

Cashman, R, 1980, *Players, Patrons and the Crowd*, Delhi, Orient Longman.

Cohn, B, 1997, *Colonialism and its Forms of Knowledge*, Delhi, Oxford University Press.

Collini, S, 1985, 'The Idea of Character in Victorian Political Thought', *Transactions of the Royal Historical Society*, 5th series, 35.

Copley, A, 1997, *Religions in Conflict: Ideology, Cultural Contact and Conversion in Late Colonial India*, Delhi, Oxford University Press.

Dimeo, P, 2001, 'Contemporary Developments in Indian Football', *Contemporary South Asia*, 10/2.

Donzelot, J, 1979, *The Policing of Families*, New York, Pantheon.

Ernst, W, 1991, *Mad Tales from the Raj: The European Insane in British India*, London, Routledge.

Ernst, W, 1999, 'Out of Sight and Out of Mind: Insanity in Early Nineteenth-Century British India', in Melling, J and Forsyth, B eds., *Insanity, Insitutions and Society*, London, Routledge, pp. 245–67.

Foucault, M, 1979, *Discipline and Punish*, New York, Vintage Books.

Fussell, P, 1975, *The Great War and Modern Memory*, Oxford, Oxford University Press.

Gandhi, M K, 1957, *Autobiography*, Boston, Beacon Press.

Guha, R, 1992, *Wickets in the East*, Delhi, Oxford University Press.

Haley, B, 1978, *The Healthy Body and Victorian Culture*, Cambridge, MA, Harvard University Press.

Harrison, Mark, 1999, *Climates and Constitutions*, Delhi, Oxford University Press.

Ignatieff, M, 1983, 'State, Civil Society and Total Institutions', in Cohen and Scull (eds.), *Social Control and the State*, Oxford, Robertson.

James, C L R, 1963, *Beyond A Boundary*, London, Stanley Paul and Co.

Khan, N, 1904, *The Ruling Chiefs of Western India and the Rajkumar College*, Bombay, Claridge.

Kumar, N, 2000, *Lessons from Schools: The History of Education in Banares*, Delhi, Sage.

Lelyveld, D, 1996, *Aligarh's First Generation*, Delhi, Oxford University Press.

Mangan, J A, 1986, *The Games Ethic and Imperialism*, New York, Viking Penguin.

McLane, J, 1977, *Indian Nationalism and the Early Congress*, Princeton, Princeton University Press.

Metcalf, B, 1982, *Islamic Revival in British India: Deoband, 1860–1900*, Princeton, Princeton University Press.

Mills, J, 2000, *Madness, Cannabis and Colonialism*, Basingstoke, Macmillan.

Mills, J, 2003 (forthcoming), *Sport in South Asia*, London, Anthem Press.

Nandy, A, 1983, *The Intimate Enemy: Loss and Recovery of Self Under Colonialism*, Delhi, Oxford University Press.

Redfield, P, 2000, *Space in the Tropics: From Convicts to Rockets in French Guiana*, Berkeley, University of California Press.

Rosselli, J, 1980, 'The Self-Image of Effeteness: Physical Education and Nationalism in Nineteenth Century Bengal', Past and Present, no. 86.

Rudolph, S, and Rudolph, L (eds.), 2000, *Reversing the Gaze: Amar Singh's Diary, A Colonial Subject's Narrative of Imperial India*, Delhi, Oxford University Press.

Sandiford, K, 1994, *Cricket and the Victorians*, London, Scholar Press.

Sarkar, T, 1992, 'The Hindu Wife and the Hindu Nation: Domesticity and Nationalism in Nineteenth-Century Bengal', *Studies in History*, 8/2.

Sen, S, 2000, *Disciplining Punishment: Colonialism and Convict Society in the Andaman Islands*, Delhi, Oxford University Press.

Sinha, M, 1995, *Colonial Masculinity: The 'Manly Englishman' and the 'Effeminate Bengali' in the Late Nineteenth Century*, Manchester, Manchester University Press.

Streets, H, October 2000, 'A Fine and Brave People', paper presented at Annual Conference of South Asia Studies, Madison, Wisconsin.

Tyndale-Biscoe, E D, 1930, *Fifty Years Against the Stream: The Story of a School in Kashmir*, Mysore, Wesleyan Mission Press.

Vishwanathan, G, 1987, *Masks of Conquest: Literary Study and British Rule in India*, New York, Columbia University Press.

Oriental and India Office Collection records: Government of Bombay Political Department files; Native Newspaper Report files (NNR), Bombay.

Notes

1. Foucault 1979, pp. 135–69.
2. Donzelot 1979; Mills 2000 and Ernst 1991, 1999. For studies on the nineteenth-century prison see Ignatieff 1983 and Sen 2000.
3. Lelyveld 1996; Metcalf 1982; Kumar 2000.
4. Alter 1992; McLane 1977; Guha 1992.
5. *The Trident*, 1 (1891), p. 6.
6. See Haley 1978, p. 4.
7. See Collini 1985 and James 1963.
8. Cannadine 2001, pp. 41–57.
9. Rudolph and Rudolph 2000, p. 233.
10. Ibid., p. 261.
11. Bombay (Political) Files, 1913.
12. See Khan 1904, p. 26.
13. See Harrison 1999, pp. 1–24, and Redfield 2000, pp. 49–108.
14. See Tyndale-Biscoe 1930, p. v.
15. Sinha 1995, pp. 1–25.
16. See also Khan 1904, pp. 11–12.
17. Streets 2000.
18. Nandy 1983, pp. 14–16.
19. Tyndale-Biscoe 1930, p. 10.
20. Rudolph and Rudolph 2000, pp. 317–51.
21. Lelyveld 1996, pp. 166–87.
22. Vishwanathan 1987.
23. Khan 1904, pp. 13–16.
24. Ibid., pp. 33–5; Tyndale-Biscoe 1930, p. 1.
25. Tyndale-Biscoe 1930, p. 52.
26. Ibid., p. 8.
27. See Copley 1997, p. 9.
28. Lelyveld 1996, p. 262.

29. See Tyndale-Biscoe 1930, p. xv.
30. Ibid., p. 11.
31. Ibid., p. 13.
32. See Cohn 1997, pp. 117–29.
33. See Cashman 1980, pp. 1–10.
34. For example *Cricket* (18 June 1896).
35. Dimeo 2001.
36. *Cricket* (31 March 1898).
37. Tyndale-Biscoe 1930, p. 14.
38. Ibid., p. 22.
39. Ibid., p. 23.
40. Lelyveld 1996, pp. 254–5.
41. Rudolph and Rudolph 2000, p. 276.
42. Gandhi 1957 p. 15.
43. See also Mills and Dimeo 2003 (forthcoming).
44. Tyndale-Biscoe 1930, p. 20.
45. Ibid., p. 23.
46. Ibid., p. 24.
47. Ibid., p. 27.
48. See Fussell 1975, pp. 26–8.
49. Tyndale-Biscoe 1930, p. 59.
50. Khan 1904, p. 118.
51. See Sinha 1995, pp. 69–99.
52. See Lelyveld 1996, pp. 256–7.
53. NNR, Bengal 1896.
54. Ibid.
55. Sarkar 1992; Rosselli 1980; NNR, Bombay 1896.
56. Khan 1904, pp. 11–12.
57. Ibid.
58. Ibid., pp. 67, 97–8. See also Mills 2000.
59. *Gujarati*, NNR, Bombay 1910.
60. *Indian Spectator*, NNR, Bombay 1910.
61. Appadurai 1996.
62. *Patriot, Indian Spectator* (February–March 1907), NNR, Bombay 1907.
63. *Gujarati*, NNR, Bombay 1909.
64. Mangan 1986.
65. See Sandiford 1994, pp. 1–2.
66. James 1963, pp. 39–46.

4

Body as Target, Violence as Treatment: Psychiatric Regimes in Colonial and Post-Colonial India

James H Mills

The asylum reduces differences, represses vice, eliminates irregularities.[1]

Introduction

This chapter will begin to consider the history of psychiatric treatment in India and will focus on the issue of violence in so-called 'therapeutic' regimes. The argument is that the body has been central to psychiatric regimes in South Asia since the nineteenth century and that this focus on the corporal has continued into the post-colonial period. A range of interventions has been imposed on the body of inmates of asylums in order to force them in the first place to submit to the authority of the medical staff. This achieved, the doctors have then proceeded with further physical interventions aimed at transforming the behaviour of the patient into something that approximated the medical officer's ideal of a useful and rational individual. In order to 'reduce difference', 'repress vice' and 'eliminate irregularities', the body was the target of the asylum.

Psychiatric treatment in India

The Asylum, I am to remark, should not be merely a place where the insane may be comfortably confined, but a hospital for their treatment and cure.[2]

There is plenty of evidence that the British authorities were intent upon providing institutions in India in which those members of the local populations that they encountered and deemed to be mentally ill would receive treatment, with recovery from their illness as the ultimate goal. The superintendent at Bareilly, for example, admitted that it was his job to see to it that 'in the management of this asylum attention is given to the comfort of the patients as well as to the cure of the disease'.[3]

It seems that, in the eyes of the British, 'recovery' or 'cure'[4] in the Indian insane was denoted by an exhibition of certain qualities in the individual linked to self-regulation and productivity, or what might be described as 'the Victorian fetishes, of 'discipline', 'routine', and 'order' and of course 'hard work'.[5] Throughout the British administration it was considered self-evident that the best way to set up institutions to effect that state was on the lines followed by model establishments in the West. Superintendents wrote: 'as we have now a good working establishment, I hope that we shall be able to carry out still further improvements, and in time bring the Asylum as near to the English standard as the circumstances of the country admits'.[6] Those nearer the top of the bureaucracy also recognized that:

> . . . everything that constitutes a remedial institution on the modern European footing has to be introduced and exercised for the first time. The classification of the insane, the regulation of their common social life under the cottage system, their recreation, their education, their cure, their employment in various descriptions of appropriate labour, all the processes of benevolence and science have to be studied and carried into effect.[7]

As such it is no surprise to see the virtues of moral management, physical treatment and the reintroduction to labour being extolled in the asylum reports.[8]

> Herein lies the foundation of the good management of a Lunatic Asylum for natives. The hope of release, avoidance of everything that might annoy or vex the patients, unremitting watching, and silent attention to their complaints and ramblings will gain perfect control over the noisiest and most troublesome. The unreal and often rude speech must be borne, because to attempt corrections or to be angry with them will only aggravate and destroy control over the patient.
>
> I believe that scrupulous cleanliness, liberal diet, affording them means of recreation or occupation, and attention to all the functions of the body are the foundation of the medical treatment and moral management of lunatics.
>
> The insane are not slow in sagacity and the power of comprehending what is done for their good and thus will appreciate kindness.[9]

The way in which the British medical officers targeted the inmate's body using the therapeutic regimes developed in the nineteenth century in order to assert themselves and their agendas over those in the asylums will be explored by examining the two stages in the process of assertion: control and reform.

Controlling the Indian inmate

It must not be supposed, because the labor of an asylum is rightly called voluntary, that the character of a Native, naturally indolent and now exalted by mania, or depressed by melancholy, is of necessity by admission to an Asylum, in a moment so transformed that industry becomes a pleasure to him. It is of the essence of his treatment that he be brought, by resolution of purpose and persistent effort, within the discipline of the place if he do not at once conform to it.[10]

The first task for the medical officer on being confronted with a new inmate was to establish authority over that individual and to ensure that his or her behaviour and body met a basic standard from which the procedures of reform could take place. The body was the first site to be prepared.

On a patient being brought to the asylum he or she is placed in a single room for two or three days, well washed, carefully fed, the state and condition of the excretions and secretions examined . . . where there is any obvious bodily disorder found to exist, appropriate medicines are prescribed for its removal.[11]

The body was to be ordered and made efficient through the regulation of its functioning, so cleanliness and eating were emphasized and the working of the body was closely observed. 'Every patient is daily bathed', insisted the superintendent at Cuttack,[12] and the superintendent at Dacca elaborated on the regime in his institution:

The lunatics, both males and females, are bathed daily . . . The dirty and intractable patients are rubbed with khullee (mustard oil culee) made into a thin paste with water and then washed under the shower bath. This cleanses the skin and leaves it soft, and is better than soap which makes the skin dry . . . one of the day keepers is particularly set apart for the bathing duties.[13]

The suggestion that cleanliness was imposed on the patients comes through even more clearly in the assertion of the Surgeon-Major at Delhi, who stressed that

. . . cleanliness is enforced both as regards the wards, the grounds and the persons of the lunatics. Nothing can prevent entirely some of the most debased of the lunatics from being guilty of filthy actions, but they are cleaned and washed and all traces of pollution at once removed.[14]

Coercive measures were also used to ensure that a patient's reluctance to feed or be fed was overcome. The superintendent at Colaba reported in 1875:

. . . there were 6 cases of refusal of food. One was of a very obstinate and protracted nature in a young Parsi suffering from acute mania; he had to be fed with the stomach pump regularly for about two months; he was in consequence very much reduced. One day he was accidentally given some beer, which had the desired effect, as he began to eat soon after of his own accord.[15]

Indeed, the administration of nutrition could be more violent still: 'Tea was also given by injection through the rectum'.[16] In other words, patients had no control over their own intake; their diet was determined by the colonial medical officer and was then forcibly administered if necessary.

The body was not just subjected to washing and feeding, it was also deliberately rested. Dr Wylie at Ahmedabad is frank in accounting for his use of certain drugs: 'Hydrate of Chloral . . . is a useful addition to the available means of controlling insomnia'.[17] The medical officer in charge of the asylum at Moorshedabad mentions 'the administration of Morphia to allay undue excitement and procure sleep', while the superintendent at Madras notes that 'a little wine or arrack at bedtime induces a quiet sleep, and I do not consider the use of opiates desirable where simple means can be employed to effect the desired result'.[18]

Vaccination of the asylum inmates also seems to have been routine in many cases. This is significant, as David Arnold has demonstrated that vaccination in the prisons of India was an unashamed assertion of the colonial will as, 'at a time when vaccination against smallpox still encountered strong resistance and evasion in India, it was compulsory for prisoners'.[19] John Murray at the asylum in Madras mentioned that 'vaccination has been carefully attended to' and Arthur Payne in Calcutta indicates that not much choice was given to the patients: 'Vaccination has been practised in every case'.[20] In the Bombay Presidency,

. . . at Ahmedabad and Hyderabad all the inmates are protected; but although the other Superintendents make no mention of vaccination,

the fact that there has not been a single case of small pox recorded
from any of the asylums even during a period when that disease was
exceptionally prevalent elsewhere, and even in their vicinity, would
seem to point to the effectual measures of protection having been
adopted by all.[21]

These processes of treating the body were all accompanied by close surveillance of the body in order to gauge its progress towards a certain standard. In
his report of 1872, Dr Penny at the Delhi institution notes the importance of
physiological monitoring, or what he calls 'carefully watching all the functions
of the body'.[22] One way to give this surveillance a scientific and empirical
footing was devised in the Madras Presidency:

> In 1874 I ordered the introduction of the system of weighing the
> patients monthly. This has been attended with great advantages, as
> an inspection of the register at once attracts attention to any patient
> needing care on account of deterioration of general health, or who
> may require a change of diet.[23]

Overall then the policy of medical officers was to tend to the patient's physical
state. This could easily be seen as an act of benevolence or just good sense on
the part of officials dealing with admissions who were often starving or ill: 'A
very large proportion, however, of our patients require no other treatment
than good feeding'.[24] It might also be suggested that the emphasis on the
physical simply reflects the limitations of doctors whose stock in trade it was to
deal with the body rather than the mind. However, it is necessary to consider
more extreme examples of the medical officer at the asylum asserting himself
over the body of the Indian inmate in order to fully comprehend the project
of treating the patient's physique. Consider, for example, treatments like that
meted out to the patients in the asylum of the Civil Surgeon of Rangoon:

> The very obnoxious practice of masterbation [sic] which is the cause
> of insanity in many cases, and which aggravates the disease, is very
> common amongst the inmates of the asylum here. I have perplexed
> myself about the vice and in former years endeavoured to prevent
> it by blistering the penis with crotenal etc., but without effect, and
> various medicines were given in vain with the view of moderating or
> repressing the desire.
>
> During the past year I have tried Dr. Yellowless's mode of preven-
> tion very recently practiced in asylums at home, and so far as it has
> gone, I am very much satisfied with the result.
>
> The suggestion was founded on the anatomical fact that the

prepuce was anatomically necessary for the erection of the penis. Its anatomical use was to give a cover for the increased size of the organ. If you prevented the prepuce going to that use, you would make erections so painful that it would be practically impossible, and emissions therefore unlikely.

The operation is very simple: the prepuce at the very root of the glans is pierced with an ordinary silver needle, the ends of which are tied together.[25]

This is an overtly and explicitly disciplinary measure in the context of which the control assumed by the medical officer over the feeding, the cleaning, the sleep and the blood of the asylum patient can be better understood. The legitimate use of the Indian's body was being decided by the British officer: the superintendent was assuming control of the inmate's physique through the infliction of pain and depriving him/her of the right to decide what to do with it. The Indian was being denied access to his/her personal physical experience of the world and was being prevented from using his/her own body to convey their own messages or satisfy their own desires. Quite simply, the Indian inmate's body had been colonized and it was to be disciplined. The doctors had their own ideas about what should be done with the body of the Indian whom they considered insane. These ideas are evident in the description of recovery on the case note of Mukhsoodally Khan, who was admitted for mania and suffered an attack of fever:

For several months past this man has improved in health, has been quiet + well conducted and assisted in the garden – he is stout and strong – all bodily functions properly performed + he does not appear to be labouring under any delusion. His relatives are anxious to remove him + I therefore, as he has been well for months, discharge him cured.[26]

There is no reason on a document containing information about an individual who was thought to be suffering from mental disorder to include all that information about the man's physical condition unless it is considered significant evidence in connection with the decision to discharge. If it is significant evidence in connection with the decision to discharge, then it must be because it is indicative of the man having achieved the condition desired by the asylum. In other words, the asylum was seeking to produce stout, strong and ordered bodies, the result of all that feeding, cleaning and chemical treating.

The production of a disciplined body was not the only end to which the efforts of the asylum were directed. The behaviour of the patient, 'exalted by mania or depressed by melancholy', needed to be similarly brought within the discipline of the asylum and under the control of the superintendent before the more complex procedures of reform could be attempted. This control was asserted through rousing or subduing the patient according to whether the patient was withdrawn and unenthusiastic or over-excited and animated.

Official policy at this period was to follow European theories of controlling the patient through kindness and coaxing. In 1877 it was written in an end of year report that

> . . . the system adopted in the asylum is what is called the 'non-restraint' system, the object of which is the humane and enlightened curative treatment of the insane. As is well known, this system was inaugurated by Pinel and Esquirol in France and by Charlesworth, Hill and Connolly in England.[27]

Almost ten years earlier the elements of 'humane and enlightened' approaches were described by an asylum superintendent in the North-West Provinces: 'Harshness and violence form no part of the system; coercion is seldom if ever resorted to; and the inmates are managed and quieted entirely by kindness, firmness, order, regularity and occupation'.[28]

Despite this rhetoric, restraint and violence in a variety of forms were sanctioned by the medical officers in charge of the institutions. There were superintendents who simply ignored fashionable opinion and went ahead with mechanical restraint: 'When refractory patients are confined in these wards it is generally found necessary to secure them with strait waistcoats, as most of them are very destructive'.[29] Surgeon-Major Payne in Bengal was similarly dismissive of non-restraint, although he was more concerned to justify his opinions:

> So much has been said and written of late years respecting the treatment of lunatics without personal restraint, and popular feeling has been so largely enlisted in its favour, that non-restraint has given its name to the modern system and has come to be an expression for every thing that is kind and humane, while all that savours of restraint is condemned in the popular mind as belonging to an age of barbarism . . . It would seem however that the time has now come when it may be said, without fear of outside indignation, that personal restraint is good or bad in the absolute, precisely as it is good or bad in the individual subjected to it.[30]

He goes on to describe 'fixing the maniac on a mattress, with a broad sheet covering his entire body' and 'a long canvas bag with a collar fitting loosely on the neck, sufficiently wide to prevent any active or dangerous movement of limbs . . . this bag envelopes the whole person except the head, and its edges are made fast by strong tapes to the cot on which the mattress is placed'.

Other officers decided to devise alternative ways of achieving control over the excited patient's behaviour and effecting desired changes in the inmate's conduct. In the asylum at Colaba the superintendent exposed in a sentence how medical officers could overcome the restrictions on restraint and devise acceptable ways of punishing errant behaviour in patients: 'No mechanical restraint is adopted in the treatment of violent or unruly patients. Such patients are placed in one of the dark, boarded cells, or merely shut up for a few hours in an ordinary room until the excitement subsides'.[31] Exclusion and isolation, rather than direct physical contact, were adopted to chastise and frighten the inmate.

Indeed, medical officers had recourse to other strategies to temper and restrict the physical behaviour of the inmates. These strategies were available in pharmaceutical form. The superintendent at Calicut admitted that 'the treatment has consisted in subduing great mental excitement by large doses of bromide of potassium, hydrate of chloral, morphia, and lately tincture of digitalis has been tried'.[32] There was a similar enthusiasm for the chemical straitjacket elsewhere in the Indian asylum system. The doctor at the Dullunda asylum near Calcutta for example reported that: '. . . digitalis and hydrocyanic acid have been largely used in the treatment of maniacal phrenzy, and the hypodermic injection of morphia has at times appeared more powerful than either. The latter is indeed seldom without beneficial effect.'[33]

Such procedures were the first step that the British officers took in asserting control over the behaviour of the Indian patients. It was the medical men who were dictating acceptable behaviour and using various means of restraint to restrict the possible modes of expression available to the Indian patient. The next stage came when the medical officers attempted to punish or attack aberrant conduct through a series of shocks. Consider the following case note:

Lalooie. f. mania. Mussul. Dullal. 30. 6 March 1862

October. This woman was sent in by City Magistrate, stated to be her first attack of insanity, but I had her as a Lunatic patient in the Jail Hospital three years ago before the establishment of the present asylum. She then suffered for months from acute mania.

On admission she was very violent + excited, would not wear clothes, tore everything to pieces + struck + bit every body approaching her. It was necessary to put her under restraint, a Blister was applied to the nape of her neck + sharp purgatives administered. Gradually the

violence of the symptoms began to subside she took to the spinning
wheel + for the last two months has been well conducted + quite
rational.
Discharged cured, October 21 1862.[34]

In the case of Lalooie, the stages between excitement and passivity and
obedience are restraint and then blistering and purging. A similar impact can
be seen in the case of Mhiboobun: 'On admission was very sulky and refused
her food. Afterwards became violent and tossed about her head and arms,
blister was applied and aperient given. Since then has been quieter and takes
her food well'.[35]

The techniques mentioned in these case notes did have medical justifications. Blistering could be defended as a 'counter-irritant' in the belief that
active disease in one part of the body would draw away morbid action from
the brain.[36] Purgatives or aperients were a means of controlling body-fluid
flows by forcing the opening of the bowels and inducing defecation. However,
the moment at which they are introduced in the case of Mhiboobun, that is,
when she has become violent, suggests that the shock for the patient of being
assaulted by a British medical officer by having him blister the neck and cause
the patient to suddenly empty her bowels was being used as a tactic by the
doctor to counter paroxysms of excitement. Pain and shame were weapons
in the armoury of the asylum superintendent in confronting behaviour he
considered undesirable.

An excellent example of the medical officer's awareness of the efficacy
of such treatments as disciplinary techniques comes from elsewhere in the
colonial system. The Commissioner of Rawul Pindee summarized the case of
the death of Mir Baz in a letter to the Punjab Government:

> Dr. Lyons caused an enema to be administered in his own presence
> to a Pathan prisoner, who pleaded epileptic fits as a reason for not
> working. It may be assumed that the man was a malingerer, and that
> he had not had any such fits. Dr. Lyons evidently considered the man
> to be shamming, and he adopted the enema, knowing it to be the
> most hateful infliction to a Pathan as a punishment and means of
> curing him of malingering. The man died three days after.[37]

The enquiry into this death conducted by the government of the Punjab
revealed further facts. It had taken two members of staff, the native doctor
and the medical dresser, to administer the enema: 'The instrument used was
Read's patent enema . . . the place where the enema was administered was
the open yard in front of the solitary cells'.[38] This last detail caused a little

unease even among the British officials of the period as a report noted that 'Dr. Lyons appears further to have acted with impropriety and harshness in having the enema administered in public, instead of within the patient's cell, or in the hospital'.[39]

Indeed, when Dr Lyons himself was asked to report his actions, he wrote a letter to the Assistant Commissioner of Rawul Pindee giving the following account:

> I considered the man was a malingerer, and applied the most disagreeable treatment appropriate for epilepsy; for this reason if the man be really ill the treatment will do him no harm; if he is malingering the treatment will still do him no harm, and be appropriate punishment. This is the orthodox rule for the treatment of malingering and has been followed by me in doubtful cases both in the Army Service as well as in this and other Jails. I ordered the man to have an injection of warm water to clear out his bowels . . . Yesterday morning I observed this man had been taken into hospital; he looked depressed and crest-fallen which I thought only natural after the treatment . . . I at once remembered that I had ordered an injection for this man about four days ago, which I am perfectly well aware is offensive to Puthans . . . the Native Doctor reported to me, at my house, that he had died about 6 o'clock, and that he did not think that he had died from illness, but from grief or shame.[40]

The enquiry decided that post-mortem examination of Mir Baz revealed signs of peritonitis in the gut and that the enema was not likely to have been the cause of death. However, what this set of correspondence does prove is that there were certainly medical officers who were not simply aware of the disciplinary possibilities of medical therapies at their disposal but were happy to use those therapies as overtly punitive measures. Dr Lyons' intention in ordering the enema was *solely* disciplinary, as he did not even consider Mir Baz to be ill and indeed exhibits a certain satisfaction at having rendered the prisoner depressed and crestfallen. The public administration of the enema was designed to shame the individual, as if being treated by Read's patent instrument was not degrading enough, and of course to inflict discomfort or even pain as a sharp rebuke to the patient's behaviour (that Mir Baz suffered physically during his ordeal is attested to in the evidence of Motee Singh, the native doctor, who pointed out that he vomited while the enema was being pumped in). Quite simply, this is an excellent example of a civil surgeon, of whom many were asylum superintendents, admitting that he had gladly used a medical procedure as a disciplinary technique and that it was certainly not the first time that he had done so. That this came to light at all was only down to the fact that the victim died in this instance.

While the case of Mir Baz is useful in providing some context for the strategies of the medical officer in the asylum, it also demonstrates that medical officers were not only concerned to calm excited individuals but also to invigorate the inactive or work-shy. In asylum practice this meant dealing with those diagnosed as suffering from dementia. 'Much active exertion has accordingly been displayed by the staff and attendants in endeavouring to rouse the listless and apathetic', declared one superintendent,[41] while another recounted some of the details of the process of 'active exertion': 'A strong water douche, by means of the hose of the small hand fire-engine pump, was tried in two cases with success in rousing the dormant senses'.[42]

Whether the patient was violent and demonstrative, or feeble and distracted, the medical officer would attempt to control and manipulate their behaviour through a series of assaults on their mind and body. These were designed to shake and shock them out of their own ways of interacting with the world and make them more amenable to the reforming programmes of the institution, or as the medical officer would have it, 'to afford in fact any means of escaping from themselves for ever so brief a period, and turn the current of their thoughts into a more natural and healthy channel'.[43]

George Smith, writing in the *Annual Report on the Three Lunatic Asylums in the Madras Presidency* in 1877, excused the use of such measures by reference to the experts:

> Even the humane Pinel did not hesitate to resort to coercive measures and the experience of men of very high authority in this department of practical medicine, have put on record many cases to show that turbulent lunatics have often been made to act in a becoming manner by treatment which assumed a more or less penal character.[44]

Bizarrely, such a passage anticipates – almost exactly – the conclusions of Michel Foucault, who wrote of the 'paradoxes of Pinel's "philanthropic" and "liberating" enterprise, this conversion of medicine into justice, of therapeutics into repression'.[45] While the seton (a strip of bandage sewn into the neck to act as a counter-irritant) and the blister, morphine and solitary confinement, the bag and the strap-down bed may have had medical justifications, there is plenty of evidence to suggest that they were used as disciplinary measures, that medical officers had disciplinary intentions and that the net effect of this violence was to control and punish the behaviour of those whom the British encountered as insane inmates in asylums. The example of Maraie

Singh, a patient at Lucknow who cried and whined 'like a baby' at the application of a seton, shows that such measures were certainly experienced as violence.[46]

Reforming the Indian inmate

Having gained control of the inmate, the superintendent's next problem was how to get the patient to 'recover', that is, as mentioned above, how to make of the patient an ordered, productive individual. Work was both the means and the measure of 'recovery' in the inmate. Dr Holmsted insisted, for example, that 'our chief means of cure is labour: if we can persuade a lunatic to labour, we have hopes of him'.[47] Through exposure to work it was thought the Indian inmates would become familiar with what were described above as the 'Victorian fetishes', or what one of the superintendents in the Bombay Presidency called 'such wholesome influences as obedience, regularity, forbearance, mutual assistance, diligence and industry'.[48] In submitting the patients to labour – 'none are allowed to be idle', insisted the superintendent at Delhi[49] – the medical officers hoped to effect their 'recovery', that is, reform them into ordered and productive individuals.

The asylum reports also indicate that 'improvement' and 'recovery' in a patient were only recognized by the British medical officers when the patient began to work. One medical officer asserted that:

> . . . all the Insanes are encouraged to engage in work as much as possible and they generally do so willingly. On first admission many sit idle but the force of example induces them speedily to join in assisting their brother unfortunates. It is indeed one of the first marked symptoms of improvement when, from sitting in an idle, listless, unobservant mood, they betake themselves to work.[50]

The superintendent at Hyderabad went further than this, stating that 'nothing looks so hopeful as regards recovery as getting them to work'.[51]

In this way work was central to the modes of treating the Indian inmate as it became both the means and the measure of 'recovery' in the patient. The British wanted patients to be 're-formed' into useful and productive individuals by learning the virtues of obedience, regularity, forbearance etc. through constant work, and the medical officers also used that constant work as an indicator of a patient's 'recovery' inasmuch as the individual's progress towards the 're-formed', 'recovered' state was signified by the frequency with which he or she willingly undertook work.

The British in the asylums wished for more from their work regimes though and were not content to have the patients simply submit to them. The fantasy was that the patient would be, in the above-mentioned words of the superintendent of Dullunda, 'so transformed that industry becomes a pleasure to him'.[52] This fantasy is expressed elsewhere, John Balfour, the Inspector General of Hospitals in the Dinapore Circle, deciding that 'I need only add that not only should there be nothing penal in the work undertaken, but the patients should learn to look on it as a privilege'.[53]

This fantasy can also be seen in asylum reports which produce images of the patients 'singing blithely at their task', or which exclaim 'I must say I never saw a more happy or contented looking set of lunatics; they work both in the gardens and at the looms with pleasure to themselves'.[54] With such an end in mind it was stressed that within the work regimes

> . . . compulsory efforts and punishment for not working have been studiously avoided; at the same time every inducement by humour-ing their fancies, and granting them some coveted indulgence in diet, extras etc. have been employed so as to form a habit; sometimes, when other means have failed, they have been kept with the working party unemployed, and have of themselves taken to work from seeing others employed.[55]

In other words the patients were expected not to have to be compelled to work but to wish to work and to learn to want to work, and this was to be achieved through the tactics of peer pressure or the offering of incentives. The ultimate aim was a *self*-disciplined Indian.

Violence and the body in post-colonial psychiatry

The examples provided so far in this article are all of British medical officers and their designs for the bodies of the Indians in their charge. In other words these are clear-cut studies in the use of the power given by the colonial relationship to the colonizer over the colonized. These examples show the imposition of one set of standards of behaviour through violent physical means by a group that has assumed the power to do this. Psychiatry in this context appears to be a tool of empire which simply serves the wider designs of the political context.

Yet the evidence from Para Brahma's case file at the Thane Mental Hospital in Maharashtra suggests that violent physical interventions cloaked as psychiatric treatments continued to be used after the departure of the British colonizers. What makes the post-colonial context of the case note interesting is that it was Indian doctors who were planning and executing these violent interventions. Para Brahma's particular story is all the more intriguing as the psychiatric interventions were made to control and trans-form behaviour that other Indians found perfectly reasonable and acceptable.

Para Brahma was admitted to the Thane psychiatric hospital on the same day as the Magistrate's Court at Victoria Terminus in Bombay decided that he was unfit to stand trial (for an assault on an Indian Railways official) because of his mental state. The police surgeon was in no doubt that 'in my opinion he is a certifiable lunatic', as he had observed that 'the patient remains in an excited state, is non co-operative in nature, eats haphazardly, sleeps irregularly but sufficiently, dirty in habits and at times aggrassive [sic]. He has exagerated [sic] ideas of false grandeur'.[56] The admission document to the asylum contained little more detail, simply that he was male and about 35 years old, and that he was excited and likely to be dangerous to others.

It transpires however that Para Brahma was more than a wandering nuisance and was in fact a Hindu mystic with a devoted following in Chikmagalur. One of his following, a coffee-plantation manager called P S Venkata Subba Rao, kept up a regular correspondence with the superintendents of the Thane institution through which it is possible to trace Para Brahma's history and his status in the minds of his followers.

> I had been to Sringeri somewhere during March 1956. My uncle informed me that here is an Avadhuta Yogi staying in the Guest quarters of the Mutt, who does not care even for the ordinary comforts, just eats whatever that is offered to him and is always jovial, some of the Pandits of Sringeri mutt who visited him said he is a practical philosopher.[57]

There were those in the town who did not welcome the appearance of Para Brahma, 'while at Sringeri he was it seems stoned by some',[58] but he came under the protection of an ex-municipal councillor, a Muslim called Ibrahim. Gradually, however, there came to be general agreement about the stranger's identity. The above passage shows that some of the townsfolk validated the idea that Para Brahma was a mystic. The local priest also agreed that this was the case: 'the present sringeri–swamijee Shankara Charya told me that Parabrahma is a gnani and raja yogi too'. P S Venkata Subba Rao himself was convinced that 'he was a perfect Bhramhachari, perfect sanyasi, perfect avadhuta, and finally the all [sic]'.[59]

Indeed, over time it seems that the mystic attracted a good deal of attention and built a following that was not without its noteworthies. Sreenivasa Shetty, who paid for the first-class ticket that explained the swami's presence at Victoria Terminus on the day of his arrest, was 'a merchant and Municipal Councillor, Sringeri'.[60] P R Hariharan, who came to the station to receive 'darsan' of Para Brahma on the night that he was arrested and who subsequently wrote in support of the patient, was a chartered accountant with an impressive address at the Stock Exchange Building in the Fort District of Bombay, its most prestigious business district.[61] B R Shetty, a regular visitor to the swami, was an official with the Reserve Bank and had an address at the staff quarters in Bombay. Other visitors included H W L Poonja, 'who is an ex-Army officer',[62] and the man who collected together all of Para Brahma's communications with P S Venkata Subba Rao for publication was 'Sri S.N. Das [who] is from Bengal and has worked in United Nations office in America, Canada, England and other places'.[63]

These followers felt that Para Brahma's behaviour was explained by his status as a mystic and a guru. Para Brahma, to P S Venkata Subba Rao, 'is realisation itself and all his actions or work or powers are most natural, effortless, ageless. He is a perfect yogi and nothing can bind him'.[64] He was striving to reach a state of perfection; 'when one reaches this state and seeks identification [with] the force or Brahman, he will be unmindful of the consequences and will be happy whereever he is and may not be conscious of his body or the environment'.[65]

However, the Indian doctors at the asylum refused to recognize the validity of these beliefs about Para Brahma and his behaviour. The superintendents of the asylum over the 20-year period of Para Brahma's incarceration seemed entirely convinced that the patient was suffering from some sort of mental illness. In 1957, for example, the superintendent wrote: 'I have to inform you that the above noted patient [Para Brahma] was personally examined by me. He is still excited, gets violent and irrelevant in his talk. He is not in a fit condition to be tried in the court'.[66] The following year the officer in charge of the asylum, identified on the medical certificate as Dr A N Mukerjee, confirmed the opinion 'that the said Parabrahma is a lunatic and a proper person to be taken charge of and detained under care and treatment'. He went on to justify this conclusion by noting:

1. This patient has delusions of grandeur, he believes himself to be the head of the universe.
2. He is very obstinate and non-cooperative, does not like to answer questions put to him.
3. He keeps in an excited state.
4. He lacks insight and responsibility.[67]

Similar behaviour led a subsequent superintendent to come up with a more specific diagnosis three years later. B Chaudhuri, in summarizing the case for the Bombay Health Department in 1961, decided that this was 'a case of schizophrenia'.[68] In a less guarded moment, however, the superintendent in charge of the asylum in 1960 gave a rather more candid impression of the swami. One of the latter's disciples recounted that on a visit to the hospital 'we went to the Superintendent's house. He says that that patient is stark lunatic'.[69]

The point of this file for the current discussion is that this was no simple disagreement on the nature of a man's behaviour. Rather, the superintendent used his view of Para Brahma to justify subjecting the mystic's body to a series of violent and dangerous physical assaults that had as their objective a transformation of the man's behaviour and identity. Despite the fact that his view of the individual was contested, and contested from within Indian cultural idioms by a variety of respectable businessmen and dignitaries, the psychiatrist organized physical interventions to impose his world view on the individual.

These physical assaults came in two forms: electro-convulsive therapy (ECT) and the now banned insulin shock treatment (IST). Para Brahma was subjected to both forms of violence, at times on a daily basis, for the full 20 years of his stay at the hospital. The violence and indeed danger of these forms of assault were candidly recognized on the consent forms issued by the superintendents which emphasized that there was a risk of death involved in these forms of treatment.

That the objective of these assaults was a transformation of Para Brahma's behaviour is implicit in the conclusion of the file. Upon the release of the patient, P S Venkata Subba Rao recorded:

> Finally he asked me not to waste money on an escort and he would go to his village himself and it is enough I see him off at Bangalore. While at Chikmagalur he had a hair cut and got made some sets of paigama (Kurta) and some underwears, shirts and also took a shawl and said he doesn't need anything else and he wanted to travel light . . . He said he was a teacher and said he would take that profession and he likes children.[70]

It seems that the hospital authorities were only happy to release Para Brahma once he had reached this state. In other words, it was only once he had yielded to the determination of a succession of superintendents to control and transform his behaviour that he was allowed back into society. He now no longer exhibited 'delusions of grandeur', he no longer seemed 'very obstinate and non-cooperative', he seems to have passed through his 'excited state' and indeed he seemed to have become a model of 'responsibility'. In other words he now met the standards of behaviour expected by the post-colonial psychiatrists, a series of standards that they had imposed on him for over 20 years through the physical violence of ECT and IST.

Conclusion

This article has traced the violence that has been a central feature of treatment regimes in the psychiatric system in India in both the colonial and post-colonial periods. The violence is not of an undirected or casual manner. Rather it involves carefully planned physical assaults on the body that are justified by the language of therapy and cure. The objective underlying this violence is to control and then to transform the behaviour of the individual subjected to the assaults. Made to sit still, to sleep, to eat and to work to the orders of the psychiatrist, the body becomes a gateway to the mind of the individual, who in turn learns to respond to the assaults on his body in suitable ways.

In the colonial period these assaults were aimed at transforming the inmates into docile, obedient and efficient Indians. The treatment regimes in the asylums were caught up in a wider fantasy on the part of the British throughout India in this period, a fantasy summarized by Arjun Appadurai : 'The project of reform . . . involved cleaning up the sleazy, flabby, frail, feminine, obsequious bodies of natives into clean, virile, muscular, moral, and loyal bodies that could be moved into the subjectivities proper to colonialism'.[71]

Indeed the asylum certainly was not a unique place in the colonial system for experimenting with, or acting out the fantasy of, reworking the Indian. Gautam Chatterjee has argued, in the case of the institution for juvenile offenders, that it also 'provided an opportunity to intervene and restructure juvenile minds', while Mathur has observed of the transportation system that 'one of the main objectives of sending a convict to the penal settlement of Andamans was to provide opportunities to a convict to reform himself'.[72]

The post-colonial context of psychiatric violence seems rather more complex, although it is important in itself simply to note the continuity over the 1947 chronological divide. Colonial medical officers seem to have used violence in order to impose a moral order that they shared with many other officials throughout the British system. In the post-colonial context the Indian psychiatrists seemed determined to impose a moral order that was actually opposed by others in Indian society. The psychiatric assessment of Para Brahma as a 'stark lunatic' was directly contested by others in Indian society who felt that he was a preacher and mystic. Despite the lack of a clear objective endorsed by a wider social group or by a governmental agenda, the psychiatrists insisted on treating Para Brahma. As such he was subjected to the physical assaults of ECT and IST, techniques so harmful to the body that they carried with them the risk of death or permanent disability. These assaults were only withdrawn once Para Brahma abandoned the behaviour that the psychiatrists considered aberrant and adopted an identity that was deemed more 'suitable' by them.

In short, and by way of conclusion, the violence of the psychiatric system in India had colonial origins in the broad fantasies – shared across much of the British government between 1857 and 1900 – that saw them impose a new order upon the chaos that they imagined in local society. The violence has continued within the asylum walls in the post-independence period, in spite of the fact that the colonial power relations that legitimated it and that explained it have withered.

Acknowledgements

I would like to thank Satadru Sen for organizing the conference at which I had the chance to present the paper upon which this article is based and indeed to the Purdue University for meeting the costs of my participation. Dr Aditya Kumar of the Agra Mental Hospital, Drs Lavatre, Borgaonkar and Kasture of the Regional Mental Hospital at Thane, Maharashtra, Lieutenant-Colonel Daniel Saldhana at the Alipore Hospital and Professor Shridhar Sharma at the Delhi Hospital for Mental Diseases are all due special thanks for their help in locating in the hospitals of India the range of primary sources for my research. Awards from the British Academy, the Wellcome Trust, the Carnegie Trust and the Economic and Social Research Council have made various stages of my research possible and their generous help is gratefully acknowledged.

Bibliography

Primary Sources

i. Published Material

'Annual Reports of the Lunatic Asylums at Bareilly and Benares for the Year 1866 and 1867', in *Selections from the Records of the Government of the North-Western Provinces*, Allahabad, 1868.

Annual Report of the Insane Asylums in Bengal for the Years 1862, 1863, 1867, 1868, Calcutta.

Annual Administration and Progress Report on the Insane Asylums in the Bombay Presidency for the Year 1873–4, 1874–5, 1876, Bombay.

Annual Report of the Three Lunatic Asylums in the Madras Presidency during the Year 1873–4, 1875–6, 1876–77, 1877–78, Madras 1874.

Annual Inspection Report of the Dispensaries in Oudh for the Year 1872, Lucknow 1873.

Annual Report of the Lunatic Asylums in the Punjab for the Year 1871, 1872, 1874, 1876, 1879, 1880, Lahore.

ii. Unpublished Material

National Archives of India, Delhi

Government of India (GOI) (Judicial Department) Proceedings 22 May 1869, 86A. Comm. Rawul Pindee to Gvt. Punjab, 2 January 1869.

GOI (Judicial) 9 October 1869, 27A. President Committee of Jail Enquiry to Gvt. Punjab, 7 August 1869.

GOI (Judicial) 9 October 1869, 26A. Gvt. Punjab to GOI, 17 August 1869.

GOI (Judicial) 22 May 1869, 86A. Civ. Surg. Rawul Pindee to Asst. Comm. R.P., 21 July 1868.

GOI (Medical) October 1877, 18–20B. Civ. Surg. Rangoon to IMD. Burma, 15 January 1877.

GOI (Public) Proceedings 27 February 1869, 105–107A. Minute by President Madras, 29 October 1865.

(TMH) Thane (Maharashtra) Mental Hospital Archive, India

Para Brahma File/1956–1977

Medical Certificate, Indian Lunacy Act 1912, no. 413/56, 19.11.1956

From P S Venkata Subba Rao to Magistrate V.T., 21.01.1957a

From P S Venkata Subba Rao to Superintendent, 13.02.1957b

From Superintendent to Public Health Department, Gvt. Bombay, 14.11.1957c

From P S Venkata Subba Rao to Superintendent, 15.01.1959a

From P S Venkata Subba Rao to Siddeshwar Varma, 08.02.1959b

From P S Venkata Subba Rao to Superintendent, 15.08.1959c

From D R Salian to P S Venkata Subba Rao, 23.03.1960

From Superintendent to Urban Development and Public Health Dept. Gvt. Bombay, 12.09.1961

From P S Venkata Subba Rao to Superintendent, 10.10.1966

From P S Venkata Subba Rao to Superintendent, 25.02.1972

From P S Venkata Subba Rao to Sri H W L Poonja of Punjab, 20.12.1977

Secondary Sources

Appadurai, A, 1993, 'Number in the Colonial Imagination', in C A Breckenridge and Peter van der Veer (eds), *Orientalism and the Postcolonial*

Predicament: Perspectives on South Asia, Philadelphia, University of Pennsylvania Press.

Arnold, D, 1993, *Colonizing the Body: State Medicine and Epidemic Disease in Nineteenth Century India*, Delhi, Oxford University Press.

Chatterjee, G, 1995, *Child Criminals and the Raj*, New Delhi, Akshaya.

Chakrabarty, D, 1994, 'The Difference-Deferral of a Colonial Modernity: Public Debates on Domesticity in British Bengal', in Arnold, D and Hardiman, D eds., *Subaltern Studies VIII*, Delhi, Oxford University Press.

Digby, A, 1985, *Madness, Morality and Medicine: A Study of the York Retreat, 1796–1914*, Cambridge, Cambridge University Press.

Foucault, M, 1989, *Madness and Civilization: A History of Insanity in the Age of Reason* (trans. R Howard), London, Routledge.

Mathur, L Kala Pani, 1985, *History of Andaman and Nicobar Islands with a Study of India's Freedom Struggle*, Delhi, Eastern Books.

Mills, J, 2000, *Madness, Cannabis and Colonialism: The 'Native-Only' Lunatic Asylums of British India, 1857–1900*, Basingstoke, Macmillan.

Ripa, Y, 1990, *Women and Madness: the Incarceration of Women in Nineteenth-century France* (trans. C du Peloux Menagé), Cambridge, Polity Press.

Scull, A, 1989, *Social Order/Mental Disorder: Anglo-American Psychiatry in Historical Perspective*, London, Routledge.

Tomes, N, 1988, 'The Great Restraint Controversy: a comparative perspective on Anglo-American psychiatry in the nineteenth century', in W F Bynum, R Porter and M Shepherd (eds), *The Anatomy of Madness: Essays in the History of Psychiatry*, London, Routledge.

Notes

1. Foucault 1989, p. 258.
2. 'Annual Report of the Lunatic Asylums at Bareilly and Benares' [hereafter Bareilly and Benares], 1866, p. 61.
3. Ibid., 1867, p. 58.
4. For a detailed discussion of the meaning of these terms for the British in this period in India, please see Mills 2000.
5. Chakrabarty, 1994, p. 55.
6. *Annual Report of the Lunatic Asylums in the Punjab* [hereafter Punjab], 1880, p. 3.
7. GOI (Public) Proceedings 1869, 105–107.
8. These were the key concepts in Western psychiatric treatment at this period. For further details see Foucault 1989, Scull 1989, Digby 1985, Tomes 1988 and Ripa 1990.

9. Punjab, 1871–2, p. 5.

10. *Annual Report of the Insane Asylums in Bengal* [hereafter Bengal], 1863, p. 3.

11. *Annual Administration and Progress Report on the Insane Asylums in the Bombay Presidency* [hereafter Bombay], 1873–4, p. 4.

12. Bengal, 1867, p. 93.

13. Ibid., 1862, p. 29.

14. Punjab, 1874, p. 1.

15. Bombay, 1874–5, p. 13.

16. Bombay, 1873–4, p. 3. The 'tea' in question here is later detailed as 'beef-tea'. The decision to administer 'beef-tea' may have been taken because the patient involved was a Parsee rather than a Hindu. However it does seem to be an odd choice, given the attitude of certain sections of the Indian community to vegetarian diets and cow products, so that the decision to use the preparation may have reflected the ignorance of British medical officers about Indian diets or indeed may suggest something altogether more disciplinary. The superintendant may have had Eurocentric convictions about the benefits of meat in a diet and could have been attempting to force 'beef-tea' into the body against the will of the Indian patient in the belief that the Indian body must be built and formed as the British wished it to be, even if the Indian individual wanted to resist that form.

17. Ibid., p. 32.

18. Bengal, 1862, p. 66; *Annual Report of the Three Lunatic Asylums in the Madras Presidency* [hereafter Madras], 1873–4, p. 19.

19. Arnold 1993, p. 108.

20. Madras, 1873–4, p. 22; Bengal, 1868, p. 3.

21. Bombay, 1876, p. 9.

22. Punjab, 1871–2, p. 3.

23. Madras, 1875–6, p. 11.

24. Bengal, 1862, p. 66.

25. GOI (Medical) Proceedings 1877, 18–20B.

26. Case Book IA, patient no.114, 8 June 1861.

27. Madras, 1877–8, p. 12.

28. Bareilly and Benares, 1867, p. 58.

29. Punjab, 1871–2, p. 1.

30. Bengal, 1868, p. 3.

31. Bombay, 1873–4, p. 4.

32. Madras, 1877–8, p. 6.

33. Bengal, 1867, p. 15.

34. Case Book IA, patient no. 175, 6 March 1862.

35. Case Book IA, patient no. 56, 24 September 1860.

36. See Digby 1985, p. 128.
37. GOI (Judicial) Proceedings 1869, 86A.
38. Ibid., 27A.
39. Ibid., 26A.
40. Ibid., 86A.
41. GOI (Medical) Proceedings 1877.
42. Bombay, 1873–4, p. 3.
43. Madras, 1877–8, p. 11.
44. Ibid., 1877, p. 22.
45. Foucault 1989, p. 266.
46. Case Book IA, patient no. 103, 9 May 1861.
47. Bombay, 1874–5, p. 28.
48. Bombay, 1873–4, p. 16.
49. Punjab, 1876, pp. 18–19.
50. Bengal, 1862, p. 66.
51. Bombay, 1873–4, p. 44.
52. Bengal, 1863, p. 3.
53. Bengal, 1862, p. 72.
54. Respectively Bombay 1873–4, p. 29, and *Annual Inspection Report of the Dispensaries in Oudh for the Year 1872*, p. 299.
55. Bengal, 1862, p. 30.
56. TMH Medical Certificate 1956.
57. TMH Letter 1959a.
58. TMH Letter 1959b.
59. Ibid.
60. TMH Letter 1957b.
61. TMH Letter 1959a.
62. TMH Letter 1966.
63. TMH Letter 1972.
64. TMH Letter 1959c.
65. TMH Letter 1957a.
66. TMH Letter 1957c.
67. TMH Letter 1958.
68. TMH Letter 1961.
69. TMH Letter 1960.
70. TMH Letter 1977.
71. Appadurai 1993, p. 335.
72. Chatterjee 1995, p. 188; Mathur 1985, p. 64.

5

The Lotah Emeutes of 1855: Caste, Religion and Prisons in North India in the Early Nineteenth Century

ANAND A YANG

Introduction

This chapter investigates the so-called 'lotah emeutes' that erupted in the jails of the towns of Arrah and Muzaffarpur in the Bihar region in 1855. The objective here is to process the colonial archival 'negatives' of these and related events as a series of snapshots. Assembled as a collage, this composition represents and evokes the changing configuration of the colonial system of discipline and punishment. However, it also suggests resistance directed against that regime in the early nineteenth century both within the prison walls and around them. This collage highlights the place and fit of the colonial prison in indigenous society, specifically its workings as a laboratory in which the colonial state carried out various probes into the body of its Indian subjects in order to further its knowledge and power. Indeed, the prison was one site where changing colonial notions and regulations were tied to efforts aimed not only at calibrating the colonial system of discipline and punishment so as to inflict a 'just measure of pain', but also at furthering knowledge about the indigenous society generally, and caste and religion specifically, particularly as these elements were factored into its various disciplinary projects.

In addition, the discussion here will indicate that colonial attempts to regulate the body of its subjects, as reflected in its policies and actions targeting its jail populations, were often challenged and resisted. Colonial rhetoric about non-interference in matters of caste and religion notwithstanding, the government frequently sought to develop disciplinary regimens, especially in the prison, that were perceived as socially and culturally transgressive by people both within and without the walls of the prison. Finally, the picture of the riots of 1855, although organized around events that occurred in two jails, can be plotted on a wider canvas that also depicts popular *mentalités* regarding the colonial state in North India on the eve of the dramatic events of the Mutiny/Rebellion of 1857.[1] Arrah, the headquarters town of the southern Bihar district of Shahabad, became a major site of conflict in 1857, while Muzaffarpur, across the Ganges, was the headquarters town of the northern district of Tirhut, also known as Muzaffarpur District.

The lotah emeute

On 26 April 1855, Thomas C Loch, the first Inspector of Jails of Bengal, issued a circular to 'all officers in charge of jails' directing that they institute a rigorous search of the persons and wards of prisoners in their jails and remove all but the following authorized articles:

1. The Jail allowance of clothing
2. One blanket. . .
3. A piece of sacking . . . which rolled up will form a pillow [and]
4. A small earthern kuttorah [*katora*] for drinking water. . .

Everything else was to be confiscated, including 'writing materials' which, according to the inspector, 'should not be allowed to the prisoners; if they require to write an appeal, the Darogah [Indian jail official] will supply them with the means'. He went on to explain that 'there ought never to be any occasion for written petitions for if you visit the jail frequently you ought to be able to hear all complaints'. He conceded that 'books of a moral character' were to be allowed, 'but others if found should be destroyed'. In precise and great detail Loch's circular spelled out the procedures to be followed in conducting the search. It even pinpointed for scrutiny places such as 'where the plaster on the walls is loose', or the 'drains under the steps' where 'Articles of larger bulk as hookahs, pipes &c are generally concealed'.[2] Conspicuously missing from the list of authorized articles – an absence made all the more notable by the inclusion of the *katora* as the authorized vessel for drinking water – was the brass lotah, an item that many prisoners were known to have. 'Every prisoner has a lotah which he uses for water for all purposes', noted one source, 'brass being in the opinion of the Hindoos susceptible of constant purification and therefore constant use for all purposes without injury to caste which earthen vessels are not'.[3]

On 9 May 1855, A E Russell, Magistrate of Tirhut, proceeded to carry out the order in the district jail of Muzaffapur. Apparently he acted promptly on the Loch directive because he was confident that the inmates of his jail would live up to their reputation of behaving 'tolerably well'.[4] But much to his surprise and that of other local authorities, an 'unfortunate emeute' erupted, 'a furious and altogether unexpected but organized outbreak on the part of the people of the town and district, in support and sympathy with the prisoners'.[5]

The 'serious disturbance' flared in the Muzaffarpur jail shortly after the brass lotahs of the prisoners were confiscated. En masse the prisoners refused to head out to work in road gangs as they normally did every day. When the magistrate arrived on the scene and directed his *daroga* – Indian jail official – to apprehend one of the prisoners, the *daroga* was pelted with bricks. The magistrate then sought the assistance of the district judge and together they attempted to talk to the inmates, but to no avail. Meanwhile, outside the walls of the jail large numbers of opium *raiyats*, cultivators who grew opium for the East India Company, were congregating. As the local authorities reported later, these cultivators openly declared that they 'would most likely make a disturbance in the event of any attack being made by the [jail] guard on the prisoners'. The magistrate then sought to starve the prisoners into submission by denying them food unless they complied with his order to return to their wards. In his estimation he would have succeeded in this tactic had it not been for the people outside the jail feeding the prisoners. The magistrate and the judge reconvened at the jail the following morning, this time backed up by a force of 50 of the jail's guards. However, they were met by what they described as an increasingly large and hostile crowd. To continue in the words of the magistrate:

> The rioters which included almost all the inhabitants of the town as well as a vast number of opium ryots declared they would not go away unless the lotahs were returned to the prisoners and after some time seeing the state of feeling shewn by the people and that their numbers were increasing and considering it impolitic to attempt with the small force at my disposal to dislodge them by force and seeing no chance of restoring quiet to the jail and station except by returning the lotahs to the men I at last determined to do so [.] I need not say how very unwilling I was to submit to the dictation of the mob but troops being at such a distance[,] and not likely to appear for some days[,] I saw not other means of keeping the peace of the station, as I was fearful of the consequences if the mob increased much more there being a very large sum of money in the Treasury and Rupees 50000 in the opium godown as well as the houses of some of the residents being near the spot and there being danger of the mob taking to plundering. After some hesitation I consented to return the lotahs and after some time the mob dispersed and the prisoners returned quietly to their wards.[6]

Concerned that he had yielded to a 'mob' in a situation that had assumed the proportions of 'an insurrection' and a 'rebellion', the magistrate insisted on reasserting his authority by a show of force. To do so, he requested his superiors to send him 'a very strong body of troops' to enforce the lotah order and to enable him to disperse 'a great part of the prisoners' to other districts in order to restore 'the discipline of the jail'.[7]

Loch's lotah directive also triggered an 'emeute' in the Arrah jail. Inmates in this jail, in contrast to those of the Tirhut jail, had long been reputed to be of the 'higher classes', 'troublesome' and possessed of 'a mutinous spirit'.[8] Therefore the no-lotah order was implemented later and not put into effect until 12 May, and then only with special precautions. At the behest of the magistrate, the jail *daroga* first allowed the prisoners to consume their morning meal. They were then convened in the yards of their respective wards while a search of their belongings and premises was carried out. Shortly after 6 am the magistrate arrived and proceeded to conduct the search in the prescribed manner, as per the inspector's instructions. As prisoners filed out of the jail they were searched and their lotah, brass plates and other unauthorized articles confiscated. They were then organized into their customary gangs of 30 or 40 and sent out to work while their quarters were searched. That after- noon, prisoners returned to a meal served on leaves and water contained in earthen pots. The magistrate concentrated first on persuading the Brahmins to partake of their meals but without success:

Those nearest begged of me to give them their lotahs. I proceeded to explain to them that I was ordered not to give them brass lotahs, that there were earthen vessels for them to drink out of, new ones would be supplied daily, and leaves to eat from; this I did in as loud a voice and as clearly and distinctly as I was able . . . The men were generally silent, and I again desired those nearest me to take their dinners, and was again asked for lotahs. I said it was not in my power to give them lotahs but told the man nearest me to take his dinner or go to his ward[.] [H]e preferred the latter and went off; another did the same, and I think a third the next I asked, said, take the leaves, only give me the lotah. I talked with him probably for three or four minutes, again explaining very quietly that to grant the lotah was contrary to my orders, and I could not do it. The prisoners now rose from all parts of the cooking shed and began a loud murmur, I imme- diately turned round to the guard and called out, quick march, and then turned again, and now the prisoners were advancing rapidly and tiles and missiles were flying about. I turned again expecting to find myself supported by the guard but saw them coming on in no

sort of order. The prisoners had now come out from the north side of
the shed, and seemed to be endeavouring to cut us off from the
door[;] they were coming down rapidly upon us, and I felt it was
necessary for our self defence to give the order to fire: this I did, and
under the momentary check from the fire; we were enabled to make
good our flight to the jail door. . .[9]

Shortly thereafter a gang of prisoners who had been late in returning to the
jail arrived and was intercepted on the road with the assistance of William
Tayler, Commissioner of Patna Division, who just happened to be in Arrah.
One member of the road gang, said to be 'a person of some influence', was
sent into the jail 'to persuade the prisoners to submit', but without effect.
Chained together, the gang was then marched off to the civil jail where they
too joined the protest and refused to eat or drink unless they had their lotahs.
When a letter was transmitted to the inmates at the jail asking for a 'parley' it
was rebuffed, although a reply was sent by 'Mussulmans' who wrote that 'they
had nothing to do with the disturbance'. Nor would the prisoners at the jail
agree to send out their wounded.

On 14 May, with troops present, the commissioner and magistrate once
again sought to win over the prisoners, at one point recruiting Babu Kooer
Singh, an influential landholder of the district and later the principal rebel of
1857 in the region, to speak to the leaders in the jail. Their overture rejected,
the local authorities followed up this time with troops who were dispatched
into the jail to regain control and to force open the doors of the wards. The
magistrate then isolated those prisoners he 'considered to be the most influential' and commanded the rest to return to their wards. Although pushed and
shoved, the inmates continued to drag their feet, moving back 'slowly and in
a refractory manner'. Dinner that evening under the watchful eyes of the
magistrate found only about 100 inmates willing to partake; 'the rest', number-
ing almost 500, refused to eat their meals. Muslim inmates accounted for 19
or 20 of those who elected to eat supper. But the magistrate was confident
that the prisoners would 'gradually give in', particularly if the military force
was stationed there to intimidate them into submission. However, he was
also aware that 'although hunger and thirst may subdue the minds of the
prisoners, it will be some time before their minds are subdued'.[10] The 'rebel-
lious spirit' persisted in the Arrah jail for the next few days. Prisoners would
eat their meals one day but refuse to do so the next, and always they would
clamour for their lotahs. One inmate refused even to come out of his ward
when called and literally had to be carried out by the guard. He was flogged
for his act of disobedience.[11]

The Tirhut and Shahabad jails were the only two prisons in which inmates defiantly and aggressively resisted the implementation of the Loch directive. But elsewhere too there was opposition, albeit less overt in nature. In the Patna jail the prisoners resisted by submitting 'sullenly'.[12] In some jails there were no protests because the lotah directive was ignored, such as in the Behar (town) and Saran jails where inmates retained their lotahs. In the Champaran jail, lotahs had been prohibited in 1853 because of constant theft and quarrels over them and *toomras* or dried gourd shells substituted in their place.[13]

The colonial regime of discipline and punishment

On 17 May 1855, by which date all resistance had already ceased, the Bengal government sent around a brief circular revoking the lotah order, which it characterized as 'unknown to government' and 'disapproved and cancelled'. Apparently, Calcutta would have issued this order earlier but for the fact that Loch's directive of 26 April was not communicated to the government until 2 May and the Lieutenant Governor, stricken with cholera, did not see the order until 17 May, by which time the Arrah and Muzaffarpur outbreaks had already occurred. The Lieutenant Governor insisted that 'had I seen it earlier and omitted to revoke so much of it as related to the lotahs I should have considered myself responsible for it all that has occurred in consequence'.[14] He condemned Loch's circular as 'unjust, offensive, impolitic and unnecessary'. He also characterized the no-lotah order as constituting 'an infringement of caste, and . . . therefore most likely to irritate and exasperate those religious feelings and prejudices which it is my duty no less than our policy not unnecessarily to offend', concluding 'that the objection to it on the part of the prisoners and people was natural'.[15] Expressing 'strong disapprobation of his [Loch's] injudicious, inconsiderate and improper order', the Lieutenant Governor warned the inspector not to 'issue any orders [in the future] affecting the management of prisoners without first submitting them to me and obtaining my sanction'.[16]

While admitting that the 'disturbances' were an outgrowth of his order, Loch took issue with the Lieutenant Governor's views and continued to maintain that his directive was not 'wrong'. Although willing to concede that 'those Hindoo prisoners, who possessed lotahs, had a great partiality for them and felt their being taken away as a great hardship', he was not prepared to recognize this as a religious 'infringement'. Rather he attributed the events to 'prisoners [who] did not like it, and were desirous of intimidating the authorities from carrying it out'. He defended himself by pointing out that the confiscation was part of the larger scheme 'to take away all hookas and luxuries and to establish an uniform scale of personal necessaries'. Furthermore, he pointed out that he had targeted lotahs because they were 'dangerous weapon[s]'.

They had indeed previously been used with deadly effect, and this allusion was obviously to the 1834 incident in which the superintendent of the Alipur jail was lotahed to death by a group of prisoners.[17]

The record of the 'outbreaks' and the exchanges between the Lieutenant Governor and Inspector Loch made its way upwards into the highest levels of the colonial administration, both in India and in England. In government circles the debate quickly became mired in such questions as: 'Is the use of lotahs, or metal water pots, essential to the preservation of caste in the case of Hindoos of any caste, or not; and if it be so, what are the castes in whose case it is essential?'.[18] Originally framed by J P Grant, one of the members of the Governor General's Council,[19] this question was reformulated by the Lieutenant Governor to state that the issue was not so much of 'whether the use of lotahs is essential to caste' but whether they could be replaced with earthen vessels. Most of the answers sent in by local administrators from Bihar as well as throughout the province of Bengal opined that higher-caste Hindus would not drink out of earthen vessels once they had been used or touched by someone else. Lower castes, on the other hand, were said to have far less objection to their reuse.[20]

Central to the assessment of the lotah emeutes as revolving around issues of caste and religion was the conviction that the Loch directive represented an 'infringement of caste'. In other words, the no-lotah order constituted an 'unjust, offensive, impolitic and unnecessary' act that violated the colonial government's long-standing espousal of and adherence to a policy of non-interference in matters involving people's fundamental beliefs and practices. Hence the 'strong disapprobation' that was registered along the entire chain of command from the Lieutenant Governor of Bengal to the highest officials in Calcutta and London. Underlying the concern about 'infringement of caste' was the widespread belief in official circles that caste was the principal organizing institution of indigenous society, a system that was anchored in a religious bedrock defined by Hinduism. Indeed, as scholars have recently noted, caste was a central trope in the colonial imagination and acted as a metonym for Indian civilization and society. Caste in this framework con-signed India to the status of being the 'other' of the West, an other, earlier and inferior form of civilization that was characterized by a backward, rigid, static and highly hierarchical society. Such 'castes of mind' – to employ Nicholas Dirks' telling phrase – rendered caste as 'responsible for the transmission and reproduction of society in India. And caste, like India itself, has been seen as based on religious rather than political principles'.[21] From such notions of caste as the 'core and foundation of Indian civilization' and the 'other' of Western civilization stemmed the colonial policy of non-interference and non-involvement in caste and religious matters. But this imperative clearly did not consistently dictate colonial policies and practices relating to discipline and punishment, not that it ever consistently did as regards indigenous society in general either. On the contrary, because colonial punishments continued to be directed at the body, caste always loomed as a possible site of intervention, a vulnerability that jailers and jailed alike sought to recruit and deploy in their confrontations with one another. Moreover, the British utilized the colonial prison as a social and statistical laboratory. Particularly in the nineteenth century, the prison was a site of investigation because its captive population presented available and useable subjects for categorizing, classifying and compiling qualitative and quantitative data relating to everything from caste and religion to diet, health and mortality.[22]

Indeed, Loch's order was not entirely at odds with colonial penal practices. Rather, it followed on the heels of government efforts to render the prison experience more punitive by recalibrating the calculus of pain and punishment, a new equation that depended on stiffening the conditions of punishment. New attempts at discipline and punishment therefore always had the potential of stirring up social and religious concerns that prisoners invariably capitalized upon and manipulated as their 'weapons of the weak'. Loch, as Bengal's first Inspector of Jails, was in fact specifically charged with instituting this potentially incendiary mix of prison reforms. Prior to his appointment a separate and distinct jail department did not exist, and even during his tenure district jails continued to operate as 'an adjunct and responsibility of the local court, controlled by the magistrate and subject to the judges of circuit'.[23]

From the time of the Committee on Prison Discipline headed by Thomas Babington Macaulay, in the 1830s, prison reform was construed as part and parcel of a larger package of changes designed to create a new penal and criminal code. There were also to be other changes intended to institute a more effective apparatus of control, including the reorganization and revitalization of the police force.[24] Celebrated by an earlier generation of historians as representing the hallmarks of an 'age of modernizing reform', such innovations now appear to be indicative of the rising colonial state's desire to assert the authority of superior 'European intelligence and power' and to claim moral authority as one foundation of colonial rule in the subcontinent.

Penal reform embodied these seemingly contradictory impulses by taking aim at the establishment and consolidation of a new penal regime and regimen. Foucault notwithstanding, the colonial penal system that emerged in the early nineteenth century did indeed phase out some of the more sanguinary punishments prescribed by indigenous law, such as mutilation, and reduced the number of cases in which capital punishment was applicable. However, it never completely did away with punishments targeting the body, even as it developed new technologies for attacking the mind as well. This dual ambition shows up repeatedly in the recommendations of the 1838 report of the Committee on Prison Discipline, which was the first systematic exposition of a penological theory for colonial India and became the primer for the emerging 'scientific' discourse on penology.[25] Punishments aimed at the body underlay the continuing reliance on transportation as a technology of punishment in India, even as its deployment in England declined and was then stopped altogether. Indeed, the Prison Discipline Committee was attracted to transportation as a punishment precisely because it threatened to undermine the social, religious and cultural identity of 'a native'. In fact it was hailed as 'a weapon of tremendous power' because '[g]enerally over India a sentence of transportation beyond the black water is regarded with indescribable horror'.[26]

The body was also the target of efforts that keyed on developing the penitentiary as the principal mechanism of punishment in India. As the Committee on Prison Discipline put it, changes were needed in order to make 'imprisonment as severe as can properly be borne'.[27] Three major revisions were deemed critical to realizing this goal: the imposition of solitary confinement; a stiffening in the conditions of work; and a diminution in jail living standards so that they would be comparable to or no better than those of the poorest of free people.

Financial constraints, so often a roadblock to the implementation of colonial penal policies and practices, ensured that neither of the first two goals was attained by the mid-nineteenth century. As the close-ups of the Arrah and Muzaffapur jails reveal, prisoners continued to be herded together in wards, a condition far different than that envisioned in the Committee's ideal of solitary confinement. Few administrators were willing to undertake the expenses involved in building jails with individual cells. Nor were the attempts to revise the working conditions of prisoners any more successful. Macaulay's Committee had found convict extramural labour projects wanting because they were unproductive. They were said to result in high mortality rates and they were believed to be conducive to the 'worst system of discipline, or . . . no system of discipline'. Apparently their supervisors, bent on maximizing their labour output, granted convict labourers a variety of perquisites, ranging from good food and feasts to money allowances and visits from friends on Sundays. In the Committee's reckoning, intramural labour was objectionable as well because it produced a labour force that competed with widely available 'cheap' free labour. Furthermore, it violated caste taboos ('higher castes would not be able to take up all trades') and provided criminals with training to become the 'best workmen in the country'. Therefore, the Committee recommended that prisoners be assigned 'dull, monotonous, wearisome' tasks involving labour on treadmills. However, this option was never widely introduced.[28] Thus, almost two decades after the Committee had condemned convict labour, prisoners at the Shahabad and Tirhut jails in 1855 were still engaged in working in road gangs.

Far more successful were the efforts of the Committee to alter the standard of prison living, a change that had the added benefit of paring down the costs of maintaining prisons. Taking a page out of the 1834 Report of the Royal Commission on the Poor Laws, the Committee on Prison Discipline deemed the diet of Indian prisoners to be overly generous. As in the case of the indigent, for whom the New Poor Laws in England had proposed a uniform system of relief defined by the principle of 'less eligibility' (that is, conditions were to be 'less eligible' or less attractive for people seeking relief than those existing for 'honest labourers'), the diet of Indian prisoners was to be regulated along similar lines. The Committee found fault with the diet of prisoners in Bengal because it was said to be better than that of agricultural labourers eking out their livelihood outside the walls. To reach parity it therefore recommended reducing the quality of the diet: coarser grain, for instance, and switching to a system of rations rather than granting inmates a money allowance to purchase their own food. The Committee condemned money allowances because they provided prisoners with access to money that could be used for nefarious purposes. They were also said to allow inmates the privilege of 'marketing' which, according to Macaulay and others, was an especially 'great alleviation of the punishment of confinement . . . [because it was] peculiarly agreeable to the Indian character'.

Targeted for elimination as well was the related practice of allowing prisoners to cook their own meals. By denying this allowance the Committee intended to enhance 'the effect of imprisonment', because the 'cooking of his dinner . . . is . . . one of the greatest enjoyments of every individual amongst the lower orders in India'. Depriving the prisoner of the 'two pleasures of marketing and cooking', the Committee confidently declared, 'would add materially to the severity of the punishment of imprisonment, and so make it possible to reduce proportionally the terms of imprisonment, without taking away from the efficacy of the punishment'.[29]

Even before the Committee's report on prison discipline was published in 1838, the Bengal authorities began to push for the abolition of money allowances and the introduction of the ration system. By April 1838 the new system was already in place in many districts; in a few areas, rations were distributed through messes (a group dining arrangement that was introduced in the Indian prisons in the early 1840s and replaced the ration system; each mess was supposed to number 20). The government stepped up its effort in 1840 when it made a systematic attempt to introduce messes, and by mid-1841 plans were well underway to extend the messing system to all the jails of

Bihar. Prisoners in virtually every Bihar jail greeted the new measures with open hostility. In Saran District's Chapra jail in 1842 the order provoked a 'serious disturbance' among 700 inmates, supported by 3,000 to 4,000 townspeople who converged on the prison gates. Such resistance compelled the local authorities to suspend the messing experiment and to launch inquiries into caste and religious rules regarding food and its ingestion.

The body behind and beyond the walls

The Bengal government returned to the subject of messing in 1845 when it announced its willingness to impose the new regimen by force if necessary. Once again the inmates of nearly all the jails in Bihar responded to the new arrangement by committing acts of insubordination and violence. In several prisons, to use the official vocabulary, 'serious insurrections' broke out that were forcibly suppressed with the loss of life when the military was called in and opened fire. Everywhere local populations gathered outside the walls to lend support to the inmates within. A handful of Patna city residents even attempted to conspire with other influential leaders in the region and the sepoys stationed in the nearby military outpost of Danapur to foment a rebellion against the British authorities.[30]

Jail and town made common cause in 1855 as well. The jail populations of both Muzaffarpur and Arrah appeared to be united to a man in the emeutes, notwithstanding the efforts their jailers made to break up their resistance by a policy of divide and conquer. The leaders of the 'disturbances' in both jails represented a wide cross-section of the inmate population. Of the 18 prisoners singled out in Tirhut as the primary instigators, the single largest group, 6, were in prison for involvement in riots and affrays; 2 were listed as sentenced for 'wounding' and 2 were termed '*diwani*' prisoners, namely those charged with violating decrees of the civil court. The remaining eight were more the common-or-garden variety of criminal, as two were described as 'bad characters' and the rest were implicated in crimes such as theft and burglary (two), receiving stolen property (one), cattle-stealing (one), forgery (one) and homicide (one). Their caste backgrounds ranged from lower castes, Dusadhs and Ahirs, to those with names such as Singh, Rai, Misra and Thakur, suggesting a high-caste status. Significant also is the fact that 18 townspeople were singled out in Muzaffarpur as having played a major role in the jail riot. This cohort included several men identified as 'wealthy inhabitants' of the town, for example 'Kaleepershaud, a wealth zamindar', 'Kewulkishoon, a zamindar who has a house in town' and 'Fuqeerchund Sao, a wealthy bunnyah in the town'. Others on this list included 'Hurbhungun Doss, a goshain living near the town [. . .] Hemsraj Rai, a collectory peon [. . .] Nagah Mistry, a carpenter in town

[and] Mukhun Sing, a moktear of the Foujdarry court'. Although less representative, the leaders of the Arrah emeute, who numbered eight in all, were also men whose offences covered a multitude of crimes: homicide (four), murder (one), theft (one) and affray (two). They may well have been drawn mostly from the upper castes as their names were Rai, Dubey and Sing.[31]

The extent to which the no-lotah order triggered a flood of support and sympathy from the wider community is also apparent from the public and open interrogation of government intentions underlying this directive. Distinctly audible was the cry uttered by the crowds assembled outside the Muzaffarpur jail that government actions were aimed at violating their religion and 'making Christians of the prisoners'.[32] Widespread rumours circulated locally in Bihar in 1855, as they had in 1845, of ulterior government motives and sinister plots. According to the magistrate of Shahabad, 'exaggerated reports' were current 'concerning the nature of the [lotah] order'. He had received 'information . . . that some of the prisoners' friends had sent out letters to the mufassil, stating that it was the intention of government to make all the people Christians'. He had also learnt from his local sources that there was 'deep and general sympathy outside for the prisoners, as well as a pretty general idea prevailing in the interior that [it] is the intention of government to make the people Christian'.[33] In fact, as in the case of messing, the issue of lotahs appeared to rankle many people beyond the walls of the prison because it touched on matters of eating and drinking that were central to religious and caste notions of purity and pollution.

It is little wonder then that jail guards often appeared to array themselves on the side of the prisoners. In Tirhut the *najibs* (irregular corps) of the jail refused to execute the order to fire on the prisoners unless the magistrate was willing to issue his command in writing. Recruited locally, jail guards were often in 'sympathy with the prisoners', a relationship that one administrator regarded as 'prejudicial should an outbreak ever occur'.[34] For the prisoners, caste and religion were always powerful and effective 'weapons of the weak'. Caste and religion defined and shaped their fundamental beliefs and practices but also served as the bases from which to challenge any innovations made in their existing system of discipline and punishment. In the words of one inspector of jails, who claimed considerable familiarity with prisoners and their understanding of caste, inmates were always

> . . . most tanacious [*sic*] and suspicious on the subject, but perfectly disposed to listen to any argument . . . It is never prudent suddenly to carry out any new measure with natives, even where it is itself unobjectionable and intended for their benefit. They are naturally indisposed to change, and in many instances would resist every

attempt at innovation incautiously made without making them fully acquainted with its real object and intention. The most extravagant popular errors exist among the uneducated classes of natives upon the subject of caste. I seldom enter a jail in which some plea of exemption from prisons rules on the score of caste is not made, but as they are most utterly untenable and erroneous, I have as yet experienced no difficulty in refusing a compliance with them. . .[35]

Notwithstanding the obvious colonial colouring of these observations, this administrator correctly recognized that prisoners often resisted efforts at discipline and punishment in the early nineteenth century on the grounds of caste and religion. In the colonial imagination, caste was an institution that incarcerated Indians in an earlier time and less civilized place. In the hands of prisoners it could be used on occasion to resist the new technologies of punishment that sought to discipline them into facing a more punitive existence.

Conclusion

The lotah emeutes of 1855 represent one in a long string of acts of resistance by prisoners in the face of the emerging system of colonial discipline and punishment in the early nineteenth century that was aimed at inflicting a just measure of pain. Directed against the body and, increasingly, against the mind as well, the colonial deployment of new technologies and imposition of new regimens were, at times, deliberately constructed and wilfully construed by their target populations to be socially, culturally and religiously transgressive. Resistance to them was therefore fierce and often united prisoners and the local inhabitants of the areas in which the jails were situated. In engendering a common cause between town and jail populations, the prison riots of 1855 anticipated the events of 1857–8, when the North Indian countryside was rocked by a rebellion that also unified a diversity of groups and that was sparked in places by rumours of colonial corporal policies aimed at religious pollution. The collage of events reproduced here also reveals that the walls dividing prisons and the rest of local society were far less concrete than those separating the colonial state from all of its subject peoples, whether they were lodged behind or beyond the walls of its carceral institutions.

Bibliography

Primary Sources

Loch, T C, 1856, *Report on the Jails of Bengal, Behar and Orissa, for the Year 1854–55*, Calcutta, Calcutta Gazetteer Office.

Mouat, Frederick J, 1856, *Reports on Jails Visited and Inspected in Bengal, Behar and Arracan*, Calcutta, Military Orphan Press.

Report of the Committee on Prison Discipline, 1838, Calcutta, Baptist Mission Press.

Loch Circular: T C Loch, Inspector of Jails, Lower Provinces, to all officers, circular no. 22, 26 April 1855, Board's Collections, 1854–5.

Outbreaks: 'Outbreaks in the Mozufferpore and Arrah Jails', compiled in *Bengal Judicial Proceedings*, 31 May–7 June 1855, nos 1–38.

11 May 1855, R A Forbes, Sessions Judge Tirhut, to W Grey, Secretary Government of Bengal (GOB), no. 78.

18 May 1855, 'Minute', F J Halliday, Lieutenant Governor.

10 May 1855, A E Russell, Magistrate Tirhut, to Hon. R Forbes, Judge, no. 185.

15 May 1855, F B Drummond, Magistrate Shahabad, to GOB, no. 270.

13 May 1855, F B Drummond to GOB, no. 200.

22 May 1855, T C Loch, Inspector of Jails, to GOB, no. 91.

17 May 1855, GOB to Magistrate.

Papers regarding Lotahs: 'Papers regarding the question as to whether the possession of Brass Lotahs is essential to the Preservation of the Caste of a Hindoo Prisoner'.

21 January 1857, 'Minute by the Lieutenant Governor'.

28 February 1856, C Beadon, Government of India (GOI), to GOB, no. 426.

January 14, 1856 'Minute by the Hon'ble J. P. Grant'.

12 May 1856, F J Mouat, Inspector of Jails, to GOB, no. 93.

Bengal Judicial (Criminal) Proceedings:

28 July 1855, Russell to Sessions Judge, no. 358 in August 30 1855, no. 33.

2 July 1856, Offg. Magistrate Shahabad to GOB in July 17, no. 18A.

16 June 1856, H Richardson, Magistrate Tirhut, to GOB in July 17, no. 14.

22 May 1855, Loch to Secy, GOB no. 91 in June 7, no. 30.

Bengal Public Proceedings:

27 June 1855, W Tayler, Offg. Commr, Patna, to GOB Sept. 6 1855, nos 34 & 35.

7 July 1855, Minute by Lieutenant-Governor of Bengal Sept. 6 1855, nos 34 & 35.

Secondary Sources

Arnold, D, 1993, *Colonizing the Body: State Medicine and Epidemic Disease in Nineteenth-Century India*, Delhi, Oxford University Press.

Chattopadhyay, B, 2000, *Crime and Control in Early Colonial Bengal*, Calcutta, Bagchi.

Dirks, N, 1992, 'Castes of Mind', *Representations* 37, pp. 56–78.

Foucault, M, 1977, *Discipline and Punish: the Birth of the Prison*, Middlesex, Penguin Books.

Ignatieff, M, 1981, 'State, Civil Society, and Total Institutions: A Critique of Recent Social Historians of Punishment', in M Tonray and N Morris (eds), *Crime and Justice: An Annual Review of Research*, Chicago, Chicago University Press, pp. 158–63.

Mills, J, 2002 (forthcoming), 'Review of B. Chattopadhyay, Crime and Control in Early Colonial Bengal', *Contemporary South Asia*.

Mulvany, J, 1918, 'Bengal Jails in Early Days', *Calcutta Review*, 292, p. 303.

Tobias, J, 1967, *Crime and Industrial Society in the Nineteenth Century*, London, Penguin Books.

Yang, A, 1987, 'Disciplining "Natives": Prisons and Prisoners in Early Nineteenth Century Colonial India', *South Asia*, 10/ 2 pp. 29–43.

Yang, A, 1995, 'The Voice of Colonial Discipline and Punishment: Knowledge, Power and the Penological Discourse in early Nineteenth Century India', *Indo-British Review*, 21/2, pp. 62–71.

Notes

1. See Yang 1987; Arnold 1993; Foucault 1977; Ignatieff 1981.
2. Loch Circular.
3. Outbreaks, 18 May 1855.
4. Loch 1856, Appendix, p. viii.
5. Outbreaks, 11 May 1855.
6. Outbreaks, 10 May 1855.
7. Ibid.
8. Loch 1856, p. vi.
9. Outbreaks, 13 May 1855.
10. Outbreaks, 15 May 1855.
11. Ibid.
12. Outbreaks, 18 May 1855.
13. Outbreaks, 17 May 1855; Papers regarding Lotahs, 21 January 1857.
14. Outbreaks, 18 May 1855.

15. Ibid.
16. Ibid.
17. Outbreaks, 7 June 1855, p. 30.
18. Papers regarding Lotahs, 28 February 1856.
19. Ibid., 14 January 1856.
20. Ibid., 21 January 1857.
21. Dirks 1992, p. 57.
22. See Yang 1995, pp. 62–71.
23. Mulvany 1918, p. 303.
24. See Chattopadhyay 2000; Mills 2002.
25. Yang 1995.
26. Ibid.
27. *Report of the Committee on Prison Discipline*, 1838, p. 115.
28. Ibid., p. 59; see also Yang 1995.
29. *Report of the Committee on Prison Discipline*, 1838, pp. 3–34.
30. Yang 1987.
31. Bengal Judicial (Criminal) Proceedings: June 1856, July 1855, July 1856.
32. Ibid., May 1855.
33. Outbreaks, 15 May 1855.
34. Mouat 1856, p. 93.
35. Papers regarding Lotahs, 12 May 1856

6

The Body at Work: Colonial Art Education and the Figure of the 'Native Craftsman'

Deepali Dewan

Introduction

In the latter half of the nineteenth century, concern about the declining state of Indian arts resulted in a number of debates around art education. These debates became articulated, in large part, around the figure of the native craftsman.[1] Visual representations of the native craftsman proliferated during the latter half of the nineteenth century and featured the body of the native craftsman in the process of producing his craft. They were reproduced in illustrated books and journals, displayed in exhibitions and gathered into museum collections. This essay will explore the production of these images of the native craftsman at work at the intersection of art education and colonialism. The 'native craftsman' figure was constructed within colonial discourse as both the hope of Indian art's revival and as the source of its corruption. Images of the body at work became the standard representational mode for the figure, outside of which he became unrecognizable.

Representations of the 'native craftsman' at work

In the latter half of the nineteenth century, images of the native craftsman were frequently produced within the arena of colonial art education. In general, the image featured the body of the craftsman engaged in his craft. The art object on which he worked was placed before him. His hand clutched a tool, raised or positioned as though in the process of being used. In drawings, the craftsman was almost invariably represented with his head bent forward as if concentrating on the task before him. In a few photographs, by contrast, the craftsman can be found looking into the camera's lens and out at the viewer, although these are rare as most photographs were carefully choreographed scenes. The craftsman's legs, arms and torso were represented as engaged in the act of production. The working body and the object it is producing occupied most of the picture plane, leaving little room for anything else. The lack of background context located the craftsman in a timeless space without historic referent. When context was provided, it was minimal and usually consisted of other finished products, more tools and the semblance of an indoor or outdoor setting. Finally, his position in the picture frame, gesture and facial expression suggested that he had been caught in a frozen moment in time and in the process of working. This representation of the native craftsman at work suggested an 'authentic' moment of production in which the knowledge of traditional Indian arts was captured in the process of being transferred from the craftsman's body to the object he produces.

Wood Carver. Drawn by John Lockwood Kipling, Simola, 1870.

It is important to point out that there are other ways of visually representing labourers. The Indian examples contrast sharply, for instance, with the photographs of American steelworkers taken by Lewis Hine in the 1920s. While both romanticize the figure of the worker and monumentalize the working body in the picture frame, the American photographs aestheticize the shape and metal of the machine as a celebration of the benefits of industrialization. Furthermore the lightening plays off the skin in the black-and-white photographs, emphasizing (even eroticizing) the body of the American worker, whereas the images of the native craftsman at work privilege the gesture of the worker, that is, the processes of the body engaged in work. In this way the physicality of the body, although present, is not thrust into the foreground to the same extent in the Indian images as in the American photographs.

Another instructive contrast can be made with pre-colonial images produced in India of the artist at work. In Mughal manuscript paintings the artist is often depicted as seated in a working posture and in the process of producing a painting. Unlike colonial images of the native craftsman at work, these images of the court artist in Mughal painting did not feature on the page but occupied the margins. Further, they were among a number of images that depicted aspects of court life. Also, unlike colonial representations, images of Mughal artists were self-referential, in other words they were produced by the artists themselves. In rare instances, the image of the artist appeared as a portrait in the centre frame, but these usually did not represent the artist at work and were disguised to fit the artist into the main scene on the illuminated page. Colonial representations of the native craftsman were hardly ever produced by the craftsman himself and usually depicted the working craftsman alone in a setting.

Representations of the native craftsman at work can be understood in the context of earlier visual depictions of caste from the late eighteenth and early nineteenth centuries. One of the earliest visual compilations on Indian castes, Balthazar Solvyns' *A Collection of Two Hundred and Fifty Coloured Etchings Descriptive of the Manners, Customs, and Dresses of the Hindoos* (1799), includes illustrations of people meant to represent generalized caste-types. Illustrations of the artisan castes depict a craftsman at work in the centre of the page. The body of the craftsman and the object of his production, as well as associated tools, make up the content of the composition. There is little background context save shading or minor foliage to indicate the ground. Like images of native craftsmen at work produced later within colonial art schools, these early representations depict a 'native' type in the middle of working. Yet unlike the later images the early depictions are part of a larger series of caste-types. Nonetheless, many visual elements are consistent. The craftsman is shown in the process of working and the unfinished object lies before him. A lack of context highlights the relationship between the worker's body and his output. His identity is defined by the work he does and the work marks his body as belonging to a particular caste. In the later images, caste translates into a particular artistic practice. A drawing of a carpet loom from 1850 in the collection of the India Office Library marks the transition between the early and later forms.[2] A large carpet loom is depicted with five weavers busy at work. Not part of the illustrations of caste-types, it marks the emerging interest in representations of native craftsmen in particular. Yet unlike later images, the carpet weavers are dwarfed by the loom itself, which seems to be the focus of pictorial attention.

Images of the craftsman produced by colonial art schools are striking for their increased focus on the body of the labouring craftsman. The visual and physical form of the craftsman at work gained increasing attention in the course of the latter half of the nineteenth century, when images of the native craftsman were produced by art school principals, teachers and students and circulated in a variety of media. The images were published in journals and books as illustrations accompanying texts on a particular type of Indian art. Drawings and photographs were produced for and distributed to annual exhibitions, museum displays and museum collections. They were often displayed beside actual objects in annual exhibitions and museum collections. A series of drawings by John Lockwood Kipling dated to 1870 (see illustration on p. 119) were sent to the South Kensington School of Art and Design in London, Britain's main school of decorative arts, for display beside the objects they depicted. These drawings were reproduced and further circulated in the first issue of *Portfolios of Industrial Art*, a series of photo-chromolithographic representations of examples of industrial art produced by W Griggs, one of the main publishers of illustrated literature on Indian art in the latter half of the nineteenth century.[3] This example shows the reuse of images of the native craftsman in a variety of related contexts, from exhibitions to publications. Photographs at the India Office Library, for example, were collected because they were displayed next to objects sent to London annual exhibitions, as indicated by notes added in the margins of the pictures.[4]

Illustrations in the *Journal of Indian Art and Industry*, the first journal to be devoted exclusively to the study of Indian arts, often included illustrations of craftsmen at work as well. Analogous to exhibition displays, the images were placed beside illustrations of finished objects. While they may have served as illustrations of technique they were not so specific as to allow the reader to replicate the method illustrated. Rather, they seem to serve a more general purpose. Illustrations of the native craftsman at work continued to appear throughout the run of the journal, from 1884 to 1917, often appearing in the decorative lettering on the first page of each article. In this way the working body had a relationship with the information presented in the article. While not referred to directly, the craftsman at work suggested the direct relationship between the textual content of Indian art and the labouring body of the craftsman.

The relationship between the image of the craftsman and the actual object is also present at the turn of the century. The catalogue to the 1902–1903 Delhi exhibition features illustrations of the craftsman at work at various intervals, between chapters on Indian decorative arts.[5] This was very probably a reflection of the particular focus on the native craftsman in the exhibition. The design of the exhibition certificate awarded to prizewinners depicts an architectural structure with niches featuring a native craftsman working diligently. An example in the collection of the Government College of Art and Craft, Chennai, reads 'Certificate of Merit, Third Class, Awarded to Madras School of Arts for two screens with gesso panels'. The craftsmen are distinguished by dress and manner and their regions of origin within India are indicated by a label under each niche. In this context, the working craftsmen stood for the generalized artistic practices of a particular area. His presence on an award certificate underscored the use of the image of the native craftsman at work to validate colonial efforts at the revival of Indian arts. It brought together the art object and its producers in a venue facilitated by colonial institutions. The image implied a tradition of artistic practice that had seemingly continued unchanged from the past to the present and that ensured Indian arts' continuance into the future.

On the decline of Indian art

A general perception that Indian arts were in a state of decline was formulated during the Great Exhibition of 1851. This perception developed as an undercurrent of the widespread praise of Indian arts that was generated by the first-time exposure to Indian art afforded by the Great Exhibition. This perception of the state of decline of Indian art entered into colonial narratives of Indian history and shaped much of the official policy towards Indian art education for the second half of the nineteenth century.[6]

The 1851 Great Exhibition of the Industry of All Nations was meant to bring together the industrial and decorative arts of many regions and nations of the world. Initiated by England's Prince Albert as part of a larger plan to boost the quality of and export market for English goods, the exhibition involved mostly European nations and their colonies.[7] Held in the glass-and-steel architectural wonder of its time, Crystal Palace, the Great Exhibition of 1851 was the first of its kind and spawned a series of similar exhibitions in Europe and elsewhere that continued well into the twentieth century. India's representation in the exhibition was organized by a committee which solicited works from the different regions of the Indian subcontinent through smaller committees and arts institutions that had been established in the presidencies. Local Indian royalty also participated by sending in works for display from their private collections. The India section of the Great Exhibition received praise from the exhibition judges and the British public alike. It was deemed superior even to British and French decorative arts for its spare and geometric ornamentation in contrast to the crowded naturalistic decoration of the early Victorian period.[8] The 1851 exhibition was thus the catalyst by which Indian decorative arts became the focus of European attention.

Alongside praise for Indian arts at the Great Exhibition there was concern for the seeming decline in the quality of recent production. This decline was observed in the more recently made objects and was defined in two ways. One was the incorporation of mass-produced elements such as stamping, printing and the use of synthetic dyes. Secondly, decline was defined by the inclusion of Western decorative forms such as naturalistic figures or floral imagery.[9] These two forms of decline, technique/method and style/design, were seen as the result of an influx of foreign products into the Indian market, leading to the corruption of Indian arts. The financial pressure on existing Indian art industries that resulted from having to compete with mass-produced European goods forced producers of Indian art to abandon handcrafted techniques in favour of mass production. Further, the shift in consumer tastes by both the new British patronage and existing Indian upper-class patrons, forced Indian artisans to abandon Indian designs for Western-style ornamentation.

The perception of decline in recent Indian arts encouraged official involvement with art education in India, which had emerged not long before in the form of isolated private institutions – part of the wave in establishing private educational institutions. In Madras, for example, the Resident Surgeon, Dr Alexander Hunter, had started a private art school that was given government funding in 1852 and became the colonial government's main school of art for the Madras Presidency. In Calcutta, the art school established by a committee of interested private individuals in 1852 gained state funding by 1854. In Bombay, by comparison, a member of the organizing committee for the 1851 Great Exhibition's Indian section, Sir Jamsetji Jijibhai, a Parsi industrialist and philanthropist, gave the government Rs 10,000 for an art school in the Bombay Presidency that was finally established in 1857.[10] Each art school was directly or indirectly affiliated with a museum connected to the school or located in the presidency capital. Also, the principals at the art schools were involved in the collection and distribution of objects for the local, regional and international exhibitions that took place throughout the latter half of the nineteenth century. The government became involved in the revival of Indian arts through art education partly because of the perception that British rule was responsible for the influx of foreign-made goods into the Indian market. Furthermore, the transformation or extinction of existing Indian art industries would take away a source of goods that had recently been found to be very popular on the international market for the display and use of exotic curiosities.

Despite the individual circumstances under which each art school was founded and the very different trajectories along which they developed, the shift of the art schools from private to government institutions involved each of them in an official mission to stop the perceived decline of Indian arts. Whether Indian art actually suffered a decline in quality is not at issue here. It can be argued that the assessment of a decline in Indian arts, alongside praise, was a necessary action for a state that in 1851 was assuming increasing political power on the subcontinent and would establish direct colonial control in a few years. Straightforward praise for Indian arts would have contradicted the positioning of the Indian subject as inferior and thus in need of foreign rule. The decline of Indian arts, which can be seen as part of larger colonial narratives about the decline of Indian civilization, was another manifestation of colonial discourse necessary to justify the British presence in India.

The narrative of decline that was constructed around Indian arts established the framework for other perceptions. Certain elements in Indian art became associated with decline and centred on mass production and the incorporation of Western motifs. As a result, other elements were valorized: handcrafted technique; and what became identified as 'traditional' Indian designs and motifs. These valorized qualities became the markers of an 'authentic' Indian art and the criteria for efforts intended to initiate an artistic revival. The paths taken towards this goal of revival varied in the specific details, and there was disagreement among art school officials about how they should proceed. Yet one constant thread emerged in debates about the decline and desired revival of Indian arts, and this involved the figure of the native craftsman.

'Native craftsman' as source of revival

Concentration on the figure of the native craftsman within debates about art education cannot be considered in the South Asian context in isolation. It was related to the British context as well, particularly to the ideas circulating within the Arts and Crafts movement during the latter half of the nineteenth century. The figure of the 'craftsman' emerged in British art education as part of the reaction to industrialization. The Gothic Revival in England romanticized the medieval period as a pre-industrial age of craft guilds, handcrafted techniques and village life.[11] The decline in British crafts was attributed, among other reasons, to the Industrial Age and the dominance of the machine. In spite of the general celebration of British technological–economic prowess, industrialization was perceived by many to be at the root of the social and cultural degradation of British society. The Arts and Crafts movement, which included such artists as William Morris, was an extension of the movement against industrialization that advocated more traditional modes of production and particularly celebrated the handcrafted object. Many teachers and principals of the colonial art schools, such as E B Havell and John Lockwood Kipling, received training at the South Kensington School of Art and Design during the time when the Arts and Crafts movement was emerging there.[12] The medieval period in Britain was considered analogous to traditional Indian society, based on village life, artisan communities, hereditary craftsmen and traditional handcrafted techniques. One result of the romanticization of the medieval craftsman was a focus on the indigenous artist in non-industrialized places as a source of revival for 'traditional' art. The indigenous craftsman was considered the counterpart to the medieval craftsman whom Europe had lost in the process of industrialization and modernization. The people who reacted to Indian arts at the exhibition of 1851 were those individuals involved with British art education, the collections of the East India Company, and philanthropists and art patrons from the subcontinent. Art schools were seen as one of the main avenues for the revival of Indian arts along with the related functions of annual exhibitions and museum collections. The arrest of decline and the encouragement of a revival in Indian arts was pursued through a number of means, most of which revolved around the figure of the native craftsman.

Reports by colonial art-school officials from the latter half of the nineteenth century claim the figure of the native craftsman to be a repository of traditional artistic knowledge.[13] As a living archive of traditional knowledge, the native craftsman was the hope for the revival of Indian arts. If the art schools could preserve that knowledge, traditional Indian arts were assured survival. One way was through the physical presence of the native craftsman at the art school itself. Art schools hoped to employ master craftsmen who could serve as teachers, providing 'authentic' knowledge to students who had not been sullied by the effects of inexpensive and low-quality imports. In this way art schools hoped to become a new site for the transfer of knowledge that had traditionally been practised within the family or in the context of the 'traditional' relationship between master and apprentice. The working craftsman in the art school symbolized a direct link between past knowledge and present production.

It was the hereditary craftsman who was looked upon by colonial observers
with particular interest. Manifesting a lineage in which technique was passed
down from father to son, the hereditary craftsman was perceived as a peculiar
cultural asset. The idea that inherited knowledge was an unbroken link with
the past was asserted in a report by T W Rolleston, Secretary of the Judging
Committee for the Indian Section of the 1911 London Exhibition of
the Pageant of Empire: 'In no country are the conditions for . . . revival more
favorable than in India [where] the traditions of handicrafts and the hereditary skill of the worker are maintained as yet in almost undiminished force. .
.'.[14] Because the knowledge of the hereditary craftsman linked him to the past
more directly than did the knowledge of his non-hereditary counterparts, it
carried a greater degree of authenticity and made his role in arresting the
decline of Indian arts all the more critical. Given nineteenth-century notions
about culture and race, it was assumed that artistic knowledge and skill
were transmitted not only orally but also biologically. Thus the notion of the
hereditary craftsman intersected with nineteenth-century colonial ideas about
the biological disposition of colonized people to certain occupations.

As part of the attempt to revive Indian arts, art schools also hoped to attract
Indian students, particularly those belonging to practising artisan families, in
order to train them in and guide them towards the forms and techniques of
traditional Indian arts. Although not stated directly, the hereditary craftsman
was perceived as more skilled than any other pupil. The annual reports of the
Madras School of Art, while under the direction of E B Havell, count 'sons of
craftsmen' as a separate student category.[15] An increase in the numbers was
presented as a positive development in student attendance. Having hereditary
craftsmen as students was a particular triumph of art education as a means of
direct access to the traditional knowledge that art schools attempted to impart
towards the salvation of Indian arts.

When a master craftsman could not be procured or could not be persuaded
to stay at the art school (a frequent frustration expressed by art officials
in colonial documents), the figure of the native craftsman was referred to
indirectly through the objects he produced, through his method of working
and occasionally through the recording of his voice. Colonial art schools
became one of the main sources for publications and illustrations of traditional
Indian arts in the latter half of the nineteenth century. These were produced
by art school officials and European scholars of Indian art with detailed
descriptions of technique, symbolism, style and use of art objects, survey of
artist villages and translations of the 'voice' of the master native craftsman.
The *Journal of Indian Art and Industry* is a prime example of this, in addition to
monographs on art industries relating to the nineteenth century. In this way
the publications indirectly referred to the presence of the native craftsman.

The information provided in textual descriptions of technique and use, and the visual reproductions of objects, served as a permanent record of the craftsman's knowledge that rendered his actual presence superfluous. Publications also allowed colonial institutions of art education a certain degree of control over artistic knowledge, whereas they could not be sure of controlling the flesh-and-blood body of the craftsman himself. Official documents surviving from the nineteenth century reveal a sense of frustration at the related circumstances of a dependency on native craftsmen, the inability to attract them to the art schools and the need for illustrated literature on Indian arts.[16] Illustrated publications, on the other hand, recorded and distributed visual and textual information on Indian arts taken directly or indirectly from the native craftsman and hence ensured the continuation of knowledge about traditional Indian arts.

The figure of the native craftsman was present in similar ways and for similar reasons in the arena of annual exhibitions and museum collections. In the physical absence of the craftsman, collections of Indian art objects manifested his traditional knowledge as a product of his work and could be used as examples for educational purposes. All the major art schools assembled collections of art objects for study purposes. Museum collections in India were conceived of along similar lines.[17] Displays of art objects were meant to educate a consumer public about which objects were worthy of purchase and to educate Indian artisans who visited the museums about which objects were worthy of emulation. In these instances, the native craftsman was both the subject and the object of museum collections: the master who produced the object on display as well as the target audience. Annual exhibitions were managed towards similar ends. Submission to the exhibitions was closely controlled, and only those objects fitting identified criteria of what constituted traditional Indian arts were admitted. A system of prizes was devised as an incentive for artists to produce and then submit objects in accordance with the criteria of traditional aesthetics laid out by the organizing committees. The objects which received awards were those that most closely matched what was considered traditional design; the prizes were meant unambiguously to direct both artisans and the consumer public towards what was judged good, better or best for emulation and purchase.

In each of the avenues towards revival devised by the school/museum/ exhibition arena of colonial art education, the figure of the native craftsman is directly or indirectly present. In particular, it is the body of the craftsman at work that is indexed. This occurs directly through his physical presence at the art school, through his presence as subject and object of exhibitions and museum displays, and through representation of the craftsman at work in publications. It also occurs indirectly through the art object (the result of his working body) in a collection or exhibition, through its reproduction in an illustration and through references to the native craftsman at work in textual descriptions written by art school officials. As in the case of Kipling's 1870 drawings, the image of the working craftsman was circulated from art school (where it was produced) to exhibition (where it was displayed) to several publications (where it was reproduced). In the 1910 exhibition certificate, the image of the working body of the craftsman validated the certificate, the objects to which it was presented, the exhibition space in which they were displayed and, by extension, the knowledge and expertise of the organizers that brought it all together. The working body was a container for the 'authentic' traditional knowledge believed to be in the native craftsman's possession. It was also a literal manifestation of the transfer of knowledge from the body to the object. Harnessing and preserving the information present in that transfer was a main focus of colonial education's efforts at reviving Indian arts. The image of the native craftsman at work was one way to pin down this elusive transfer.

'Native craftsman' as source of corruption

Perceptions of the decline of Indian arts due to the emulation of imported Western goods also positioned the native craftsman as the source of corruption in Indian arts. Emulation of Western aesthetics by traditional craftsmen was seen as a sign of their degradation and as a lack of discernment on their part. In this way, the 'Indian craftsman' was thought to indiscriminately imitate any and all 'outside' influences in his craft. In 'Defects of Indian Art', Thomas Holbein Hendley, the principal of the Jaipur School of Art, presented the Indian craftsman as subject to thoughtless imitation:

> The Indian art worker . . . has proved far too ready to comply with the demand . . . patterns are repeated ad nauseam . . . the principal object of many workmen has been . . . to search out in a pattern-book something which might meet the immediate want . . . In this way no thought [is] required . . . By this method balance is soon lost, styles of ornament become mixed, and the whole effect is weakened.[18]

The view of craftsmen as undiscerning and thus a source of decline also provided a justification for colonial art schools. The need for colonial guidance in India in the form of art education was also asserted by Burns: 'I have always hoped and believed that the chief purpose of Schools of Art in India was to stand between the indigenous craftsmen and all [the] disturbing influences'.[19] In a 1894 report F H Andrews, then principal of the Lahore School of Art, elaborated upon this purpose of art schools to protect against ignorant middlemen, a source of corruption as influential as foreign designs: 'the influence of [the] school is . . . in the arrest of the degeneration of the arts towards which there is a constant tendency, largely due to the influence of non-discriminating and inartistic employers'.[20]

The construction of the native craftsman as a source of corruption in Indian art positioned the art schools as institutions to police and monitor artistic production. In praising the presence of master craftsmen in the industrial workshop connected to the school, John Griffiths, a teacher at the Sir J J School of Art in Bombay, was quick to add that strict supervision was required of the craftsmen. If left to their own devices, he argued, they were quick to imitate cheap and commercial styles associated with tourist art.[21] The same guidance was found necessary for teacher and pupil alike. At the 1894 Lahore Conference, Hendley underscored the ultimate authoritative role of art schools:

> Having been thus far educated, the pupils would undergo special training in their crafts . . . and come under the training of master-craftsmen, who would work under the supervision of the local bodies, on the understanding that the authorities in the Schools of Art should have power to inspect and control them, and give advice when they had proof that degeneration was occurring or wrong methods were being followed.[22]

Again, within colonial constructions of the figure of the native craftsman as a source of decline in Indian art, it is the working body in particular that is at the forefront of colonial pedagogical efforts. The working body of the native craftsman was the focus of colonial surveillance and policing in the art schools. It was the working body that was indirectly controlled in museums and annual exhibitions through the rigid criteria with which objects for collection and display had to comply. The undiscerning native craftsman as the centre of artistic corruption fits the larger colonial discourse of the imitative Indian, lacking the mental faculties for discernment, who was necessarily different from and inferior to the colonizer,[23] not to mention his artistic counterparts in Europe. The native craftsman could not be the keeper of traditional knowledge and the saviour of Indian arts without colonial intervention in the form of education. He had also to be represented in a way that justified the colonial presence: in this case as the source of creative corruption and the need for colonial guidance.

The idea that the working body of the craftsman was a source of artistic corruption in India fits nineteenth-century notions of the role of labour and reform. Michel Foucault in *Discipline and Punish* describes how labour, in particular the naturalization of work habits within the body, became a method of reform in Europe in the eighteenth century, shifting emphasis away from physical torture to psychological reform through industrious labour.[24] In nineteenth-century England the connection between art education and reform was applied to the working class and art schools were set up in factory towns to 'uplift' the labouring poor. In the colonial context, work and reform were also instituted in the form of industrial arts. For example, early efforts at industrial art education included Mechanic's Institutes, established not along the lines of the Royal Art Academy but as institutions for adult education, particularly for the working and artisan classes. Like their British counter- parts, colonial art schools combined industrial education with social reform, that is, with the desire 'to wean artisans from improper habits, to make them moral and open doors of knowledge'.[25] By the mid-1860s, art schools had been set up in reformatory schools for boys and prisoners in jails were produc- ing carpets. Photographs of workers in jail, such as an image of convicts in Karachi Jail that is now in the collection of the India Office Library, accom- panied the objects themselves and were no different in representational mode than the images of free craftsmen at work. Kipling's 1870 drawings of weavers actually depicted the production of carpets in Amritsar Jail and accompanied an article entitled 'Carpet Making in the Punjab' in the *Journal of Indian Art and Industry*.[26] Although it will not be argued here that craft production in art schools and craft production in jails were one and the same, these images and other sources indicate that in the Indian colony the body receiving artistic instruction and the body being disciplined were not so dissimilar.

Visualizing contradiction and producing the figure of the 'native craftsman'

That the native craftsman represented both the corruption and the revival of Indian arts was, obviously, a contradiction. The image of the craftsman at work visualized this contradiction. The body at work was a manifestation of the transfer of 'authentic' knowledge about traditional Indian arts from craftsman to art object. The body at work was also a symbol of the colonial civilizing mission through education. In both cases, the body at work was a sign of the success of colonial art education at revival through reform and reform through revival.

The subject position described by the term 'native craftsman' did not and does not exist outside of the colonial knowledge that produced it. It is through and within the nexus of colonial art education that the figure of the native craftsman was produced. As a cultural–political icon, it facilitated debates about the revival of Indian art in colonial art education and in turn was produced by them. Images of the craftsman at work were produced alongside particular notions of the native craftsman, at the conjuncture of colonial knowledge and efforts to revive Indian art. In the pre-colonial period the producer of objects, whether decorative or functional, was seen alongside other occupations. If anything, it was the court painter who was romanticized in Mughal memoirs, particularly those of Jahangir. The figure of the native craftsman in the latter half of the nineteenth century was focused not on the object he produced but on his labouring body. The image of the 'body at work' became the defining feature of the native craftsman. Without it he was unrecognizable.

Conclusion

The native craftsman emerged as the focus of attention in the debate surrounding the decline of Indian art. He was thought, on the one hand, to be the last surviving link to a rapidly dying past. On the other hand, he was also perceived as an inferior colonized subject and a victim of Western imperialism, both of which made him susceptible to the influence of foreign goods. Informed by ideologies in the Arts and Crafts movement and nineteenth-century notions of reform, the body of the craftsman at work became the focus of attention for colonial art education. The colonial context is important for, unlike the European subject, the colonial subject was already in need of reform. In this way the contradiction of the native craftsman as a source of both revival and corruption could be sustained.

The representational mode of the native craftsman at work continued through the nineteenth and into the twentieth century.[27] Nationalist images, especially pictures of Gandhi spinning cotton, can be traced genealogically to the earlier art-school images of the native craftsman. Visualizations of nationalist ideology, they borrowed from the associations of cultural authenticity established by the art-school images, linking the present with a pre-colonial past. The native craftsman was further evoked by the nationalist art movement, which romanticized village and folk art as sites of Indian identity unsullied by a colonial history.[28] The native craftsman as a site of national identity continues to be invoked today at craft museums, craft villages and exhibitions of Indian folk arts. This serves as a response to what is perceived as the homogenizing (for which read 'Westernizing') impact of globalization.[29] Exhibitions of 'folk art' often feature a living craftsman at work at the opening or during the course of the exhibition. Indeed 'native craftsmen' are increasingly invited to university campuses and arts institutions to demonstrate their traditional skills. Projects initiated by Non-Governmental Organizations (NGOs) that focus on localized crafts production as a means of social and economic development can be seen in the same light. In each instance, the body of the craftsman at work is present in one form or another, as the marker of a local identity and an embodiment of 'traditional' knowledge, apparently

pre-dating the global present. The survival of the representational mode
points to the ways in which globalization cunningly absorbs, rather than is
deflected by, articulations of the 'local' or the 'traditional'. At the same time, it
is in such articulations that what comes to constitute the 'local' and the 'traditional' is produced.

Acknowledgements

This essay is developed from a chapter of my dissertation, 'Crafting and
Knowledge of Crafts: Art Education, Colonialism and the Madras School of
Arts in Nineteenth-Century South Asia', University of Minnesota, 2001.
Research used for this essay was funded by the Social Science Research
Council, the American Institute for Indian Studies and the Macarthur Inter-
disciplinary Center for the Study of Global Change at the University of
Minnesota. I would like to express special appreciation to the Government
College of Art and Craft, Chennai, for giving me access to their collection of
materials on nineteenth-century art education. I am also grateful to a number
of people whose comments at different stages strengthened the ideas present-
ed here: Frederick Asher, Deborah Hutton, Qadri Ismail, Pradeep
Jeganathan, James Mills, Gloria Goodwin Raheja, Satadru Sen and Sanjay
Seth. Any remaining inadequacies are my own.

Bibliography

Bayley, S, 1981, *The Albert Memorial: the Monument in its Social and Architectural
    Context*, London, Scolar.
Bayly, C, 1990, *The Raj*, London, National Portrait Gallery.
Bhabha, H, 1985, 'Signs taken for wonders: Questions of ambivalence and
    authority under a tree outside Delhi, May 1817', in *The Location of Culture*,
    London, Routledge.
Birdwood, George, 1880, *The Industrial Arts of India*, London, Chapman Hall.
Burns, C, 1908–9, 'The Function of Schools of Art in India', *Journal of the
    Royal Society of Arts* 57/2952, pp. 629–50.
Burton, A, 1999, *Vision and Accident: The Story of the Victoria and Albert Museum*,
    London, V&A Publications.
Chatterjee, P, 1993, *The Nation and Its Fragments: Colonial and Postcolonial
    Histories*, Princeton, Princeton University Press.
Cohn, Bernard, 1996, *Colonialism and Its Forms of Knowledge: The British in India*,
    Princeton, Princeton University Press.
Coomaraswamy, A, 1909 (repr. 1989), *The Indian Craftsman*, New Delhi,
    Munishiram Manoharlal.

Desmond, R, 1982, *The India Museum 1801–1879*, London, HMSO.

Dewan, D, 2001, 'Crafting and Knowledge of Crafts: Art Education, Colonialism and the Madras School of Arts in Nineteenth-Century South Asia', PhD thesis, University of Minnesota.

'Draft Scheme for the Promotion of Industrial Arts in India', 1884, *Journal of Indian Art and Industry*, 1/1.

Foucault, M, 1979, *Discipline and Punish: the Birth of the Prison*, New York, Vintage Books.

Greenough, P, 1995, 'Nation, Economy, and Tradition Displayed: The Indian Crafts Museum, New Delhi', in Carol Breckenridge (ed.), *Consuming Modernity: Public Culture in a South Asian World*, Minneapolis, University of Minnesota Press.

Griggs, W, 1881, *Portfolio of Indian Art, Parts 1–10*, London, South Kensington Museum.

Hendley, T, 1913, 'Defects of Indian Art', *Journal of Indian Art and Industry*, 15/117.

Hunter, A, 1850–51, *Indian Journal of Art, Sciences, and Manufactures*, 1, pp. 1–8

Hunter, A, 1856, *Indian Journal of Art, Sciences, and Manufactures*, 2nd series, 1, pp. 1–4.

Latimer, B A, 1917, 'Carpet Making in the Punjab', *Journal of Indian Art and Industry*, 17/131.

Macdonald, S, 1970, *The History and Philosophy of Art Education*, London, University of London Press.

Metcalfe, T, 1994, *Ideologies of the Raj*, Cambridge, Cambridge University Press.

Mitter, P, 1977, *Much Maligned Monsters: History of European Reactions to Indian Art*, Chicago, University of Chicago Press.

Mitter, P, 1994, *Art and Nationalism in Colonial India, 1850–1922: Occidental Orientations*, Cambridge, Cambridge University Press.

'Papers Relating to Maintenance of Schools of Art in India as State Institutions (1893–96)', 1898, in *Selections from the Records*, 341, Calcutta.

'Reports on Public Instruction in the Madras Presidency (1854–1901)', in *Selections from the Records of the Madras Government*.

Rolleston, T W, 1913, 'Report of the Jury', *Journal of Indian Art and Industry*, 15/117, pp. 28–30.

Royle, J Forbes, 1852, 'The Arts and Manufactures of India', in *Lectures on the Results of the Great Exhibition of 1851*, London, David Bogue.

Solvyns, B, 1799, *A Collection of Two Hundred and Fifty Coloured Etchings Descriptive of the Manners, Customs and Dresses of the Hindoos*, Calcutta.

Tarapor, M, 1997, 'Art and Empire: The Discovery of India in Art and Literature, 1851–1947', PhD thesis, Harvard University.

Watt, G, 1903 (repr. 1987), *Indian Art at Delhi, 1903: Being the Official Catalogue of the Delhi Exhibition 1902–1903*, New Delhi, Motilal Banarsidass.

Notes

1. The terms 'artist' and 'craftsman' artificially separate different types of visual production along lines defined by Western art academies in the eighteenth and nineteenth centuries. These are used here because no adequate replacement has yet been suggested and to provide one here would divert focus away from the main ideas in the essay.
2. Bayley 1981, p. 196, fig. 235.
3. Griggs 1881.
4. India Office Library, Photograph Volume 52, Nos 4891–4980, entitled 'Trades and Occupations'.
5. Watt 1903.
6. Dewan 2001.
7. Desmond 1982; Burton 1999.
8. Royle 1852.
9. Ibid. See also Birdwood 1880; Tarapor 1997, p. 55.
10. Mitter 1994, pp. 30–31.
11. Macdonald 1970.
12. Mitter 1977.
13. Hunter 1850–51, 1856; 'Reports on Public Instruction in the Madras Presidency (1854–1901)'; 'Papers Relating to Maintenance . . .', 1898.
14. Rolleston 1913, p. 30.
15. 'Report on Public Instruction in the Madras Presidency', 1887–8, p. 127.
16. Hunter 1850–51; 'Report on Public Instruction in the Madras Presidency', 1886–7; 'Papers relating to Maintenance . . .', 1898.
17. *Journal of Indian Art and Industry*, 1884.
18. Hendley 1913, p. 49.
19. Burns 1908–9, p. 649.
20. 'Papers relating to Maintenance . . .', 1898, p. 43.
21. Ibid., pp. 35–42.
22. Ibid., p. 4.
23. Bhabha 1985; Metcalfe 1994; Cohn 1996.
24. Foucault 1979.
25. Mitter 1994, p. 31.
26. Latimer 1917.
27. Coomaraswamy 1909.
28. Chatterjee 1993.
29. See Greenough 1995.

7

Making a Dravidian Hero: The Body and Identity Politics in the Dravidian Movement

Nimmi Rangaswamy

Introduction

This essay examines the Dravidian movement in Tamil Nadu and the diverse writings it threw up in a bid to construct the notion of a Dravidian identity among Tamils. It will focus on the movement's propagandist political rhetoric, on the pamphlets, books, journals and newspapers authored by its prominent leaders, ideologues and spokespersons that were specifically intended to propagate and disseminate a particular political consciousness and create a political identity for the Tamil public. Overall, this set of texts represents a multi-layered attempt to weave together sometimes contradictory ideological positions in the project of successfully creating a political identity. This attempt touched all aspects of 'being a Dravidian' and sought to unite a variegated Tamil people as a Dravidian community that subscribed to common, constructed notions of a Dravidian culture, a Dravidian citizen and a Dravidian body.

The study covers a period from the 1930s to the 1960s, which is the historical phase that saw the movement develop outside of, and in opposition to, the formal political machinery of the state. This development was made possible by the mass media – media that were shaped by the prevailing political conditions and artistic traditions of local society. In an era that was still dominated by personal communication and a tradition of orality, the media through which messages spread were largely the stage and the podium. The leaders of the Dravidian movement attracted large crowds for their speeches in huge makeshift *pandals* (tents), in spaces such as Marina Beach, Madras, which became a particular favourite for hosting these spectacles.

From the late 1930s another method of communicating party ideals was found in the form of public agitations, such as those centred on the anti-Hindi campaign between 1937 and 1940 that generated significant advances in the mobilization of people around a political identity. What is directly relevant here is the reporting of agitations in the movement's own print media. This reporting lent a mythic resonance to leadership and created political narratives around leaders who went on to rule the state, it entrenched the movement's hold over Tamil politics and, most importantly, it secured the mass media as an indispensable asset for 'creating' a political life for the Tamil people. Books, pamphlets and newspapers captured live speeches and public events in print, recasting, reconstructing and even reinventing what might have happened on the streets and in other public places. In the process it gave birth to a community of participants and created a heightened sense of belonging to a political phenomenon in the making. These 'snapshots' of the movement were captured for posterity, becoming 'history' – as the movement proclaimed – for future generations of Dravidians. This history was intended to promote a sense of belonging to the cause, which was the creation of an authentic and politically autonomous Dravidian community.

The creation of the Dravidian community was contingent on the construction of a legitimate self to challenge 'colonial' rule. This was a reference to a perception of Aryan/Brahmin domination and, by extension, North Indian rule over the south. The self was presented as emasculated and as shorn of its 'pure Dravidian traits'. The rhetoric of the Dravidian movement was, accordingly, an attempt at restoring the Dravidian self by dramatizing and elevating a heroic body that would live and die in the process of recreating its country. The movement's print media used vivid images of the body, especially the mutilated and injured body, in the effort to rouse the targeted subjects to act in accordance with its social mission. This essay examines the textual strategies of identity creation with a focus on the body as a key trope in the processes of discursive construction that Tanika Sarkar has described in another context as the 'mixed baggage of representational strategies and ideological maneuvers' that make up the means of identity formation.[1]

These discursive manoeuvres rested on two foundations. The first was the retelling and selection of history so that the new position appeared to be grounded in the past. This is familiar from other case studies and has prompted the observation that 'identity creation is not the product of pure fantasy but an attempt at, and a product of, the embellishment of reality'.[2] The second was language. Sumathi Ramaswamy's study of the transformation of Tamil language into several signifiers, passionately prompting Tamils to act in particular ways, is immensely helpful in understanding and locating the cultural registers affecting the analysis of Tamil identity politics.[3] Her research identifies a potent link between the 'poetics and politics' of 'devotion for the Tamil tongue' and the ideological devices and strategies of persuasion developed by

Tamil subjects to rouse themselves to the point where they would lay down their lives. The matter of passionate attachment to language became central to Tamil identity politics and Tamil nationalist discourse. Again, this is familiar from other studies. It has been noted in the case of the Sikhs, for example, that language in these contexts functions more to 'produce a particular reality than to represent it'.[4]

The body, politics and rhetoric

To begin with, it is necessary to identify certain signifying practices used by the movement that provided a normative account of what the Tamil person ought to resemble. The movement's rhetoric, authored by prominent leaders and writers of the party such as E V R Periyar, C N Annadurai (referred to hereafter as Anna) and M Karunanidhi, proposed specific strategies of political mobilization which prescribed action, participation and rules that were instrumental in injecting and stabilizing a Dravidian identity in each and every Tamilian.[5] It was firmly propagated that the Tamil country was under the alien rule of North Indians who despoiled its natural, economic and, most importantly, its cultural resources. This collapsed into one another the demands of reclaiming self, community and country. Once the Tamilian possessed the reacquired Dravidian self, he would soon inhabit a space called *Dravida Nadu*, the Dravidian country. Rhetoric was thus geared towards dramatizing the heroic self that might be sacrificed in the process of recreating its country.[6] Dravidian lives were for the *enam*, the community, to take up weapons and go to war. The singular mission of 'liberation' propelled the embodied community of freedom fighters whose voices would echo, 'If I win it will be the garland of victory, if I lose it will be the garland of death'.[7]

The Dravidian movement insisted that the authentic/heroic self could be created and the necessary proofs for a Dravidian candidature could be acquired. Although there remained a parallel rhetoric of being Tamil by birth, blood and kinship, this did not interfere with the project of 'becoming Dravidian' through appropriate enculturation. This figuring of the Dravidian, linked as it was to an agenda of radical social reform, was also connected to the emergence of a political aspiration and it was in the electoral arena that Dravidian politics attempted to inscribe and register its cultural claims. Since the inauguration of the Self-Respect League in 1925, Periyar remained the fountainhead of reform and protest against the Brahminical 'pall of doom' encircling the Dravidian country. As long as Periyar led the movement, the Dravidian self was also a radical self, imbued with a reformist zeal for creating critical consciousness.

For Periyar, the project to reconstruct the Dravidian self was to reject certain entrenched social realities. These included all received notions of being Tamil stemming from Hindu religion, philosophy and social structures. The Brahmin/Aryan notion of the Tamil was devoid of historical sensibility, social standing and cultural ingenuity. Tracing the cultural history by which the Tamilian had been made into a *Shudra*, Periyar introduced the notion of reclaiming the Tamil self as a project in his politics of self-respect and social reform. Though Periyar acknowledged the multi-faceted process of this rendering of the Tamil as outcaste, his critique culminated in radical inversions of texts that were seen as creations of high Brahminism. For him, the *Ramayana* was a Brahminical text par excellence, consolidating Brahmin hegemony while leaving others menial, outcaste, illiterate, dependent and subhuman.[8] However, Periyar went beyond tracing the origins and sustenance of caste in society and proclaimed another project that would inject self-respect and introduce human equality and dignity in society. The Dravidian must reclaim his lost standing in society:

> He must be able to say he is not a Hindu but a Dravidian, that he loves his *Kural* [a revered Tamil text], be able to rub off his *vibuthi* and *namam* [both upper-caste markers], debunk the *puranas* and Hindu rituals, uphold the human doctrine of *Kural*, and to say all of these out of thought and reasoning and not coercion.[9]

As such, the creation of the *nadu* – the country – was a project not only to drive out the alien but also to redeem and reform Dravidian society and its component individuals. Anna hailed the Self-Respecters in an idiom that linked individual, country and history by entwining images of the body and its fate, the country and the past:

> The light that shone from their eyes, their voices full-throated, the sight of their chests forward, the shoulders raised . . . Symbols of an *enam* on the rise! The dust on the gem has to be wiped. The light has to shine forth . . . Come to toil. Do not ask when, where, how are we going to. Do not even ask yourselves if you have the will, the power . . . Come to war! . . . The Tamilian has crossed the seas, scaled the Himalayas, sold silk to the Romans . . . He has the courage that will stun the enemy.[10]

In this vision the individual body and an imagined history are made central to the possibility of communal redemption and salvation. The body was the link between a glorious past and a glorious future as work and war (the occupation of bodies), not questions or reason (the occupations of the mind), were the means of tackling the enemy.

The staging of a community identity and the privileged sites for its invention had to proclaim action strategies for the common man so as to render him uncommon and extraordinary. New subjectivities were fashioned and propagated by dipping into the available cultural idioms and popular culture of Tamil society. The concepts of *thondu* (selfless work) and *veeram* (courage) were deployed to construct a politicized 'Tamil' ethos. A *thondan* was the quintessential 'self-respecter', willing to lay down his life for the cause. He was the 'hero' who entered the society 'wading against the tide', withstood the floods and the spears of opposition, his selfless work making the organization grow from a drop to a flood. He will be 'teased and taunted, corrupted with heaps of gems, a bed of jasmines and velvet, a web of seduction, anything just short of paradise'. But the *thondan* was a renouncer, his mind, like 'burning camphor . . . lighting a wet log of wood . . . to destroy the unwanted'.[11] He belonged to the long list of heroic and crucified historical figures:

> Men who told the truth, demystified unjust social reality, destined to live in degradation, banished to the forests, burnt at the stake, nailed to a cross, poisoned. . . What happened to Galileo, Socrates, Luther, Lenin, who fought for the worker, Marx who demystified the atrocity of capitalism, Kemal Paccha who shattered Turkey's blind faith, Lincoln who fought for black rights . . . All of them had suffered atrocities upon them[selves].[12]

Taking cues from these great lives, the party had to 'set a time bomb to the mountain of casteism even if the boulders are sure to fall on them'.[13] The body was not just to be the means of liberation through work and war, it was to be the site at which the commitment of the Tamil was to be most severely tested.

Suffering, sacrifice and the body

The *thondan* had to carry visible scars. His mission would put his body through the roughest of experiences 'out of which he emerges cleansed, purified, like gold from the embers'. It was imperative for him to suffer bodily abuse that elevated his spirit and made him tough in battle even if 'knifed from both the sides with his intestines spilling out'. The enemy might cut the body and throw it to the wolves, but they never could destroy the 'revolutionary thoughts, striking roots in the country, creeping into its heart'.[14]

This discourse of physical injury was a mainstay of party rhetoric, as it established the Dravidians as a community of rebels and liberators who had been 'given poison, jailed for life, stoned to death, nailed in a cross, fed to the lions, wrung by the neck, hacked to pieces. These but happen to those who stand in the midst of a revolution, and speak of reform'.[15] The appeal of this language was its dual functionality. On the one hand it could serve as a series of heroic examples and as a corporal link with historical experiences. On the other it served as a test of the individual Dravidian's physical commitment to the *nadu* by asking: 'Do we have the guts? Can we face the bruises of freedom struggles? Do we possess the culture and tradition of freedom struggles?'.[16]

The army of heroic bodies primed for self-sacrifice had luminous predecessors. The archetypal *thondans* were Natarajan and Talamuthu, who died during the language revolt of 1940. Their deaths in police custody at the height of the revolt against the imposition of Hindi fuelled the movement's critique of the state's abuse of power. (The colonial state, in this case, was perceived as an extension and amalgam of Brahminical socio-economic interests as C Rajagopalachari, a Brahmin, presided over the Madras Presidency.) In the deaths of the two martyrs Dravidian activists visualized a convergence of the finest Dravidian traits, making the pair a potent locus of physical mobilization. Their 'unvanquished bodies' filled 'the eyes of every Tamilian at the very recollection of their martyrdom'.[17] Propaganda texts linked their sacrifice to other heroic bodies 'until the last Tamilian lives, until the last drop of his blood is shed, their names will be remembered'.[18] Their bodies, once mythologized, belonged to all (and only to) real Tamils:

> They did proud to the Nadar and Dalit communities that had nurtured them to adulthood, but breathed their last orphaned in jail, with no kith or kin beside them. Death did not frighten them, nor disease hurt them. . . The prison sent out its invitation to the two Tamil bulls, who willingly knocked on its doors and entered . . . They came home, not in flesh and blood, but a corpse to their parents and loved ones.[19]

It was explicitly stated that when the Tamil state became a reality and Tamil children went back to studying Tamil it would be 'over the bodies of the two heroes', a metaphor that once again places the body at the heart of the transition from past to future. The statue of Periyar would be erected in a free Dravida Nadu with the 'two Tamil bulls ordaining his sides'.[20]

Physically charged with the imagery of masculine strength and virility, such symbols of martyrdom as Talamuthu and Natarajan were the highlights of propagandist literature as they could be used to signal a code of ethics and action for all Dravidians to emulate. Inspired by their life histories, Anna urged his men 'to light the lamp of freedom through their *aattral* (potential), abandon skepticism and sprout a lion's heart'.[21] He called out to his men to come together 'laden with this strength, alongside Tamil brothers, with cries, with looks that will transform a coward into a lion: "Come, my dear brother . . . Walk like an *arima* [tiger]"'.[22]

The suffering body was also extensively used in order to make vivid the burden of colonialism. It was the enslaved body that most readily lent itself to propaganda of this type. It was this body that was deployed in depictions of Kallakudi, a village that had been renamed Dalmiapuram. This latter name reminded Tamil activists of their collective humiliation under the northern Baniya's economic colonization of the *nadu*'s resources (Dalmia was a North Indian entrepreneur with a cement factory in Kallakudi who had pressured the village to change its name in his honour). It was evident that 'Dalmia' had to be removed from Dalmiapuram and its original name reinstated. In the memoir 'Six Months in Rigorous Imprisonment', Karunanidhi carefully constructed an image of bonded bodies, bodies that included the earth itself, which assumed life through a corporal metaphor:

> There were at least 2000 Dravidians working down there, their sweat mixing with the mud of Kallakudi. All of the sweat will go into the white cement that will be sold in every Dravidian street. Kallakudi is the earth that gives riches, but her sons will live in huts . . . Dalmia set foot on it and made a permanent slave of the land. Now they want to etch their alien name on our earth . . . It was time to wipe the stigmata . . . The crown of shame adorns the head of the mother and chains imprison her arms to her very earth.[23]

Kallakudi, as such, was ready for revolt and the body would be the means of liberation. The *arrappor* (righteous war) was described as a clash of body parts and a sequence of miraculous physiological functions. The army of Dravidian activists would march ahead to block the Hindi tongue from entering as much as a single Tamil home. The bugle would roar to wipe the alien name from the Dravidian soil, the cymbals would clash, with the army registering its zeal by making the deaf hear, the dumb sing, that they 'were not banana babies, but banyan trees'.[24] The army of 'pure Tamilian thondans' was ready to stop all trains entering Dalmiapuram. This they would achieve with their bodies, laid out on the train tracks.

The dawn of 15 July 1953, when the Kallakudi episode began, 'saw the unfolding of a valourous saga, with the sea roaring to wake the entire Tamil country'. The lions began their march, the bent Tamil head under the alien rule now lifted high. The eyes saw a vision of the army raising a cloud of dust from the very earth on 'whose belly their honourable mother had shed tears of bitter sorrow'. It was the place of death, a symbol of shame, a crown of thorns on the mother's head, with blood oozing from the wounds. The army would wipe away the blood as they would the name Dalmiapuram, the act of wiping being the balm they apply to the mother's wound. They would place their heads on the rail tracks. The rest of the world would, at the very least, hear bones being crushed as the brave *thondans* got ready to embrace death.[25] The first to succumb to a police bullet at Kallakudi was the *thondan* Kesavan, the 'mother earth's lap drenched with his blood, the lap that nurtured crores of Tamilians'. Karunanidhi called it the 'dance of horror' unleashed by the forces in power who 'drank blood, till their stomachs burst, and chewed on the bones . . . But did the hunger end?'.[26] The outcome by the end of the day was 6 corpses and 5,000 in prison.[27] The epic of Kallakudi, created by the memoirs of Karunanidhi, remained a favoured text of heroic valour for party *thondans*, reminding them of the historic year of 1938 and the language revolt. Kesavan, through the sacrifice of his body, was their new Talamuthu.

Into this passionate rendition of a violent, public configuration of the body nested a self-imposed imprint of non-violence. The movement believed that it never planned arson, killing or destruction. The idioms of social reform and reconstruction were aimed primarily at changing consciousness. The *thondan* subscribed to codes of conduct that were bound by *kadamai, ganniam, kattupadu*: duty, dignity and self-control. He would shed his blood but not 'lift a finger against another human'.[28] Violence, for the party worker, was opposed to humanity and a death knell to the democratic spirit he had so honourably inherited. Anna, in his newspaper column, insisted that 'a look at his party's history would reveal the purity of intentions. They would beseech even the Brahmin to fight for his freedom'.[29] If their pleas did not bring success, they were prepared to shed blood, to accept the call with courage in body and mind. After all, the Dravidians were:

> . . . people with a heightened sense of shame and honour [who] will never stand the slightest bit of indignity and humiliation. They were men with a wild passion and a zeal to reclaim what was theirs. But they did possess a heart to withstand all. Blood shed for a cause never bothered the Dravidian heroes.[30]

Interwoven into such 'heroic accounts' was a trenchant critique of the state's abuse of power, articulated in terms of assault and mutilation:

> The thondans could have cried out bitterly about the injustice and abuse meted out to them by the state, run amok when the police wielded the lathi . . . They were lions of self-respect. Let the thumb go, the finger too. We have a mouth to speak, and an active stage

ready for it. They can even put locks to our mouths, even cut our tongues. We will not stop. We will stage silent plays.[31]

Conclusion

The concept of the body is crucial for understanding Tamil identity and Tamil politics since the 1930s. The land that was claimed by political activists was imagined as the body of the mother. The body was identified as the key to transition from a glorious past to a bright future in its potential for work and war. The fate of the group under the rule of others was captured in images of the bound and enslaved body. These others were also constructed in corporal terms, although their bodies were evil because they were given to excess, voracity and cannibalism as they 'drank blood till their stomachs burst and chewed on the bones'. The sacrifice of the body elevated the individual to the status of hero. Liberation would be a bodily experience as the free Tamil would 'walk like an *arima* [tiger]'.

To begin understanding the importance of the body in the construction of the Tamil political project and the Tamil political identity between the 1930s and the 1960s it is of course important to remember the point made in the introduction about the nature of the media used. Public performance was at the heart of the creation of these identities and projects, and the body has an immediacy and importance in the oral creation of any story for an audience. The body is as much a part of the performance as the voice, and it lends itself readily to gestures that give the story both dramatic impact and meaning. To this extent, then, the written propaganda that remains the source for the historian is simply an incomplete trace of performances that would have carried immediacy and vigour through a corporal medium. The body as metaphor in the writing is in fact a ghost of the body as vehicle in the performance.

Related to this point is that made by Arjun Appadurai in his analysis of sport in South Asia.[32] He argues that cricket has taken on a range of meanings in post-colonial India as it offers a corporal experience, however fleeting and partial, of imagined identities and historical processes. This may well be important for understanding the significance of the body to the Tamil project. By invoking physical experience, endurance, suffering and potential in their political activities and visions, Tamil propagandists were inviting those whom they sought as followers to feel the politics rather than simply to think about them. By making their programme a physical encounter they gave their politics the immediacy and the thrill of bodily experience. The body was not simply the chief metaphor of the Tamil propagandists or one of their key tropes. It was, in fact, their target.

Bibliography

Aanaimuthu, V, 1974, *Periyar E V R Sinthanaigal*, vol. I, Tiruchirapalli, Thinkers Forum.

Annadurai C N, 1963, *Thambikku Annavin Kadithangal*, vol. II, Madras, Pari.

Annadurai C V, 1974, *Viduthalai Por*, Tiruchirapalli, Dravida Pannai.

Annadurai C V, 1981, *Thambikku Annavin Kadithangal*, vol. IX, Madras, Pari.

Annadurai C V, 1985, *Ilatchia Varalaru*, Madras, Pari.

Annadurai C V, 1986, *Thambikku Annavin Kadithangal*, vol. XI, Madras, Pari.

Annadurai C V, 1989, *Inba Dravidam*, Madras, Pumpuhar.

Appadurai, A, 1995, 'Playing with Modernity: The Decolonization of Indian Cricket', in C Breckenridge (ed.), *Consuming Modernity: Public Culture in a South Asian World*, Minneapolis, University of Minnesota Press.

Das, V, 1995, *Critical Events*, New Delhi, Oxford University Press.

Dravida, P, 1960, *Dravidam Draviddarukke*, Madras, Noor Padippu Kazagam.

Elamchezhian, M, 1986, *Tamilan Thoduttha Por*, Madras, Viduthalai.

Jeganathan, P, 2000, 'A Space for Violence: Anthropology, Politics and the Location of a Sinhala Practice of Masculinity', in *Subaltern Studies XI*, New Delhi, Ravi Dayal.

Karunanidhi, M, 1950, *Kovayil MK*, Madras, Munnetra Pannai.

Karunanidhi, M, 1953, *Viduthalai Por*, Tiruchirapalli, Dravida Pannai.

Karunanidhi, M, 1990, *Aaru Maadha Kadumkaaval*, Madras, Bharati.

Maran, M, 1962, *Een Vendum Inba Dravidam*, Madras, Muthuvel.

Ramasamy, E V, 1959, *Ramayana: A True Reading*, Madras, Viduthalai.

Ramaswamy, S, 1998, *Passions of the Tongue: Language Devotion in Tamil Nadu, 1891–1970*, New Delhi, Munshiram Manoharlal.

Sarkar, T, 1999, 'Pragmatics of a Hindu Right Politics of Women's Organization', *Economic and Political Weekly* (31 July), pp. 2159–67.

Sunder Rajan, R, 1993, *Real and Imagined Women: Gender, Culture and Post Colonialism*, London, Routledge.

Venu, A S, 1954, *Dravidasthan*, Madras, Kalai Manrum.

Vettriveeran, 1951, *Ethirpil Valarntha Kazhagam*, Madras, Selva Nilayam.

Notes

1. Sarkar 1999, p. 159.
2. Sunder Rajan 1993, p. 131.
3. Ramaswamy 1998.
4. Das 1995, pp. 118–21.

5. The formal definition of who was a 'Tamil' recorded shifts as it charted its course through the various stages in the movement's political life. Early descriptions attempted to incorporate a larger geographic area covering Kerala, Karnataka, Andhra Pradesh, parts of Orissa and Maharashtra as Dravida Nadu. When Tamil was deployed in several contexts to denote Dravidianhood, the other three southern languages became its 'uterine sisters'.
6. Annadurai 1974, 1989; Maran 1962; Dravida 1960; Venu 1954.
7. Annadurai 1985, p. 12.
8. Periyar 1959.
9. See Aanaimuthu 1974, p. 1463.
10. Ibid. [*sic*], pp. 12–13.
11. Karunanidhi 1953, p. 56.
12. Vettriveeran 1951, pp. 25–6.
13. Annadurai 1985, p. 69.
14. Vettriveeran 1951, p. 27.
15. Annadurai 1985, p. 70.
16. *Dravida Nadu* (2.1.1949), p. 9.
17. Ibid., p. 8.
18. Elamchezhian 1986, p. 170.
19. Ibid., pp. 169–72.
20. Ibid., p. 176.
21. Annadurai 1963, p. 20.
22. Ibid., pp. 22–3.
23. Karunanidhi 1950, pp. 50–60.
24. Ibid., pp. 60–61.
25. Ibid., p. 63.
26. Ibid., pp. 74–5.
27. Ibid., p. 77.
28. Annadurai 1981, p. 186.
29. *Dravida Nadu* (10.8.1958), p. 6.
30. *Dravida Nadu* (2.1.1949), pp. 10–12.
31. Karunanidhi 1950, p. 14.
32. See Appadurai 1995.

8

Describing the Body: The Writing of Sex and Gender Identity for the Contemporary Bengali Woman

SRIMATI BASU

Introduction

This paper considers the idea that simply raising questions about the sexual body can be a radical gesture. The Indian women's movement has addressed a broad range of issues, including political participation, labour, legal status, reproductive rights and sexual violence, but it seems that there has been little discussion of the politics of the sexual body and the sexual woman per se. The topic has instead been raised mainly in the media, in what claim to be radical articles in women's popular magazines. Popular media, reach a large variety of women in ways that are beyond the reach of individual groups and may be able to raise feminist issues non-didactically, making them part of everyday conversations. However, such popular women's magazines are often viewed as troubling feminist spaces, as they can be accused of propagating patriarchal desires rather than subverting them. The question arises then of whether it is possible to have a radical conversation about sexuality if the topic is to be packaged within a glossy magazine which must defer to dominant ideologies about gender, sexuality, capital or nation as a condition of its survival.

This article will explore this question by looking at the Calcutta magazine *Sananda*. Given the claim of the magazine to speak the truth on 'women's issues', representations of sex and gender in its pages can be seen as significant arenas for interrogating the limits of talking about sex in popular culture, and for examining the ways in which norms of gender can at once be both recuperated and challenged within progressive social and political constructions of Bengali identity and alongside the economic imperative to sell consumer products.

Locating Sananda in multiple spaces

If Indian women's magazines are divided on the basis of their subjects, formats and target audiences it seems that there is a continuum of feminist awareness: film magazines such as *Stardust* are largely oblivious to women's socio-economic and cultural problems and form one end of the spectrum, with English-language women's magazines such as *Femina* and *Eve's Weekly* close by. *Manushi*, an ad-free progressive magazine focusing on issues of gender and class, appears at the other extreme. At the *Stardust* end there are no pretensions to subvert, and at the *Manushi* end there are no attempts to provide fashion or cooking tips. The subject of this paper, *Sananda*, falls somewhere in the middle. It is squarely within the glossy commercial genre and shares its market with *Stardust* and *Femina*, but it claims to be 'feminist' since it covers topics that are otherwise considered taboo for women and includes a range of subjects not coded in the wider culture as properly within the female sphere.

This is only the first of many complexities contained in *Sananda* that are significant for examining the writing of female sexuality within popular culture and for the construction of sexuality within the writing of 'Indian' cultures. A further consideration is that while a magazine like *Sananda* sees itself as having a different voice than *Femina*, it is enmeshed in relations of production that are similar to those of *Femina*. The typical consumer is projected as female, urban, wealthy (or at least upper-middle-class), young, deeply appreciative of the depth and variety of 'Bengali culture' and yet an informed consumer of global news and products. A glance at any 'Table of Contents' page points to this multiple positioning. The page shows a variety of issues that are often broader in scope than most women's magazines as they include travel, politics, fiction (rarely in the romance genre) and health/environment. Alongside this list of contents, however, looms an image of a giant fashion model that visually dominates the page and dwarfs other images. The model is magnified several times in proportion to the others (though her body is waif-thin in itself) and best captures the economic exigencies that govern a glossy magazine brought out by a commercial publishing concern. As Gloria Steinem demonstrates in 'Sex, Lies and Advertising',[1] articles and images in women's magazines are often forced to reflect the ethos of femininity portrayed in adverts if magazines are to retain major advertisers; that is, they are ultimately not just complementary but supplementary to the ads. In *Sananda*, the giant model on the 'Table of Contents' page amplifies the significance of the numerous other clothing and cosmetics adverts filling the magazine and underlines the conditions of the magazine's continued existence. This image is often not selling a product directly, but it is constructing certain forms of consumption – normative and utopian – and thereby 'affirming the values of late capitalism yet inverting them into symbols of primitive simplicity and pure emotionality', as Eva Illouz puts it.[2]

A further complexity is added by the editor. Aparna Sen is a film director and regional film star who draws mass appeal from having starred in numerous commercial movies and yet also claims intellectual credibility from starring in the art film *Teen Kanya*. In certain editorials she emphasizes her position within the world of film criticism as a daughter of a well-respected film critic and as someone who has worked with the director Satyajit Ray, the ultimate source of prestige in the cinema of Bengal. Her films, such as *36 Chowringhee Lane, Parama* and *Sati*, have dealt respectively with the alienation of an Anglo-Indian woman teacher, the erasure of sexual desire and markers of selfhood in an elite housewife, and the material significance of forced marriage in the story of a poor woman married to a tree. These have been important feminist films in Indian cinema and the authority derived from her roles adds ballast to the claim that the magazine speaks about transgressive topics related to women.

She is careful in her editorials to construct herself in terms of her readership. On the one hand she is a political progressive, expressing anti-fundamentalism and adopting such causes as *Fire*, Deepa Mehta's film about a lesbian relationship in a middle-class family that was the subject of virulent protest by Hindu fundamentalist groups who objected to the sexualized portrayal of women. On the other hand she is keen to portray herself as a discerning consumer of international trends in advocating such fads as vitamin E and no-starch diets. Simultaneously, however, she shows herself as a product of a loving 'traditional' Bengali family by writing on such topics as her grandparents' mutual love. Overall, she portrays herself as an intellectual who is capable of challenging undesirable norms while remaining firmly in tune with local culture, thereby apparently capturing in an individual the spirit of *Sananda* and its difference from other kinds of women's magazines at both ends of the continuum, and a potentially unique space for feminist conversation.

Because of such complexities, *Sananda* cannot simply be dismissed as adopting a superficial feminist packaging that is really intended simply to sell products to a particular market. Rather, it is more productive to analyse the magazine in terms of the various discourses it attempts to negotiate as it interprets the challenge of feminism, meets the more traditional reader's expectations, preserves elite and middle-class values, sells an ideology of consumption, embellishes and celebrates symbols of Bengali culture and embraces cosmopolitanism in its coverage of national and international issues. These discourses often complement but also contradict each other, producing zones of unease. This conflict and unease go to the heart of the question about popular magazines as feminist vehicles and the extent to which they can oppose dominant ideologies and offer liberatory alternatives. I argue that such zones of unease often fail to develop in these directions and instead read as mild heartburn and queasiness, soon forgotten amid the numerous temptations of consumption.

Sananda as a product for post-colonial Bengal

A study of *Sananda* cannot just be located in the comparative literature that features studies of women's magazines elsewhere. The Indian, and indeed the Bengali, context means that quite specific discourses are part of the picture. As historians, sociologists and legal studies scholars have repeatedly argued, gender was an overdetermined subject in colonial relations of rule.[3] Issues centring on women, such as *sati* and widow remarriage, were at the heart of ideological and political struggles in the earlier part of the nineteenth century, forming the rationale for colonial legal intervention in the interests of 'civilization' as well as the grounds for Indian resistance to colonial interference and impetus for reform within Indian communities. However, in the latter part of the century, as the nationalist project occupied centre stage, the 'woman question' appeared to fade away. Partha Chatterjee argues in an influential essay that this fading away was not merely due to a set of new political priorities but was a consistent approach to gendered norms by Indian reformers. 'Western' material resources and practices were seen as beneficial for the new nation, but 'Eastern' spirituality was preferred as superior: i.e., the 'outer' forms of the colonizer's world were to be embraced, but the 'inner' Indian world was to be sacrosanct from external intervention. Reform for women, who were associated with the 'inner' world, was thus to come from within the community. The 'new woman' (educated, middle-class, refined, modest) was to be nothing like a *memsahib* or Englishwoman, but nevertheless a vast improvement over other Indian women of previous generations and of poorer classes:

> . . . superiority over the western woman for whom, it was believed, education meant only the acquisition of material skills in order to compete with men in the outside world and hence a loss of feminine (spiritual) virtues; superiority over the preceding generation of women in their own homes who had been denied the opportunity for freedom by an oppressive and degenerate social tradition; and superiority over women of the lower classes who were culturally incapable of appreciating the virtues of freedom.[4]

Chatterjee contends that the brilliance of the argument lay in the notion of symbolic interiority, as it implied that women could move into the public sphere and receive all its material advantages while embodying a particular form of femininity internally. Male conduct had no corresponding prescriptions for modesty and purity. As Himani Bannerji demonstrates in her analysis of nineteenth-century Bengali women's writings on appropriate dress, the modestly clad figure of the *bhadramahila* ('gentlewoman' being Bannerji's preferred translation) was thus a significant mode of entrenching class relations and regulating sexuality as well as 'the Bengali males' response to European accusations of their 'barbarism'.[5] This ultimately confirmed patriarchal control and 'counterbalanced the anxiety of being faced with radically transgressive possibilities'.[6]

Sananda as a contemporary magazine can be read as an heir to this local cultural heritage. The reader is called upon as a descendant of the *bhadramahila,* constantly interpellated through a discourse of sexual modesty and decency, and counterposed against the 'over-Westernized' and the 'old-fashioned woman'; the outer/inner dichotomy that delineated colonial relations is mapped on to the present and on to the ways in which Bengali women are described as being different from Euro-American women. Active sexual engagement is associated with Western women (spectres include the so-called sexual revolution and lesbian feminism), low-class women (whose language and sexual practices are not seen as being 'modest') and elite women (who are out and about in high society and business and may be morally lax). As the following analysis of the articles shows, conversations about the sexual body and its practices are pitched as being the sorts of topics that modern women ought not to avoid, but the scope of discussions is contained in ways that do not overly challenge patriarchal norms of sexuality and marriage. The contemporary *Sananda* reader appears to embrace new and taboo topics, but ultimately sexual modesty is a sacrosanct marker of respectability for the middle-class Bengali woman. Also, resistance to Western hegemony is asserted, even while hegemony among Indian cultures is claimed and class and urban hegemonies are reinforced.

While *Sananda* reproduces a post-colonial version of the *bhadramahila* codes, it also refers to versions of other Bengali pasts. Analysis of contemporary sari advertisements by Dulali Nag has shown that ad-makers consistently attempt to invent a nostalgic, 'essential' Bengali tradition.[7] This is marked by rural utopias, women's domesticity and female beauty that are to be consumed by the wealthy urban elite. In these ads, an imaginary rural habitus (actual rural women are not part of the imagined readership) as well as local literary and artistic 'high' traditions (invoking distinguished elite and middle-class Bengali poets) seem very important in establishing that Bengali culture has a unique spiritual location and intellectual profundity (different from both Western and

other Indian cultures). Therefore when *Sananda* locates itself in Bengali culture it draws upon this Bengali-ness of the utopian (poetic, rural, nostalgic)
imaginary as well. However, it also tries to manipulate more radical imagin-
ings of Bengal, and invokes the alleged histories of political and intellectual
progressiveness that draw on the role of Bengalis in the nationalist movement,
and the nineteenth-century cultural efflorescence of the so-called Bengal
Renaissance. At moments when *Sananda* might push the limits of what can be
talked about in public, it justifies that overreaching by claiming that the trans-
gressions are only to be expected in the contemporary milieu, given Bengal's
radical intellectual and political traditions.

Careful answers: rendering sex docile

The focus of this paper is on *Sananda* articles that deal explicitly with the
sexualized body and sexuality, subjects that might seem wildly transgressive
given the history of prescriptive sexual modesty for the Bengali *bhadramahila*. It
is easy to be surprised simply to find discussion of these taboo topics on the
printed page, but it is not clear that such moves are in fact rupturing established norms of understanding sexuality. Foucauldian analysis, one of the
most important apparatuses for talking about constructions of sex and the
sexual body, indicates both the power and the limitations of such discussions.
On the one hand, Carol Smart has argued that 'Foucault's insights into what
we might call ways of knowing and his insistence that these are modes of
deployment of power has provided a new focus of political action'.[8] That is,
the notion of discursive power is in itself a crucial tool, and simply to examine
the ways in which sexuality is discursively constructed makes power and
politics evident. On the other hand, Meryl Altman has pointed out that 'the
claim that [the modern discussion of sex] breaks the sound barrier of repression is made again and again with no cumulative gain, in order to validate
and create a discourse that may or may not be equally repressive'.[9] She
critiques Foucault's idea that the mere fact of talking about sex imbues one
with the 'speaker's benefit'; 'if sex is repressed, that is, condemned to prohibition, nonexistence and silence, then the mere fact that one is speaking about
it has the appearance of a deliberate transgression'.[10] Transgression may be
negated through speaking, so that by bringing certain forms of sexual behaviour into discourse, one may render them 'docile' by defining and regulating
them, incorporating them into the ideologies of dominant discourse. However,
it is also useful to recall Blix's use of the notion of 'excess': the idea that
something may be left over even if most things are appropriated into
hegemonic discourse.[11] If sex talk is not a substantive blow to patriarchal
structures, it may still cause a few cracks.

The May 1998 *Sananda* article on sex education, 'How to inform your child about the mystery of birth',[12] makes the claim to be a modern and radical move. The editor introduces it as an important resource for *adhunik* (modern) men and women who need to be able to tell their children about men's and women's bodies and the 'mystery' of birth. 'Experts' in various fields (doctors, child psychologists, teachers, poets) are summoned up as authorities in a telling example of creating disciplining/disciplinary authority. But the headlines of the articles themselves shift the terms of the discussion. The narrative is cast in terms of a child's questions regarding sex on television, but crucially the responses are immediately framed as being about the 'mysteries of birth'. The questions 'What were Sharon Stone and Michael Douglas doing? Why weren't they wearing any clothes?' were met with the following response in *Sananda*:

> The vessel/jug in the mother's stomach has an egg in it. When the father and mother love each other and want to have a child, then the egg hatches and a child is made in the stomach . . . People are naked when they do private things like bathing, and when they caress each other with love (*aador*) to make a child then clothes cannot be worn either [the passive voice is part of the text].

The effect is to bypass non-reproductive sexual behaviour altogether. The meeting of the American movie couple is designed by the film-makers to represent a moment of lustful sexual behaviour in which the bodies involved were seeking stimulation and gratification (it is difficult to argue that Douglas and Stone were shown in a scene in which she was trying to get pregnant). This meaning is completely ignored in *Sananda*, and the Indian responses are intended to contain such physical behaviour in terms of reproductive sex. In doing this, lust and the sexual body are dismissed and sex becomes a specifically heterosexual act completely framed within the implied context of marriage. The hypothetical question concerns a television moment rather than the primal scene of one's own parents, creating an alienation from the topic that need never be related back to the parents' bodies or to the child's own.

Note that the only actor in the babymaking piece is the uterus in the female body; it is described as a *kolshi*, a jug, that is a receptacle with a specific shape. The uterus mysteriously blossoms in response to *aador*; the vulva, the vagina and even the penis are absent as delivery routes, let alone as sites of pleasure. There is simply no connection between the genitalia and sex or reproduction. There is also the mysterious concept of *aador*, which can be variously translated as 'respect' or 'love' or 'hugging' or even 'making out'. While this *aador* is used to characterize sex, the child is also reassured that parents perform *aador* towards children too and this latter is described as the best kind of *aador*.

Such information, which is supposed to be timely and correct, provides completely non-useable data. Armed with this information, one would have absolutely no possibility of having sex or even recognizing it, largely because critical bodily zones had vanished in the description. Framing the conversation in terms of marriage, reproduction and the distant future renders invisible the many forms in which children may actually encounter a penis or a vagina, or witness sex acts, or experience their own sexuality. Instead the article is an exercise not in sexual education or debate but in confirming sexual mores considered desirable. It denies the female body the experience of erotic pleasure, instead constructing it as the site of compulsory reproduction and asserting that women ultimately derive pleasure from mothering, given that *aador* towards children is said to give supreme satisfaction.

Marriage: bad practice and mystical necessity

The article on 'Marriage versus living together' (the actual phrase 'living together' is transcribed in Bengali) also appears to make a transgressive move by its very nature because it suggests the possibility of an alternative space to compulsory marriedness.[13] In advertising the article, the monthly editorial frames the two options as roughly equal alternatives, comparing the love and happiness of two longtime unmarried Indian couples who are well known actors and authors with that of the editor's married grandparents, who are described as having a 'profound companionship'. The author of the article, Mallika Sengupta, describes herself as an oppositional (*pratibadi*) writer and uses a slough of historical details and sociological studies as well as interviews to make her point that there is really not much 'difference' between the two options, as they both involve love, strife, companionship and responsibility. She describes Sartre and de Beauvoir as the archetypal cohabiting couple, emphasizing their aversion to owning and possessing spouses. She characterizes Adam and Eve as the first couple who 'lived together', because societal shame and prescribed 'artificial' codes of behaviour had yet to come to dominate. Interviews with various Bengali couples who have lived together are used to show that living together may be 'marriage in waiting' for those waiting to be divorced, or a period of figuring out the other person's reliability, or a means of getting together in the midst of very busy schedules.

Perhaps most importantly, Sengupta emphasizes a materialist feminist critique of marriage, arguing that women's economic and emotional independence is a necessary precondition for cohabitation to be viewed positively, given patriarchal ideologies whereby a woman is deemed a whore if she relies on a man for economically while single but an ideal role model if this reliance is within marriage. She shows an awareness that marriage is an economic necessity for women based on their dependence, rather than a mystical status, and she also points to the sexual double standard whereby female sexuality is commodified and subjected to moral censure when not bound within patri- archal property relations. She points to the class dimensions of the debate, to the irrelevance of the particular issue for non-elite women, as well as to the violence that can befall poor women who have few economic alternatives. Sengupta cites a Swedish study showing that the majority of couples living together continued to do so long-term without marrying, given that the 'legit- imacy' of children was not a concern within that system, i.e., that legal paternity was not juristically or morally significant. She hypothesizes that, if Bengali women express an interest in living together with partners rather than marrying, this may be an index of their dissatisfaction with marriage and that the rise in divorce rates is another aspect of this dissatisfaction. She concludes that as long as there is a hierarchical relationship between the husband and wife:

> Women will be confined, dependent; they will be beaten and they will be burned in tandoors. Then, they will look for alternatives. If a marriage can be an abode of love between equals rather than a pyramid of hierarchy, then marriage may last a few more centuries. Otherwise women will want to look for alternatives. It is quite likely that this alternative may be living together or marriageless companionship.

Overall, the article thus makes no overt attempts to condemn the practice of living together for those who do it. Moreover, it ends on the explicit feminist threat that the onus for preserving marriage is on men, who need to relinquish and to share power.

The cultural assumptions that frame this critique in the article, however, show some significant cracks. Perhaps most remarkable is the pervading sense of the mystical inevitability of marriage, the constant reiteration that living together is just fine and all sorts of great people do it, but that for some mysterious and not quite explicable reason, marriage represents a preferred closure. The article opens with a question posed to the author by a famous poet colleague who asks her why, as a writer who favours a persona of protest, she is getting married rather than living with her partner. Sengupta admits that the thought intrigued her, but never answers it in the article. Given that the audience is aware that she is married, the indicated answer seems to be that ultimately marriage is prescribed and pleasurable, although one can consider the theoretical possibility of alternatives.

The desirability of marriage is implied in further arguments and evidence produced. The poet Joy Goswami and the film director Gautam Ghose both insist that there is no difference between marriage and cohabitation but that they got married because of 'societal injunctions' or 'people saying bad stuff'; the social pressure to marry is never challenged. An element of sweetness and solidity in the institution of marriage is demonstrated through further facts about the Swedish study of long-term cohabiting couples, whose children are attracted to marriage despite there being no stigma to cohabitation. Even the feminist threat in the conclusion – that women may prefer cohabitation if marriage continues to be hierarchical – is based on the assumption that women as a group would ultimately prefer heterosexual marriage, but that the institution needs to be reformed. The idea that there are alternatives in other forms of sexuality or even alternative expressions of heterosexual desire is never considered.

The child also makes its appearance to safeguard the necessity of marriage. While living together is seen to be comparable to marriage for childless couples, the argument changes entirely with the child in the picture. Sengupta contends that 'there are very few instances of living together with a child or having a child while living together, because no parents want the risk of bringing a child into such uncertainty, or at least we don't have those conditions in our country yet'. This 'uncertainty' is never explained and no explicit connection is drawn to the stigma of illegitimacy as being a consequence of patriarchal norms of descent and property ownership, despite Sengupta's articulation of the connected argument that marriage inscribes women as forms of property. Marriage is depicted as an important path for safeguarding a child's economic rights and legal expert advice is cited to demonstrate the difficulties of obtaining maintenance for children of non-married couples. There is the acknowledgement that 'marriage is socially imperative because of the extreme dependence on the stamp of paternity', but there is no attempt to analyse the economic or moral basis of this prescription, or to envisage liberation from this norm in the same way that divorce is visualized as liberation for the dissatisfied married woman.

Sengupta's argument is also complemented and fractured by the visual images and the short interviews that frame her piece. The article is illustrated with photographs of two young, urban, wealthy and happy couples in various poses, seeming to represent marriage versus cohabitation. In one set, the woman appears to be coded as 'Bengali' through the adornment of her body in saris, bangles and long hair, while the other woman is marked in an opposite way in shorts, a skirt and a nightie that identify her as 'Westernized'. The male pictured with the first woman is in a *kurta-pajama* in one image but in the others wears a shirt and trousers, while the man with the second

woman wears shorts and singlet, and just a towel in one picture. The easy
assumption to make would be that the first couple represent the married unit
and the other the cohabiting unit: that is, living together is represented as
Western and ultimately alien, while marriage is the true Bengali arrangement,
visually validated by the docile Bengali female body in 'traditional' attire. This
reading fits well with Partha Chatterjee's analysis that the male may be
unmarked by cultural specificity in attire and can incorporate Westernization
without dismantling societal norms, whereas the woman is expected to
embody and express internalized cultural traditions. However, there is no
specific label attached to these pictures and, given the assertions in the article
that both forms are equal with respect to love and companionship, perhaps
the images attempt to invert easy expectations by mixing up assumptions of
who might subscribe to marriage or cohabitation.

Similarly, the short interviews play with the meanings of the central essay in
various ways. These statements on the topic at hand come from painters,
singers, dancers, actors, directors, writers and feminist organizers, and the
sample includes an equal number of men and women. Some of the inter-
viewees express virulent opposition to the concept of living together, notably
including all the film actors, who are most wont to be characterized as morally
lax and sexually promiscuous. They characterize cohabitation as blind imitation of the West, as temporary and non-monogamous, as a futile attempt to
escape social duties, as a spectre against which marriage looks wholesome,
responsible and emotionally meaningful. However, even as the dancer and
actor Mamata Shankar calls cohabitation 'slimy, dirty . . . self-indulgent . . .
about suspicion and bodily lust', she says 'I don't believe in wedding vows
and in society. I want to remain true, pure and faithful within myself'. If she
does not believe in weddings or social norms, then it is not clear what exactly
makes cohabitation slimy and dirty. There is no guessing what makes up her
'pure and faithful' third alternative. In other interviews, even where the
speaker is theoretically unopposed to cohabitation, there is always the ultimate
move whereby marriage is recuperated as a stable social norm. For example,
the singer Indrani Sen declares that 'I believe the auspicious occasion creates
a beautiful intimacy between the two people', the photographer Raghu Rai
states that 'if one lives in society one has to follow its laws', and the feminist
activist Madhu Kishwar believes that 'in societies where the matter is viewed
as being entirely between two individuals, marriage or living together are
irrelevant. But here [with families involved] there are many people to put
moral pressure on husbands, who then cannot break the relationship and run
easily'. The trope of the child appears again and again to justify marriage,
although there is never any explanation of how exactly cohabitation is supposed to harm a child physically or emotionally. From Kishwar again: 'The

issue is also connected with giving the gift of an emotionally and physically protected life to the next generation. I would never advise women who want children to live together [with a man]'. And from several others: 'Still, there is the question of the children's future'. If read together with the first article above, a more troubling image emerges. If marriage is necessary for the child's correct development, and if the female body is simply a jug designed to carry the child and her ultimate corporal pleasure comes from embracing her offspring, then marriage suddenly carries with it a physical imperative. Whatever the social and emotional grievances of individual women, the two articles together construct a logic that adds the authority of physical satisfaction in the 'correct' female body to the side of marriage.

The second article poses a more complicated puzzle than the previous one and seems to exemplify the core of contradiction that scholars of popular culture have talked about with respect to women's magazines: the immutability assigned to heterosexuality and marriage paired with explicit discontent and critique of patriarchal structures, the pleasures and intimacies associated with marriage that hint at its ideological attractions counterposed against the betrayal and grief of numerous 'bad' marriages. There appears to be a complex acknowledgement of marriage as an economic coping strategy that is also a hegemonic signifier of utopian intimacy. It is possible for readers to identify with the discontent *and* the pleasure. They may negotiate dominant definitions of the regulation of sexuality in a resistant, troublemaking voice, but they may also recover the dominant definition of marriage as optimal when it is not too bad a marriage, i.e., they may conclude that the problem with marriage may be bad practice rather than the concept itself.

Beyond this particular article, *Sananda*'s message about marriage is infused with contradictions and compromises, with moments of acquiescence as well as of rupture. Just a few months before the 'Marriage versus living together' article came the humorous and nostalgic piece 'Why it is necessary (*jaruri*) to get married' by the male author Parthasarathi Talukdar,[14] which talks about the pleasures of marriage in terms of wedding rituals and bonds of kinship, developing intimacies and sharing life-cycle rituals. Brightly coloured folk art illustrates the article, signifying the association with allegedly ancient, unchanging and culturally unique traditions. Significantly the advertisement facing the article, placed by a jewelry firm, features a young girl bedecked in gold and gems as a bride in waiting plus another smaller picture of her along with other married women, also heavily bejewelled, who are meant to represent family members. The combination of the article and advertisement perfectly exemplifies Gloria Steinem's arguments about the ways in which the 'content' in women's magazines sells the products that fuel its economic sustenance through advertising.[15] The advert in question invokes the same nostalgia about the stability and attraction of 'tradition', but it is selling a commodity central to marriages and patriarchal notions of 'women's wealth', drawing upon the nostalgia of the article to sell its product. Steinem describes similar advertising strategies used by advertisers for women's magazines in the USA.

On the other hand, there is the letter sent to the feature 'In your ear' (*kaane kaane*), an advice column on sexual behaviour. This was purportedly from an anonymous 35-year-old Bengali woman, who described herself as leading an 'ordinary domestic life' as a housewife with two children, married to a man working for a computer agency. She narrates a sexual encounter with her husband's friend (the two families are described as being very close), who came over when the husband was out of town on work. She characterizes herself as remorseful about this one-time episode and contemplating a confession to her husband. The response from the 'expert' was as follows:

> It will be very hard to convince your husband that a deviation like that was an accident. An excess of alcohol takes our inhibitions away and creates episodes which we would probably not be part of if we were not high. So be careful about alcohol. And forget that episode as an unfortunate accident. Since it's not part of an ongoing relation-ship, turn to lying. The lie will save your husband and family from needless grief. And make sure your husband's friend does not take further advantage of you based on that episode.[16]

This response, along with numerous columns on legal advice, is part of a pragmatic discourse about marriage. Like other responses in agony columns described by researchers,[17] it appears to conserve dominant cultural norms while being non-judgemental. In this case the 'actor' becomes alcohol and the woman is carefully denied direct blame while being told to maintain the stability of the domestic order. The stress on adultery as an accident, a mishap, does not confront the ways in which adultery is viewed as deviant, based on the notion that marriage creates exclusive forms of bodily property and par-ticularly marks women's bodies as sites of purity. There is no explicit feminist critique of the guilt over adultery. However, the advice to lie is powerfully subversive even as it is conservative, since it validates (and perhaps thereby encourages) the self-preserving silences of women who do act on corporal impulses in forbidden ways and who therefore deny the prescriptions made for their bodies elsewhere in the very same magazine.

Conclusion: discourse and discipline

Along with – and indeed through – health and shopping tips, political commentary and celebrity gossip *Sananda* serves up discourses of femininity and sexuality that are both compliant and subversive. By manufacturing consent and pleasure from a wide spectrum of readers through invoking both Bengali cultural specificity and a rational modern self, it enables the conditions for its continued existence to the satisfaction of advertisers and readers. Yet it incorporates contradictions in style and content and so makes space for rupture and discontent. Some of the contradictions are in the play between words and images, while others subvert the overt agendas of articles. The effect of trying to package outrageously different or oppositional topics in terms that will fit standards of Bengali cultural modesty usually goes only as far as the acknowledgement of diversity and at best a call to tolerance and understanding. Further, elite and middle-class privileges are solidified and global hegemonies challenged through the assertion of gendered norms for the Bengali woman. But while loud announcements of seemingly modern and oppositional topics often refer to modest if not conservative analyses, gaps of logic and expressions of discontent within statements that seem overtly culturally prescriptive can be subversive. Moreover, raising questions may in itself open up room for interrogation in readers, even if the article draws a less than radical conclusion on the topic.

In any case, there is no reason to expect *Sananda* to be other than it is. It does not address itself to a feminist audience but to a 'general' readership of women, after all, and makes no claims to be radical in its approach to gender or class or capitalism. As the editor's persona and voice make clear, the primary goal is to appeal to middle-class, urban Bengali women, suggesting a savvy cosmopolitan self as a preferred contemporary identity by invoking a purported Bengali legacy of being 'modern', yet 'different'. However *Sananda* does repeatedly cast itself as a venue where hitherto taboo issues are discussed for the edification of today's Bengali women, drawing upon the film-maker editor's reputation for having raised some startling questions about marriage and gender, its controversial front covers and its claim to being as frank as possible on a variety of subjects. In the absence of a Bengali equivalent of the American magazine *Ms.*, *Sananda* does lay claim to defining the nature and limits of feminist discourse (although not necessarily in radical ways). While the economic exigencies and cultural expectations that govern the success of *Sananda* make it suspect as a feminist space, because it cannot really reach beyond sexual modesty or afford to minimize the creation of ever-growing consumer needs, it is significant that the magazine's accessibility and normative tone of social consensus make it possible for it to raise unprecedented transgressive issues about sex without seeming prurient or culturally gauche. *Sananda*'s existence thus reveals the inevitable contradiction of radicalizing through a commercial, popular medium that demands acknowledgement of cultural norms while containing within it the means of destabilizing such assumptions.

Acknowledgements

I would like to say 'thank you' to Meryl Altman and Sabarni Das for their generous help with resources and ideas. This paper draws upon the argument made in 'The Blunt Cutting Edge: The Construction of Sexuality in the Bengali "Feminist" magazine Sananda', *Feminist Media Studies*, 1/2 (2001), pp. 179–96; my thanks to the editors and to Routledge for their help with that piece.

Bibliography

Altman, M, 1984, 'Everything They Always Wanted You to Know: The Ideology of Popular Sex Literature', in C Vance (ed.), *Pleasure and Danger: Exploring Female Sexuality*, Boston, Routledge.

Bannerji, H, 1994, 'Textile Prison: Discourse on Shame (Lajja) in the Attire of the Gentlewoman (Bhadramahila) in Colonial Bengal', *Canadian Journal of Sociology*, 19/2, pp. 169–93.

Blix, J, 1992, 'A Place to Resist: Reevaluating Women's Magazines', *Journal of Communication Inquiry*, 16/1, pp. 56–71.

Chatterjee, P, 1989, 'The Nationalist Resolution of the Women's Question', in K Sangari and S Vaid (eds), *Recasting Women: Essays in Colonial History*, New Delhi, Kali for Women.

Hegde, R, 1995, 'Recipes for Change: Weekly Help for Indian Women', *Women's Studies in Communication*, 18/2, pp. 177–88.

Ho, M, 1984, 'Patriarchal Ideology and Agony Columns', *Studies in Sexual Politics*, 1, pp. 3–13.

Illouz, E, 1997, *Consuming the Romantic Utopia: Love and the Cultural Contradictions of Capitalism*, Berkeley, University of California Press.

Kumar, R, 1993, *The History of Doing: An Illustrated Account of Movements for Women's Rights and Feminism in India 1800–1990*, London, Verso.

Nag, D, 1991, 'Fashion, Gender and the Bengali Middle Class', *Public Culture*, 3/2, pp. 93–112.

Nair, J, 1996, *Women and Law in Colonial India*, New Delhi, Kali.

Parashar, A, 1992, *Women and Family Law Reform in India: Uniform Civil Code and Gender Equality*, New Delhi, Sage.

Smart, C, 1995, *Law, Crime and Sexuality: Essays in Feminism*, London, Sage.
Steinem, G, 1990, 'Sex, Lies and Advertising', *Ms.* (July-August), pp. 18–28.

Notes

1. Steinem 1990.
2. Illouz 1997, p. 86.
3. Chatterjee 1989; Nair 1996; Parashar 1992; Kumar 1993.
4. Chatterjee 1989, p. 246.
5. Bannerji 1994, p. 188.
6. Ibid., p. 183.
7. Nag 1991.
8. Smart 1995, p. 8.
9. Altman 1984, p. 116.
10. From M Foucault, *The History of Sexuality*, vol. I, *An Introduction*; quoted in Altman 1984, p. 117.
11. Blix 1992.
12. *Sananda* (22 May 1998), pp. 26–32.
13. *Sananda* (3 April 1998), pp. 28–35.
14. *Sananda* (30 January 1998), pp. 47–8.
15. Steinem 1990.
16. *Sananda* (15 January 1999), p. 51.
17. For example, see Ho 1984.

9

A Perfect 10 – 'Modern *and* Indian': Representations of the Body in Beauty Pageants and the Visual Media in Contemporary India

SHOMA MUNSHI

Introduction

When Sushmita Sen, daughter of an Indian Air Force officer from Delhi, clapped her hands to her mouth in ecstasy at becoming the first Indian to be crowned Miss Universe, the image sizzled off of television screens into the collective Indian consciousness. She was followed almost immediately by Indian supermodel (and now top Hindi film actress) Aishwarya Rai, who won the Miss World crown for India for the first time since Reita Faria's victory long ago in 1966. Both Sen and Rai enjoyed a triumphant homecoming to India that involved victory processions, carriage rides down New Delhi's Rajpath with cheering crowds lining the sidewalks, countless interviews in the media and gala parties across the country. They were personally received by the President and Prime Minister of India and other political leaders, who showered accolades on them for bringing glory to the country. Their victories also launched an unprecedented run for the global beauty titles on India's part. Between 1994 and 2000, five Indians won the coveted Miss Universe and Miss World crowns and four others were runners-up. It is almost mandatory now that an Indian is among the final five finalists vying for the crown on the international stage.

Sen and Rai's victories illustrated the assertion of a new confidence among Indians about the body. The last decade in India has witnessed an obsession with the body, arguably to an extent not seen before, where the 'desirable' body is now on display through the constant circulation of images in the media. The 'look' meets the international blueprint for beauty – glamorous, healthy, taut and worked-out – and in an increasingly globalized world it connects India to the 'outside' world. This body is on display not just on our beauty queens but also on film stars, models, television celebrities and an increasing number of middle-class urban Indians. This investment in the body and its physicality coincides, not unnaturally, with the period of India's economic liberalization. This was set in motion by Rajiv Gandhi's government in the mid-1980s and has been gathering pace since 1991 with Manmohan Singh's path-breaking budget that opened the doors to foreign investment in India on an unprecedented scale.

This chapter tracks the changing visual mediascape in India over a decade of economic reform and the growth of a middle-class, urban consumer culture in which the 'beauty industry' has become a hugely profitable one. Representations of beautiful bodies constantly circulate in media images found in films, television, the print media of magazines and, more recently, on Internet sites as well. What is new in this rapidly changing urban socio-economic climate is how representations of the body of the woman in particular now span both the national and international as a site of identification, being instilled with notions of India's 'modernity' and increasing visibility on the international arena; and how at the moment(s) of consumption, leaning 'toward habituation through repetition',[1] they have become a major subject of the debate surrounding notions of 'Indian' values.

The Indian media landscape

'A decade of reform has raised the level of competition in most of the economy, lowered barriers to trade and foreign investment, and given greater scope to the private sector'.[2] In this climate, India in the 1990s witnessed sweeping transformations in the information and communications landscapes, with the boom in media industries becoming practically unstoppable. A few landmark events in the media sphere resulted in an open-skies policy signalling the final break with Nehruvian socialism. One was the introduction of the Prasar Bharati (Broadcasting Corporation of India) Act 1990, which came into effect in September 1997. This facilitated the creation of an autonomous body, the Prasar Bharati Corporation, to replace the system of government control over Doordarshan (the government television channel) and Akashvani (All-India Radio). Another was the beginning of live broadcasting of the proceedings of the Indian Parliament, 'wherein the saga of democracy at its best in the making and unmaking of governments was witnessed by millions of people. . . .'.[3] A third was the Broadcasting Bill of 1997, designed to replace the Cable Television Networks (Regulation) Act of 1995 in order to facilitate and regulate broadcasting services. Most importantly, two ministries completely new to India were set up at the turn of the century. After the general elections in October 1999 a new information technology ministry was created, along with a task force for reforms in the telecommunications industry. Perhaps nothing better underlines the growing importance of the Mumbai/Bombay film industry ('Bollywood') and the chances for profitable investment there than the fact that it was recently accorded ministry status, with Information and Broadcasting Minister Sushma Swaraj declaring that the Industrial Development Bank of India (IDBI) would now be allowed to fund films. As a result, IDBI 'made an allocation of INR (Indian Rupees) 1000 million for the film industry for 2001–02'.[4]

The media scene in India has changed both quantitatively and qualitatively as a result of these measures. Currently there are more than 70 television channels in India. A third of these are government-owned, while the rest are privately run with Indian and foreign ownership. The state-controlled Doordarshan and private channels such as Zee, Star, Sony, EL, ATN etc. compete fiercely for viewers, these rose in number from 17 million to over 300 million in less than 15 years.[5] The private company ZeeTV recently claimed to have access to 225 million viewers worldwide and 32 million homes in India.[6]

In the critical area of viewership preferences, the National Readership Survey shows that:

> . . . the upper and middle-income urban audiences prefer STAR, ZEE and Sony to the entertainment channel DD2 or Metro. Doordarshan's revenues have dipped as a result, from Rs 570 crores in 1996–97 to Rs 395 crores in 1998–99. Channels less widely received in the country meanwhile have registered increasing profits: Zee's annual revenue is Rs 325 crores, Sony's Rs 275 crores, and Sun is touching Rs 170 crores.[7]

Advertising on television is a major source of income for these companies. TV channels and advertisements 'bombard Indian TV sets with over 10000 thousand commercials every day (including free-spots and self-promos) . . . More than 3,300 new ads hit screens in 1999 and some 2,914 (in 2000)'.[8] The total spend on advertising is estimated at about Rs 8,400 crores.[9]

The booming beauty business

Beauty is big business and the market for related products has gone from a worth of Rs 100 crores in the 1980s,[10] to Rs 1,500 crores in 1994, to over Rs 3,000 crores by the close of the century.[11] A combination of several factors accounts for this tremendous boom in the beauty business. There are increasing numbers of women in the professional and service-sector workplace in cities such as Mumbai and Delhi, and increasingly in smaller towns as well. There is also the sheer diversity and range of products from indigenous cosmetic companies (Lakme, Elle, Tips and Toes, Ayurvedic Concepts, Shahnaz Husain etc.) and multinationals such as L'Oreal, Revlon and Maybelline, with Indian beauty queens endorsing their products.

The simultaneous emergence of the new cosmetics market and the cult of the beauty pageant is not accidental, of course. Market researchers questioned in the course of this study replied consistently that India's presence on the international beauty circuit has had a dramatic impact on the beauty business.[12] Studies done on visual media flows in the West have shown how changes in the definitions of femininity have been linked to the development of consumer culture. The most notable change was a shift from the representation of women in terms of their roles as wife and mother to an increasing emphasis on tropes of glamour, sexuality and appearance.[13] A similar pattern has been observed in the representations of femininity in the Indian visual media.[14] Advertisements of the 1960s and 1970s in India mainly featured women in their roles as homemakers, that is as mother, wife and daughter-in-law (the last being important in the context of joint families). Motherhood as a vocation was prominent in advertising at a time when women were generally homebound and advertising discourse adopted a serious, almost righteous air while targeting mothers as consumers.[15] Advertisements from the 1960s and 1970s typically showed the woman as anxious for the approval of her husband and mother-in-law. Even in the 1980s, television commercials for Sanifresh (a household cleaner) depicted the daughter-in-law holding her breath in terror while her mother-in-law checked every corner of the house for offending dirt. Military music playing in the background clearly underscored the mother-in-law's superior hierarchical position.[16]

Women's preoccupation in India with what Janice Winship famously called 'the work of femininity' has followed a somewhat different route from Western representations. As Susan Bordo argues in her work on the body in Western contexts, 'at different historical moments, out of the pressure of cultural, social, and material change new images and associations emerge'.[17] In this context, Arjun Appadurai's argument about the consumer revolution is persuasive:

. . . [if] we define *consumer revolution* as a cluster of events whose key feature is a *generalized* shift from the reign of sumptuary law to the reign of fashion [then] it . . . detaches consumer revolutions from specific historical sequences and conjunctures [and] opens up the possibility that large-scale changes in consumption may be associated with various sequences and conjunctures of these factors. Thus in India department stores are a very late development, coming after advertising had been for at least forty years a well-established commercial practice.[18]

To extend Appadurai's argument for the purposes of this paper, as far as advertising in India went, there were very few beauty product advertisements before the 1990s. The few advertisements for beauty products, in a socio-economic climate in which there were far fewer nuclear families and women in the workplace than today, were mainly in the print media of women's magazines. In back issues of such magazines as *Femina* (in English) and *Sarita* (in Hindi), publications that have been around since the 1950s and 1960s, products were limited mainly to hair oils and face creams. Long hair, worn braided or in a bun, was the general fashion norm as evinced on the film stars and models of the 1970s and 1980s. Most skin-care adverts were for creams and powders with whitening and smoothening properties: a smooth, fair skin was (and still is) considered a hallmark of good looks. Very importantly, these ads also underlined the need for masculine appreciation. The herbal soap Margo stressed the natural properties of the product and told the woman that it left her with 'a naturally glowing complexion and exhaustive compliments from your man'.

With the gradual decline in the numbers of joint families in urban India and an increase in the numbers of women in the workplace, the wife and mother living for her husband and children was transformed into the partner and friend carving out her own patterns of consumption.[19] The cosmetic company Modi-Revlon, for instance, is building its brand through a series of profiles of professionally successful women who radiate confidence about their achievements. Maruti Udyog now market their popular Maruti 800 as the car which helps the woman balance home and career with the byline 'Helps you speed between two worlds'. She also seems less dependent on male judgement than before. Indeed, the byline for Anne French hair remover went from the 'Don't you want his approval?' of the 1970s to the 'I feel soft and silky and woman all over' of the 1990s.[20]

The influence of global advertising campaigns is most potently visible in advertisements for makeup[21] and fitness items. Leading global brands are sometimes priced at the top end of the spectrum, but their makers are aware that a market for their product exists. More affordable brands swamp the marketplace. For instance, there is a war on to corner a segment of the nail-enamel market that is being fought out between companies such as Modi-Revlon, Lakme, Maybelline, Elle and others.[22] Most recently, the competition is between different brands of fairness creams. The market, estimated to be anywhere between Rs 500 and 700 crores and growing at double-digit pace, has over 20 players in the organized sector alone. Fairness products, including creams, soaps and lotions, make up almost 50 per cent of the total skincare market, which stands at Rs 1,200 crores. Hindustan Lever's brand Fair and Lovely, launched in 1976, can be credited with creating the market for fairness creams in which it continues to boast a 75 per cent share today.[23]

Fitness fever: fat is out, fit is in

In the Western context Bordo has argued that:

> . . . the bulging stomachs of successful mid-nineteenth century businessmen and politicians were a symbol of bourgeois success, an outward manifestation of their accumulated wealth. By contrast, the gracefully slender body announced aristocratic status; disdainful of the bourgeois need to display wealth and power ostentatiously, it commanded social space invisibly rather than aggressively [. . .] subsequently, this ideal began to be appropriated by the status-seeking middle class, as slender wives became the showpieces of their husbands' success.[24]

This appears to parallel the urban Indian situation until the late twentieth century. Middle-class Indians had long accepted that marriage brought women a few spare tyres and men a comfortable pot belly and these were taken as signs of prosperity, good food, children and marital bliss. Hospitality meant stuffing family and friends with rich food and sweets. Veena Merchant, one of the country's fitness gurus, is known to have famously remarked: 'Indians have such beautiful faces . . . but what gross bodies'.[25]

If 'corpulence went out of middle-class vogue (in the West) at the end of the (nineteenth) century',[26] it took another century for the same to happen in India. Slender 'trophy wives' are very much a late-twentieth-century adoption in urban India. Physical exercise and working out, for both men and women, is relatively new in India. Several factors coalesced in the 1980s when the concern for fitness crystallized into action. In 1982 India hosted the Asian Games and for the first time, and very publicly, the fact that Indians were by and large 'unfit' was driven home. A direct result was the creation of the Sports Authority of India (SAI), which included a massive nation-wide fitness blitz. This included run-for-fun, jogathons, pay-and-play schemes and interest-free loans to anybody wanting to set up a gym. Major O P Bhatia of the SAI remarked at the time, prophetically as it turned out, that 'by 1990 the dent will be seen'.[27]

By the 1980s, the impact of big-city living and sedentary lifestyles had also begun to manifest itself as a serious concern and obesity – a problem not commonly associated with India in the Western imagination – had become a problem. The BBC carried an article entitled 'India Faces Weighty Problem' which stated that 'nearly half of all high-income women in Delhi are over-weight . . . Like their counterparts in the West, Indian professionals are increasingly falling victim to the combination of too little exercise and too much food'.[28] Jane Fonda's aerobics became hugely popular in India in the 1980s (as VCR ownership boomed), followed by film star Rekha's *Mind and Body Temple*. Rekha, who had always been fat, now reinvented herself through diet and exercise and became one of Hindi films' most enduring and visible icons of how a body could be transformed. Gymnasiums sprang up, not just in the big cities but also in smaller cities like Chandigarh and Lucknow.

In the streets, in parks and on the beach in cities like Mumbai and Thiruvananthapuram, in health clubs and nature-cure centres and in the privacy of their own homes, increasing numbers of (urban) Indians did what few had done before: they pursued fitness. Perhaps nothing appealed more to a wide cross-section of people than jogging and walking. Given the Indian propensity to socialize, walking in parks, particularly in the early hours of the morning, became (and continues to be) a good place to meet people regularly, discuss work and play. In the new millennium, novel ways of working out and staying fit have arrived, including martial arts. From taekwondo to t'ai chi and kickboxing, combat fitness is the most fashionable way to burn fat, with salsa music an added incentive. Yoga, now doffing its hat to popular culture, has taken on the soubriquet of 'power yoga'. The fitness fever has become 'literally a running battle, this obsessive desire to keep fit and young looking. It becomes even more of a battle to keep up with the latest trends and fitness programmes'.[29]

The 'perfect 10' body beautiful

The new norms of beauty make few concessions to older ideals of the female body in India. Sculptures on temple walls, paintings of any period, even films and advertisements until the 1980s defined 'beautiful' body proportions voluptuously, in terms of what is often termed the 'hourglass' figure. This emphasized breasts and hips, the markers of reproductive potential, against a tiny, fragile waist and reflected male fantasies rather than any 'real' female body.[30] Throughout the 1990s, Indian cinema and advertising rejected this image and instead embraced the arrival of a differently sculpted body to meet exacting international standards. It no longer matters that the international blueprint for beauty does not match the older, indigenous one: it is taller than the average Indian woman, with never-ending legs. If international beauty contests are anything to go by, then India is all set to replace Venezuela in producing lean, mean international beauty queens.

During fieldwork in India I interviewed Pradeep Guha and Sathya Saran, members of the *Times of India* group which hosts the Miss India contest. It is quite true that the *Times* media group, one of India's oldest and wealthiest,

> . . . can single-handedly take credit for the boom in India's beauty industry. It not only discovers new hopefuls every year, but also makes sure they never leave the public eye through its glossy big city supplements which are devoted solely to designer-do's, designer clothes and beautiful people.[31]

The *Times* media group is responsible for grooming the beauty-pageant winners to perfection before dispatching them to compete with the best from the rest of the world. Both Guha and Saran averred that India is a huge market with enormous potential and that they are well equipped to produce winners from such a huge crop of young hopefuls. The only two prerequisites were that the women be 'reasonable pretty and taller than average'. The rest was 'positioning and packaging: two factors of utmost importance'. The formula which they described to me had been worked out to perfection:

> . . . after an initial screening, personalized food plans, fitness workouts to shape up and lose weight from 'trouble spots' like hips and thighs, plastic surgery if necessary, sartorial and physical groom-ing, etiquette, diction and general knowledge sessions, tossing difficult questions around and coming up with politically correct answers to be delivered while sashaying up that aisle victoriously.[32]

The winning makeover is expensive and time-consuming. If Cinderella had one fairy godmother, today's contestants have a battery of them, referred to as 'the A-team', who help in the transformation from basic raw material to export-quality finished product. They range from 'beauticians, nutritionists, hair stylists and designers to cosmetic surgeons, dentists, dance instructors and speech therapists'.[33] As market-research professional Kiran Tandon of the Indian Market Research Bureau (IMRB) explained to me, 'around this beauty factory has mushroomed an entire industry that takes care of packaging, branding and marketing. The bottom line is of course big bucks. Sponsors like Palmolive spend crores on beauty pageants in return for free and prolific publicity'.[34] Media personality, author and one of Mumbai's best-known names on the social circuit, Shobha De, put it tongue-in-cheek but with a ring of truth when she said, 'earlier we exported gurus and yoga from India, today we export glamorous beauty queens'.[35] Guha and Saran take the product more seriously when they say 'it's not just about glamorous, beautiful girls or empty-headed beauty queens. It's much more about the search for the complete modern Indian woman'.[36] Film-maker Mahesh Bhatt recently told me:

> The modern Indian woman is a truly global person today, good looking, intelligent and articulate, without losing the charm and grace of her grandmother and mother. The concept of the 'body beautiful' has finally penetrated the Indian psyche. A few decades earlier, the Indian psyche only accepted the 'simple' woman as the 'good' woman. This celebration of beauty, body and brains came just about a couple of decades ago. Not many people now care about those who brand beauty contests as a show of 'breast and buttock'. These beauty contest winners now are called combinations of 'brains and beauty'.[37]

The 'tyranny of slenderness', as Kim Chernin termed it,[38] has now become an important feminine preoccupation. This desirable and narcissistic body is on display not just on our beauty queens but also on film stars, models and television celebrities. The neighbourhood barber now offers manicures and pedicures, and many housewives offer services as beauticians and hair stylists in the afternoon hours, working out of an extra room in the house. Nutritionist Anjali Mukherjee says that 'a sizeable percentage of my clients are women who want to get into shape post-pregnancy or post-lactation' and cosmetic surgeon Vijay Sharma is on record as saying that 'my business has grown 600-fold since 1988 . . . looking good has become an obsession with people'. Sharma terms this 'hyper-aesthetic tension'.[39]

Clearly, discourses of physical appearance and body care have shifted from the private to the public space. In contemporary India, the onset of the new physical perfection has rightly been termed 'the arrival of the professional body; a body acquired, shaped and toned like any other professional skill'.[40] Nowhere is this more visible than in the case of the successful stars of Hindi cinema today 'for whom the display of the body and the body-in-performance are integral to the spectacle'.[41] What is beyond debate is that today the worked-out, taut body has become a cultural icon in India: a statement to the world that its owner cares for herself and about how she appears to others. Implicit

Priyanka Chopra, Miss World 2000: 'Export-quality finished product'.

in the statement is the assumption that one does not so much shape the body through subscription to fitness and beauty regimes as transform life itself.

As in the West, there is a negative side to this in India, as numbers of young girls now fall prey to anorexia and other eating disorders in their desire to meet the new standards. Also, the desire to break through to the 'beauty elite' and become the next Sushmita Sen or Aishwarya Rai sometimes forces women into unsavoury situations on the casting couch or at the dubious modelling institute.

The body beautiful and beauty pageants as a site of identification and contestation

Between the processes of actual lived realities and consumption of media images the body itself has become a site both for identification and for contestation. The anxieties surrounding larger sociocultural transitions in India have found expression in media-centred discussions. Quite simply, due to the pervasiveness and scale of televised images in India today, it looms on the urban mind as a dark, threatening presence.[42] Context here is all important. The specificity of cultural and social practices in India has lent a particular direction to the ways in which both the Hindu Right and the women's movement have dealt with the issue of beauty pageants and countless images of beautiful bodies circulating in polysemic media texts.

The Hindu Right opposes beauty pageants as well as print media, film and television representations of the 'body beautiful' on the grounds that these are corrupting 'foreign' influences that threaten to destroy the fabric of 'Hindu' culture and traditional 'Indian' values.[43] The women's movement in India has a different history and trajectory than in the West.[44] However, as with feminist discourses elsewhere in the world, the women's movement in India too has 'privileged the analysis of the forms in which the female body is constructed in societal discourses as an important source of women's oppression'.[45] Ideological differences apart, the women's movement finds itself aligned (uncomfortably) with the Sangh Parivar in its critique of beauty contests and feminine representations in the media.[46] While the objection of the Hindu Right is based on a desire to protect the modesty and 'Indian-ness' of women with reference to a glorious Hindu past,[47] that of the women's movement is aimed against the objectification and commodification of women in beauty pageants and in the media in general.

It is well known by now that moral panics occur in societies when unresolved social anxieties focus on agents which are perceived in some form as threatening.[48] Instances of the media determining social mores are also well documented.[49] In contemporary urban India, perhaps the first major controversy

Aamir Khan in Lagaan: 'The display of the body and the body-in-performance are integral to the spectacle'.

around notions of 'decency' versus 'obscenity' arose over the picturization of the song *Choli ke peechey kya hai* ('What do you have behind the blouse?') in the film *Khalnayak* (The Villain) of 1993. Then came the furore over the staging of the Miss World contest in Bangalore in 1996. In 2000, when Priyanka Chopra was crowned Miss World, the chief minister of Uttar Pradesh, Rajnath Singh, banned beauty contests in the state saying that they violated Indian culture. As Shohini Ghosh points out lucidly in her analysis, 'beauty pageants justifiably present a problematic terrain for feminists. While the sexist and heterosexist assumptions of a pageant provide little resistance to traditional representations of women, they are not singularly oppressive to women either'.[50] Contrarily, 'they extricate exhibitions of the female body from within the private domain and locate it in the public sphere'.[51]

I have argued elsewhere, borrowing from Foucault, that 'in the realm of femininity in particular, we need an analysis of power "from below" . . . an analysis of the mechanisms not which subdue, but rather which multiply and generate our energies, and help in the construction of notions of normalcy and deviance'.[52] Nowhere is this argument more illuminating than where it comes to a social and historical analysis of femininity (and masculinity) and the politics of appearance. What is to be made of the many women who are not only enthusiastic supporters of such cultural practices but also willing participants? Almost all the women and young girls I spoke with found the objections (both by the Hindu Right and the women's movement) against beauty contests and the mediatization of beautiful bodies 'reactive', 'backward-looking' and 'quite unnecessary when these girls were highlighting India's presence on the international stage'.[53] Undoubtedly, such media representations, particularly the beauty pageants in their engagement with global media flows and international standards of beauty, instill a sense of 'Indian-ness' and a nationalistic pride in the image of India. The visual media in India now echoes post-liberalization India with the youthful, Westernized-yet-Indian-at-heart persona, in which London and New York are nearby, but the heart is in the right place, being unflinchingly Indian.[54] Also, the urban, middle-class Indian now comfortably straddles two worlds. This is due, in large measure, to how 'questions of multiple citizenship and multicultural education' have gained priority in today's transnational world and 'hyphenated identities'[55] or 'double coded identities'[56] have become the order of the day. Two things are evidently happening in tandem: both the producers of visual media and the consumers/audiences feel that India has arrived on the 'global scene' and both are afraid of forgetting one's Indian roots.

How then is 'Indian-ness' signified? Reams of print are given over to interviewing the beauty-contest winners, their families and those responsible for their success on the international arena. Over and over, they speak of how 'modern' the girls have become, able to hold their own against the best from the rest of the world, yet how 'our girls' have not forgotten the importance of 'traditional Indian values'. Apart from the rigours of working out, training, physical fitness and beauty makeovers, those who prepare the contestants talk of the importance of 'a Vedic lifestyle, replete with yoga, mantras and meditation'.[57] So *prana shakti* is skilfully juggled with Christian Dior, Estee Lauder and the 'Firm and Full' bust developer. All the contestants are on record as telling how their parents are responsible for their mindset and how they have been 'driving forces in their rise to fame'.[58] The mother of Yukta Mookhey (Miss World 1999) in an interview with the *Times of India* insisted that 'Indian women . . . are modernizing themselves without uprooting from traditional Indian values. The Indian woman of today represents a healthy blend of the modern and the traditional'.[59]

The image of the 'modern-*and*-Indian' woman is reinforced by other visual media representations as well. The 'face' of the music-driven Channel V, Ruby Bhatia-Bali, a former Miss India who came from Toronto to work in the Indian media industry, is a perfect example. Dressed in shorts and T-shirt and with close-cropped hair, she typifies a youthful Westernized image. Yet in interviews she says:

> I had a nose ring for five years in Canada . . . I was really attached to my culture, that's why I don't have a problem living in India, I love it. 'Cause I'm so Indian . . . I'm vegetarian, I'm very religious, I can quote our ancient scriptures . . . I was raised very Indian . . . I wasn't allowed to date. . .'[60]

Furthermore, as Butcher notes, 'the Indianness of Ruby is signified (by placing) the body in context to remind the viewer that it is an Indian body: speaking Hindi and Hinglish, surrounded by Hindi pop and film music, and the station identification logos'.[61] The nose ring completes this 'migratory-yet-rooted' Indian body.

Popular Hindi cinema and advertisements are also responsible in large measure for keeping this 'modern-*and*-Indian' woman alive and well.[62] *Femina* insists that it regards 'a creche, a ma-in-law and a good maid as the best support systems one can have',[63] and Aishwarya Rai mouths such platitudes as 'if an Indian girl wears western clothes, it does not mean that she ceases to have Indian values'. This is reflective of the media's eagerness to appeal to all sections of opinion as, on the one hand, it is winking at a younger generation with skin-tight Lycra ensembles and overseas-educated heroes and heroines in today's Hindi 'NRI films',[64] while at the same time it sounds reassuring to nervous conservatives (who are not necessarily a different set of people) by upholding 'Indian values'. It is testimony to the fact that economic imperatives have to pay attention to social and cultural standards in order to reap rewards.

Certainly, there is truth in the observation that women are being commodified in the media. But in a competitive economy, as is India's today, it is not necessarily the case that the commodification of beautiful bodies is worse than the commodification of other people or other things.[65] I am aware that feminist scholarship is always politically informed. Any focus on cultural production 'begs the question of representation in its two senses: political (who speaks for whom) and aesthetic (what images, strategies, genres, etc. are used)'.[66] Much feminist analysis is inadequate in its failure to admit female responsibility. My own research and writing on representations of femininity in the Indian media locate my argumentation at a distance from the viewpoint which holds that the burden of 'good' (Indian) modernity always falls on the shoulders of the Indian woman, 'perennially and transcendentally wife, mother and home-maker, who saves the project of modernization-without-westernization'.[67] My argument was, and remains, that this implies that Indian women somehow need rescuing from this burden. I adhere more to the modified Foucauldian approach, which states that:

> . . . even if we want to act for the liberation of women, we must acknowledge that women, as such, have neither been liberated nor repressed. Rather there has been a succession of discourses about femininity . . . that have displayed knowledge and power differently at different periods. The pattern of these discourses have been . . . patriarchal . . . the constitution of man as subject has been a power ploy. So must the constitution of woman as subject be.[68]

Conclusion

In recent writings on beauty pageants and their critique I agree with the pithy observation that 'rescue operations are legitimized only if those in need of rescue desire to be rescued. In this case, no such desire was expressed by the participants. On the contrary, they repeatedly insisted that their participation was voluntary and consciously made'.[69] So, by way of conclusion, I quote Rabindranath Tagore, who wrote in his memoirs:

> . . . the powerful always seek to limit freedom by talking about its misuse, but freedom cannot be called freedom unless one has the right to misuse it . . . More than evil itself, I have learnt to fear the menace of good that garbs itself in the guise of improving others.[70]

Acknowledgements

The research and fieldwork for this paper were carried out in 2000 and 2001 when I worked as a post-doctoral Research Fellow at the Amsterdam School for Social Science Research (ASSR), University of Amsterdam, also affiliated to the International Institute for Asian Studies (IIAS), Leiden, in the Netherlands, on the project 'Transnational Society, Media and Citizenship', funded by WOTRO (the Netherlands Institute for Research in Tropical Countries). This paper is part of a larger ethnographic process, and I would like to express my gratitude to those in the media and market-research industries in Mumbai who always made time for me in their busy schedules and the people in Delhi and Mumbai of whom I asked questions and opinions regarding the Indian beauty business and beauty pageants while on fieldwork for this project. Special thanks to my parents, Sreela and Anil Munshi, for the translation and referencing of Tagore's work and to my sister, Poroma Rebello, and Kishore Singh of Business Standard, a friend of long standing, both of whom helped supply the pictures for this article.

Bibliography

A&M, 2001 (15 October).

Agrawal, B C, 1997, 'The Meaning of Hinglishness: Liberalisation and Globalisation in Indian Broadcasting', in K Robins (ed.), *Programming for People: From Cultural Rights to Cultural Responsibilities*, Italy, RAI.

Appadurai, A, 1997, *Modernity at Large: Cultural Dimensions of Globalization*, Minneapolis, University of Minnesota Press.

Asia Times Online, 2000 (25 May).

Banet-Weiser, S, 1999, *The Most Beautiful Girl in the World: Beauty Pageants and National Identity*, Berkeley and Los Angeles, University of California Press.

Banner, L, 1983, *American Beauty*, New York, Knopf.

Bordo, S, 1993, *Unbearable Weight: Feminism, Western Culture and the Body*, Berkeley, University of California Press.

Bourdieu, P, 1977, *Outline of a Theory of Practice*, Cambridge, Cambridge University Press.

Brosius, C, and Butcher, M (eds), 1999, *Image Journeys: Audio-Visual Media and Cultural Change in India*, New Delhi, Sage.

Brownmiller, S, 1984, *Femininity*, New York, Ballantine.

Business Standard, 2000 (22–28 January and 1–7 April).

Butcher, C, 1999, 'Parallel Texts: The Body and Television in India', in C Brosius and M Butcher (eds), *Image Journeys: Audio-Visual Media and Cultural Change in India*, New Delhi, Sage.

Chernin, K, 1981, *The Obsession: Reflections on the Tyranny of Slenderness*, New York, Harper and Row.

Cohen, S, 1980, *Folk Devils and Moral Panics*, Oxford, Martin Robertson.

Doordarshan 1997, Audience Research Unit, New Delhi, Directorate General Doordarshan.

Douglas, M, 1966, *Purity and Danger*, London, Routledge.

Douglas, M, 1982, *Natural Symbols*, New York, Pantheon.

Dowling, R, 1993, 'Femininity, Place and Commodities: A Retail Case Study', *Antipode*, 25/4, pp. 295–319.

Federation of Indian Chambers of Commerce and Industry (FICCI), 2002, *The Indian Film Industry: A Structuring and Financial Perspective*, FICCI, New Delhi.

Foucault, M, 1980, *Power/Knowledge*, New York, Pantheon.

Foucault, M, 1981, *The History of Sexuality*, vol. I: An Introduction, Harmondsworth, Penguin.

Foucault, M, 1983, 'The Subject and Power', in H Dreyfus and P Rabinow, *Michel Foucault: Beyond Structuralism and Hermeneutics*, Chicago, University of Chicago Press.

Ghosh, S, and Bose, B, 1997, *Interventions: Feminist Dialogues on Third World Women's Literature and Film*, New York and London, Garland Publishing.

Ghosh, S, 1995, 'The Challenge of Communalism', *Journal of Peace Studies*, 2, p. 80.

Ghosh, S, 1999, 'The Troubled Experience of Sex and Sexuality: Feminists Engage with Censorship', in C Brosius and M Butcher (eds), *Image Journeys: Audio-Visual Media and Cultural Change in India*, New Delhi, Sage.

Ghosh, S, and Kapur, R, 1996, 'Beauty Queens: What a Drag?', *Forum (APWLD)*, 9/4 (December).

Golding, P, and Middleton, S, 1982, *Images of Welfare*, Oxford, Martin Robertson.

Goldman, R, 1995, *Reading Ads Socially*, London, Routledge.

Hall, S, and Jefferson, T, 1976, *Resistance Through Rituals*, London, Hutchinson.

Hansen, T B, 1999, *The Saffron Wave: Democracy and Hindu Nationalism in Modern India*, Princeton, Princeton University Press.

India Today, 1988 (15 February).

India Today, 1999a (12 December).

India Today, 1999b (20 December).

India Today, 2000 (29 May).

Internet, 1999, H-ASIA Discussion List (August).

Jaffrelot, C, 1996, *The Hindu Nationalist Movement and Indian Politics*, New York, Columbia University Press.

Jaffrelot, C, 1998, *BJP – The Compulsions of Politics*, Delhi, Oxford University Press.

Jaggar, A, and Bordo, S (eds), 1984, *Gender/Body/Knowledge: Feminist Reconstructions of Being and Knowing*, New Brunswick, Rutgers University Press.

Jha, S, 1997, 'The Beauty Contest and the Politics of Liberalization', *Ghadar*, 1/1 (1 May).

Kapur, Ratma and Cossman, 1996, *Subversive Sites: Feminist Engagements with Law in India*, New Delhi, Sage.

Kellner, D, 1995, *Media Culture: Cultural Studies, Identity and Politics Between the Modern and the Postmodern*, London and New York, Routledge.

Kishwar, M, 1990, 'Why I Do Not Call Myself A Feminist', *Manushi*, 61 (November–December).

Kumar, N (ed.), 1994, *Women as Subjects: South Asian Histories*, New Delhi, Stree.

Lury, C, 1996, *Consumer Culture*, Cambridge, Polity Press.

MacDonald, M, 1995, *Representing Women: Myths of Femininity in the Popular Media*, London, Edward Arnold.

McRobbie, A, 1991, *Feminism and Youth Culture: From 'Jackie' to 'Just Seventeen'*, London, Macmillan.

Menon, U, 2000, 'Does Feminism Have Universal Relevance? The Challenges Posed by Oriya Hindu Family Practices', *Daedalus* (April), pp. 77–99.

Munshi, S, 1997, '"Women of Substance": Commodification and Fetishization in Contemporary Advertising within the Indian "Urbanscape"', *Social Semiotics*, 7/1, pp. 37–53.

Munshi, S, 1998, 'Wife/Mother/Daughter-in-Law: Multiple Avatars of Homemaker in 1990s Indian Advertising', *Media, Culture & Society*, 20/4, pp. 573–91.

Munshi, S, 2000, 'Media, Consumption and Identity Politics in South Asia: The New Globalization', *Asian Studies*, 36/1, pp. 183–212.

Munshi, S, 2001, '"Marvellous Me": The Beauty Industry and the Construction of the "Modern" Indian Woman', in S Munshi (ed.), *Images of the 'Modern Woman' in Asia: Global Media, Local Meanings*, Richmond, Curzon Press.

Munshi, S, forthcoming, 'Enabling the Migrant's Return via-Bollywood's "NRI Films": Transnational Cultural Flows and Diasporic Construction of "Indian-ness"', *Contemporary South Asia* [2003].

Nandy, A, 1995, *The Savage Freud and Other Essays on Possible and Retrievable Selves*, New Delhi, Oxford University Press.

Outlook India, 1999 (11 December).

Outlook India, 2002 (18 February).

Pathfinders India, 1997, P:SNAP Polls.

Philip, K, and Gopal, P, 1997, 'The Beauty Contest and the Politics of Resistance Against Liberalization', *Ghadar*, 1/1 (1 May).

Puwar, N, 2000, 'Making Space for South Asian Women', *Feminist Review*, 66 (Autumn), pp. 131–46.

Sarkar, T, and Butalia, U, 1995, (eds) *Women and the Hindu Right*, New Delhi, Kali for Women.

Sengupta, S, 1999, 'Vision Mixing: Marriage-Video-Film and the Video-walla's Images of Life', in C Brosius and M Butcher (eds), *Image Journeys: Audio-Visual Media and Cultural Change in India*, New Delhi, Sage.

Standard & Poor, 2001, *Ratings Direct Research: India*, Standard & Poor, New York.

Sundaram, R, 1998, 'Recycling Electronic Modernity', in *Automedia*, USA.

Sunder Rajan, R, 1993, *Real and Imagined Women: Gender, Culture and Postcolonialism*, London, Routledge.

Tagore, R, 1961, 'Jibansmriti', in *Rabindra Rachanabali*, vol. X, Calcutta, Government of West Bengal.

Time, 2000 (7 August).

Times of India, 1999 (12 December).

van der Veer, P, 1988, *Gods on Earth*, London, Athlone.

van der Veer, P, 1994, *Religious Nationalism: Hindus and Muslims in India*, Berkeley, University of California Press.

van der Veer, P, 1999, 'ICTs: The Political Dimension', unpublished paper.

van der Veer, P, 2001, 'Postmodern India: Engineering and Communalism', unpublished paper delivered at the Center for the Advanced Study of India, University of Pennsylvania, 5 November 2001.

Viswanath, K, 1997, 'Shame and Control: Sexuality and Power in Feminist Discourse in India', in M Thapan (ed.), *Embodiment: Essays on Gender and Identity*, Delhi, Oxford University Press, pp. 313–33.

Weeks, J, 1991, *Against Nature: Essays on History, Sexuality and Identity*, London, Rivers Oram Press.

Wilson, E, 1992, 'Fashion and the Postmodern Body', in J Ash and E Wilson (eds), *Chic Thrills: A Fashion Reader*, London, Pandora.

Winship, J, 1987, *Inside Women's Magazines*, London, Pandora.

Wolf, N, 1991, *The Beauty Myth*, London, Vintage.

Zee, n.d., *Always Better, Always Ahead*, Mumbai, Zee.

Notes

1. Appadurai 1997, p. 67.
2. Standard & Poor 2001.
3. Doordarshan 1997.
4. FICCI 2002, p. 25.
5. Zee, n.d.
6. *A&M*, 2001.
7. *Business Standard*, 2000.
8. *A&M*, 2001.
9. *Business Standard*, 2000. One crore of Indian rupees equals close to US$205,000.
10. *India Today*, 1982
11. *Outlook India*, 1999.
12. Interviews with Kiran Tandon, Indian Market Research Bureau (IMRB), and other market-research professionals in MARG, Probe Qualitative Research, *Mode*, while on fieldwork in 2000 and 2001.
13. Winship 1987; Wolf 1991; McRobbie 1991; Wilson 1992; Dowling 1993; MacDonald 1995; Lury 1996; Banet-Weiser 1999.
14. See Munshi 1997, 1998, 2001.
15. Munshi 1998, p. 578.
16. Ibid., p. 582.
17. Bordo 1993, p. 4.
18. Appadurai 1997, pp. 72–3; emphasis in original.
19. P:SNAP Polls 1997.
20. Munshi 2001, p. 83.
21. Munshi 2001.
22. *Business Standard*, 2000.
23. *Outlook India*, 2002.
24. Bordo 1993, pp. 191–2; see also Banner 1983, pp. 53–5, 232.
25. *India Today*, 1988.
26. Bordo 1993, p. 192.
27. *India Today*, 1988.
28. *BBC News Online*, 23 October 2000.
29. *India Today Plus*, September 15, 2000.
30. Bordo 1993.
31. *Asia Times Online*, 2000.
32. Personal interviews with Pradeep Guha and Sathya Saran.
33. *India Today*, December 20, 1999.
34. Personal interview with Kiran Tandon, IMRB, New Delhi.

35. Personal interview with Shobha De.
36. Personal interview with Guha and Saran.
37. Personal discussion with Mahesh Bhatt.
38. Chernin 1981.
39. *Times of India*, 1999.
40. Ghosh 1999, p. 22.
41. Ibid.
42. Nandy 1995.
43. See Ghosh 1999 and Sundaram 1998.
44. Kishwar 1990; Sarkar and Butalia 1995; Viswanath 1997; Ghosh 1999; Menon 2000; Puwar 2000.
45. Viswanath 1997, p. 313.
46. Philip and Gopal 1997; Jha 1997; Ghosh 1999.
47. Kapur and Cossman 1996.
48. See Weeks 1991; for the Indian media context, see Brosius and Butcher 1999.
49. Cohen 1980; Golding and Middleton 1982; Hall and Jefferson 1976; Weeks 1991; Bordo 1993; Goldman 1995.
50. Ghosh 1997, pp. 246–7.
51. Ghosh and Kapur 1996; see also Munshi 1997.
52. Foucault 1980, pp. 94, 136.
53. Discussions on beauty pageants with women between the ages of 18 and 50 while on fieldwork in Delhi and Mumbai.
54. Munshi 2000, 2001.
55. van der Veer 1999, p. 7.
56. Kellner 1995, p. 242.
57. *India Today*, December 20, 1999.
58. Ibid.
59. *Times of India* (12 December 1999).
60. Quoted in Butcher 1999, p. 174.
61. Ibid. The term 'Hinglish' refers to a mixture of Hindi and English (see Agrawal 1997 for details).
62. Munshi 2000, 2001.
63. *Femina*, 1998.
64. See Munshi 2001 and forthcoming [2003].
65. Ghosh 1999, p. 252.
66. Ghosh and Bose 1997, p. xxxi; Banet-Weiser 1999.
67. Sunder Rajan 1993, p. 133.
68. Kumar 1994, p. 9.
69. Ghosh 1999, p. 250.
70. Tagore 1961

10

Demographic Rhetoric and Sexual Surveillance: Indian Middle-Class Advocates of Birth Control, 1920s–1940s

SANJAM AHLUWALIA

Introduction

Beginning in the late nineteenth century, India witnessed an explosion of public interest and debates on birth control. The early framing of birth control as a 'solution' to India's perceived demographic increase constructed the issue within an oppressive trajectory, ensuring preservation of the class, caste and gender status quo. The predominantly elite demand for wider dissemination of contraceptive information in colonial India did not challenge the inequitable class/caste distribution of resources or seek to empower Indian women to exercise control over their sexuality and reproductive functions. Instead, middle-class male proponents of birth control represented 'overpopulation' as India's unquestionable demographic reality. They argued that one of the principal tasks for India to ensure development, progress and independence was to secure lower fertility rates among the subaltern groups in society. To this end, birth-control advocates outlined a strict prescription of sexual conduct for the lower classes, the aristocracy and the emerging middle class. Besides a distinct class, caste and community bias, there was also a strong patriarchal understanding that shaped their demands for wider dissemination of contraceptive information. In order to make a convincing argument in favour of birth control, Indian male supporters eclectically borrowed from intellectual traditions as diverse as Malthusianism, eugenics, demography, nationalism and sexology.

There were numerous actors in this public debate, including middle-class Indian men, international advocates, middle-class Indian feminists, biomedical practitioners and colonial officials. The demand for wider dissemination of contraceptives in colonial India, as articulated by various supporters, was primarily an elite discourse that sought to 'improve' the national/racial stock. Moreover, although the debates on birth control in colonial India allowed for public discussion of sexual issues, the dominant discourse that emerged was strongly heterosexual and patriarchal. Most interlocutors framed sexual expressions for women, particularly middle-class women, within the confines of matrimony and did not allow for any suggestions of female sexual auton-omy outside 'legitimate' heterosexual relationships.

This chapter examines the writings of early middle-class male advocates of birth control in colonial India. It highlights the eugenic patriotism of those who articulated the national procreative imperative in specific class, caste and community terms and argues that instead of emphasizing the liberating influ-ences of birth control, these men regarded birth control as a modality of socio-sexual power that could be used to invent 'truths' about sex and sexuality and function as an useful apparatus for policing subaltern and female sexuality.

Intellectual and political background

From the late nineteenth century to 1947, numerous intellectual and political traditions influenced discussions on India's population and its health. In their articulation of the discourse on birth control, Indian male advocates reflected their hybrid intellectual and cultural positions as colonial subjects, drawing as much from indigenous as from Western systems of knowledge.[1] These advocates – Gopaljee Ahluwalia, Aliyappin Padmanabha Pillay, Raghunath Dhondo Karve, Narayan Sitaram Phadke, Praye Krishan Wattal and Radhakamal Mukherjee – all espoused the need for wider dissemination of biomedical contraceptive information. Before looking at the overlaps and divergences in their specific positions it is necessary to understand why, in the 1920s–1930s, these middle-class and upper-caste men began to call for wider dissemination of contraceptives in colonial India. It is also important to consider how they were successful in deploying numerical and statistical inform-ation to present a scenario of declining national health, increasing poverty and arrested social, cultural and political development. They did this in a wider context that gave their negative assessments legitimacy in public debates, making room for their sometimes alarming articulations of over-population.

The 1920s and 1930s were marked by increased popular participation in a mass-based Gandhian nationalist movement. There was at this time a cor-responding anxiety about the future and about the outcome of nationalist agitation. Among the middle classes, there were public debates on the nature of *swaraj* (home rule) and on the social reforms that needed to be implemented to ensure freedom from British rule while ensuring the stability of the normative societal hierarchy. During this period India witnessed unrest among peasant, labour and lower-caste groups as well as exacerbation of communal tensions. These conflicts disrupted and challenged the existing social and cultural fabric from within, calling into question many of the privileges based on class and caste distinctions. Simultaneously, leaders such as Gandhi provided strong critiques of Western modernity and constructed 'Indian-ness' to contrast with Western liberal ideals of individualism, industrialization and biomedical traditions.[2] At the same time, strong lower-caste movements emerged in Maharashtra and Tamil Nadu. Many of the upper-caste advocates of birth control, such as Phadke, Karve and Pillay, came from these regions. Phadke and Karve were Maharashtrians and Pillay, a Tamil Brahmin, was based in Bombay during the 1920s and 1940s. It is not irrelevant that the caste movements in these regions were strongly anti-Brahminical. The Satyashodhak movement in Maharashtra and the Self-Respect movement in Tamil Nadu both challenged the caste privileges of Brahmins and other upper castes. In both these areas there were incidents of public burnings of the *Manusmriti*, a canonical text compiled from about CE 200 to 400, which combines legal injunctions and moral prescriptions to place women firmly within the patriarchal structures of family and marriage.[3] Not coincidentally, Phadke quoted extensively from this text in his work *Sex Problem in India*[4] in order to support his claims that eugenics was indigenous to Indian intellectual tradition.

Birth-control activism should also be viewed in the context of rising communal tensions between Hindus and Muslims in contemporary India. There was a violent millenarian outburst in 1921 among the Moplahs of Malabar. Hindu communal opinion read this episode as an expression of Muslim aggression against Hindus, and it resulted in the Arya Samaj response of conversion and reconversion know as *shuddhi* (purification) and *sanghathan* (systematic organizational effort). These movements were particularly strong in the Punjab and in parts of the western United Provinces.[5] The United Provinces also formed the stronghold of Madan Mohan Malaviya's communal organization, the Hindu Mahasabha.[6] In response, there were similar movements among Muslims, especially *tabligh* (propagation) and *tanzim* (organization), to reassert the hold of Islam among the poorer groups.[7] During this same period India witnessed an increasing communalization of organized politics. As Sumit Sarkar has noted, the Government of India Act of 1919 heightened divisions and tensions based on community affiliations.[8] The extension of electorates based on religious affiliation gave the anxiety of numbers a new lease of life within Indian public-sphere politics. The politics of numbers also underlined caste conflicts; the Justice Party in the Madras Presidency made demands for separate electorates and reservations for non-

Brahmins. The criterion of numerical representation became important once again in the Communal Award of 1932. This time the issue was the creation of a separate electorate for Untouchables.

It was within this unstable political, social and economic context that upper-caste men articulated their agenda for population control, with both a Malthusian vision of reducing the size of the population and an emphasis on eugenics aimed at improving the racial/caste composition of the Indian nation. Wattal, a Kashmiri Pandit, and Mukherjee, a Bengali Brahmin, both raised the issue of high fertility among aboriginal tribes, lower castes and Muslims. The communalization of demographic issues, one might argue, was a result of the communal rhetoric that was dominant in nationalist politics from the 1920s onwards.[9]

Ideological convergence: Neo-Malthusianism and eugenics

Unlike their British and American counterparts, middle-class male advocates of birth control in colonial India did not find it difficult to combine Neo-Malthusian and eugenic arguments in support of their demands.[10] Since both intellectual currents were available in India at the same time, each provided urgency to the cause of birth control. The proponents of birth control in India moved freely between these two ideologies, giving them a different import from what they had in the West.

The title of Ahluwalia's 1923 essay, 'Indian Population Problem: Selective Lower Birth Rate, A Sure Remedy of Extreme Indian Poverty',[11] supports the argument for the existence of an alliance between Malthusian and eugenicist ideas in Indian birth-control activism. In this article Ahluwalia claimed that the primary cause for India's poverty was 'thoughtless, irresponsible and extensive breeding, particularly among the middle and poor classes'. The eugenic elements were dominant in his analysis of the composition of the population, as he lamented that:

> . . . racial defects and poisons are multiplying from day to day. The physique of the people was surely deteriorating. The tall, stout and strong is being fast replaced by persons lean, lanky and bony, objects fit and proper for the study of a student of medicine. The extent and pace of growing degeneration justify a speedy cure.

The cure for this malaise, he argued, was to be found in spreading knowledge about sex hygiene, eugenics and birth control. He complained that 'India resembled a vast garden literally choked with weeds, fine roses being few and far between'.[12] Here is an alarmist construction of population as a problem both in numerical terms and in its caste and class composition.

Pillay's eugenicist ideas were clearly stated in his article 'Eugenic Birth Control for India'.[13] This article also reflected his Malthusian disdain for philanthropy. Pillay argued that the indiscriminate efforts of welfare workers to keep alive all who were born were helping the unfit to survive. He complained that philanthropy was being practised with very little regard to racial safeguards and the result was that the 'unfit' were 'allowed' to survive, multiply and leave behind 'tainted descendants'. Guided by eugenic principles, Pillay called for the prevention of the 'unfit' and the converse encouragement of the reproduction of the 'fit'.[14]

Phadke, in an early article on birth control, presented an environmentalist plea common among Neo-Malthusians, arguing that even though *swaraj* could achieve much it would not be able to neutralize the dreadful consequences of 'foolish procreation indulged in by its subjects without regard to the natural resources of the land'.[15] Like Ahluwalia, Phadke emphasized the need to 'improve' Indians so that they might become physically stronger. He argued that the 'stalwart physique of the people is one of the greatest assets of a country and an important instrument of its uplift'.[16] Combining eugenic and Neo-Malthusian positions, Phadke made a case for spreading knowledge about birth control to improve Indian physiques. According to him, the use of new contraceptive technologies would ensure healthy males for the development and modernization of the embryonic nation. In a chapter entitled 'The Mother of the Race', Phadke assigned women the sole responsibility of producing and parenting healthy sons for the nation: 'Like the sun from which all light radiates the mother is the root source of the strength or weakness of the race'. This explains his focus (and that of other birth-control activists) on the need to improve women's health and stem their physical decline.

Writing as late as 1927, Phadke articulated a stance that was different from the classic eugenicist position, arguing for an increase in the numbers of the 'fit' as opposed to the 'unfit' by encouraging the former to multiply while controlling the population of the latter. For Phadke in the India of 1927 the problem of an eugenically unfit population was compounded by the Malthusian problem of overpopulation. As an eugenicist in India, he was not content with merely providing for the mating of the fit. In *Sex Problem in India* he stressed the need for 'fit' married couples to adopt birth-control methods to limit their progeny, since any increase in population would have a deleterious effect on the nation's well-being. By the 1920s and 1930s overpopulation had become a politically and culturally constructed problem that led to an increasing concern with managing reproduction. Reproduction and conjugal sexuality were no longer regarded merely as belonging to the 'private sphere'. Instead these were viewed as directly impacting on the public life and prosperity of the nation.

This new understanding of marital sex called for its 'scientific' management within the discourse of birth control. The social agenda of the speakers at the first All India Population Conference in Lucknow in February 1936 indicated an alteration in the traditional Malthusian position, along with an acceptance of some of its tenets. Malthusian prudery and the reluctance to advocate birth control were absent from the lectures at the conference. In his introduction (and also in a paper) at the conference, Mukherjee asserted the importance of 'the diffusion of knowledge of birth control'. What was needed were 'appropriate and cheap devices of birth control derived by the rural population from materials in its own domestic surroundings . . . so that contraception can be applied until the man has attained the age of say 21 or 23 and the woman the age of 20 or 22 in India'.[17]

Debendra Nath Ghoshe, one of the participants at the Lucknow Population Conference, argued in his presentation 'Social Background to Pauperism in India' in favour of curbing welfare measures for the poor. Like Pillay, Ghoshe reiterated the traditional Malthusian position on charity.[18] Although the poor deserved some support, Ghoshe cautioned that 'humanity should not be carried too far' and advocated a formula to deal with paupers where 'liberty was regulated by law, rights by discipline and leniency by rigor'. He elaborated a scheme for helping the poor whereby the 'hopeless destitutes' would be turned into 'normal' men capable of helping themselves and society. He suggested that arrangements should be made with tea gardens or coal fields so that able-bodied paupers could be sent there to work.[19] The poor were denied control over their own bodies and labour, and in the name of 'reform' they were to be transported to some of the most extreme sites of labour exploitation in colonial India.[20] It is clear, then, that Indian middle-class/upper-caste male advocates of birth control attempted, in the name of the nation and the Hindu community, to institute various 'reforms' aimed at marginalizing subaltern groups while simultaneously preserving the existing structures of elite privileges.

National demography and partial citizenship: bodies and difference in India

Birth-control activists were especially keen to project a 'modern' image of India and *swaraj* was imagined as an inauguration of modernity. Phadke argued that for India to be a free nation it needed strong, sturdy, well-clad men and women. This, he argued, could be achieved only if 'scientific' thought was given to procreation, so as not to produce a single unwanted child. Although Phadke wrote of the exploitation of Indian resources by foreign imperial forces, he also lamented the 'foolish procreation indulged in by its subjects'. According to him, the need for birth control was far greater under colonialism since there was a danger of 'foreigners' exploiting India's population for their own imperialistic uses. By bringing forth more children than they could take care of, Indians were only creating a 'race of slaves who will too readily fall a prey to the designs of the foreign rulers and exploiters'.[21] The logical extension of an argument that tied the national well-being to sexual practices was to call for a strict surveillance of reproductive functions, particularly among those represented as undesirable citizens, such as the working class, the lower castes and also, within the predominantly Hinduized nationalism of these advocates, Muslims.

Wattal's analysis of the 'population problem' betrayed the communal, caste and class biases of an upper-caste Brahmin. According to Wattal, high fertility among the Indian aboriginal tribes was an indication of a lack of civilizational dignity and the low worth of individual life. Similarly, the high fertility rate among Muslims was for him a sign of the intellectual backwardness of that community. According to him, 'Muslims' cerebral (capacity) was so much less (compared to the Hindus) and as a consequence their fecundity so much greater'.[22] Likewise, he sought to argue that lower-caste Hindus were more fecund than the higher castes. Unfortunately, Wattal the statistician could not locate the data to support his thesis about the lower castes or Muslims from the Indian Census, and the relationship between class and fecundity had to be proved by citing figures from the Census of Scotland for 1911. This census 'proved' that members of the labouring classes, those engaged in the agricultural and fishing occupations, workers in mines and quarries, and transport workers, were more fertile than those in the legal, medical and teaching professions.

The demands for wider dissemination of birth-control information and technology allowed middle-class men to examine the intimate domain of procreation and conjugal relations of subaltern groups. Middle-class advocates typically expressed great suspicion of working-class sexuality. Phadke argued that it had been scientifically proven that 'specific type of environments were productive to prolific progeny, and it had also been shown that this peculiar type naturally obtained in the homes of the poor'.[23] In his chapter 'Higher Living', Phadke elaborated his views on the hypersexuality of the working class as reflected in high fertility within this socio-economic group. He represented the private spaces of working-class homes as breeding sites and his middle-class observer's gaze was hostile, impatient and incriminating. His distinctly middle-class discourse represented working-class sexuality as animal-like:

And if you could brave a visit to the dark, dusty, dingy slums of the mill operatives you will find that almost in every family the woman is either carrying or in confinement. And when our eyes fall on street loafers who find their food on the dunghill and make their bed in the gutter we find them bearing more children than the rags with which they cover their shame and are reminded of the bitch that breeds kennelfuls of puppies four times a year.[24]

Ridicule was also heaped on over-wealthy aristocratic families and their lifestyles and they were reprimanded for not fulfilling their eugenic duty of producing 'fit' sons for the nation. According to Phadke:

> . . . the prospect of a child is as impossible as the nut tree yielding an apple in the case of those over-wealthy people whose daily life is divided only between eating and sleeping and who have no other occupation than rolling in knee-deep cushions all day long and who visit the beach in the evening, as if with the object of giving exercise, not to their own bodies but to their horses or automobiles.[25]

The middle-class advocates were thus anxious to define themselves in opposition to the social classes both below them and above them.

Mukherjee and other participants at the first Population Conference presented an alarmist projection of India's population growth and argued that this demographic increase placed a tremendous burden on national resources.[26] Documenting his case with statistics which he assumed told an 'objective' story, Mukherjee stated that 'the outstanding feature of the population situation is India's chronic and increasing food shortage. By 1941 India's population will number 400 million, while her population capacity, estimated on the basis of her present food supply, cannot exceed 330 million'.[27]

Citing data, Mukherjee made a case – as had Wattal before him – for higher fertility among the lower castes and among Muslims. Representing both groups as sexually degenerate and deploying statistics to support his case, Mukherjee argued that:

> As in the West, the most fertile social strata in India are inferior but nowhere is the disparity between fecundity and culture greater than in Northern India. In the United Provinces the Brahmins and Rajputs have diminished by about 5 and the Kayastha and Kurmis by about 10 and 12 percent while the Chamars and Ahirs now aggregate more than the total number represented by the four upper castes, who have increased by 6 and 2 percent respectively. Among other lower castes, the Pasis, Gadarias and Lodha have increased by so much as 18, 9 and 5 per cent respectively.[28]

Statistical information, as Urla has argued, came to be regarded as a 'uniquely privileged way of "knowing" the social body, becoming a central technology in diagnosing its ills and managing its welfare'.[29] Mukherjee once again utilized an alarmist numerical narrative in discussing the case of Indian Muslims:

> The Muhammadan, who is less literate than all upper caste Hindus everywhere and in Bihar and Bengal less than even some of the backward castes such as the Santhals, Mahisyas and Namasudras, increased by 51 per cent., in Bengal and Punjab during the last 50 years while the Hindu has declined by 6 per cent in the Punjab and increased by about 7 per cent., in the United Provinces and 5 per cent. in Bihar and 23 per cent in Bengal. . . The enormous growth of the Muslims is no doubt due to widow remarriage, polygamy, and later consummation of marriage than among most Hindus and probably also due to the differences of food and economic habits.[30]

'Muhammadans', represented as a homogenous social group, were seen as universally less literate than all upper-caste Hindus and the community as a whole was castigated for its 'uncivilized' reproductive behaviour.

Disciplining the sexual body

As a sexologist, Pillay saw himself as a guardian of middle-class sexual well-being, defining and labelling appropriate sexual expectations for men and women of this class within matrimony. He accepted that the sex urge varied in women just as it did in men but insisted that desire in middle-class women had a definite periodicity. He contrasted this periodicity with chronic copulation among working-class women, poor rural women and also Western women, who were all represented as hypersexual 'others'. According to Pillay:

> . . . the poor women are ordinarily robust and though they have much manual labor to do are not tired out by the evening. Their husbands are also robust and do not suffer from lack of virility. It has therefore to be assumed that they enjoy sexual intercourse, according to their interpretation of the term. I may as well mention here that the majority of these people copulate almost daily.[31]

Even though the rural poor copulated daily, their sexual relations did not provide emotional satisfaction to either the husband or the wife. Pillay regarded sexual relations among the poor as a monotonous physical act aimed only at providing relief from nervous tension. Sexual pleasure in its 'true' essence, defined by Pillay as 'recreation, mentally stimulating and physically invigorat-ing', was believed to be the preserve of the educated middle classes.

Elaborating on working-class fertility in 1934, Wattal too argued that this class possessed a heightened sexual life compared to the educated middle class:

> Communities and occupations which are concerned with intellectual pursuits and have a relatively high standard of living show a smaller rate of fertility than occupations connected with manual labor and communities whose standard of living is relatively low or whose outlook on life is more material and physical than intellectual and spiritual. The well to do have many interests in life and more than one outlet for their nervous energy; but the poor have few. Sex life for the poor means much more than it does for the well to do.[32]

Nothing in the working-class lifestyle could be identified as 'cultural', since that was the sole prerogative of the 'well to do'.

Agreeing with Wattal's and Mukherjee's analysis of working-class sexuality, Ghoshe recommended forced sterilization to ensure that 'propagation of pauper species may not be possible'.[33] Nowhere in this literature is there a trace of a critique of social relations, the need for land reform or more equitable distribution of resources. The existing hierarchical social structure came under scrutiny only to express middle-class anxiety about its possible displacement. Employing Malthusian slurs, Mukherjee rebuked people of the subaltern groups for 'breeding like field rats, rabbits and fruit flies'.[34]

In their debates on birth control, middle-class male advocates established the parameters for defining the rights of citizens in independent India. The social aggregate whose interests they defended and promoted through such constructions were upper-caste, middle-class, Hindu and male. The discourse on birth control is therefore a useful lens for understanding how the intersect-ing politics of class, caste, community and gender shaped political rhetoric in colonial India. It is important to recognize that the advocates of birth control were not writing in a political or cultural vacuum. Their own elitist vantage positions clearly marked their discourse on the subject of birth control and population.

Roy Porter and Lesley Hall have argued that books and articles by Marie Stopes were instrumental in constructing a new understanding of sexuality, particularly of sex within marriage, in Britain.[35] Indian male advocates and sexologists, especially Pillay and Phadke, were also interested in rethinking ideas of sexuality and in presenting strict prescriptions of normative sexual practices for subaltern groups, the declining aristocracy and the emerging middle classes. The subject of birth control presented a legitimate platform for the articulation of new discourses on sexuality and conjugality. Here it is important to stress that colonial India during the 1920s and 1930s witnessed heightened public interest and veritable discourses on the body and sexuality. Issues of the 'private domain' were not repressed, resolved or absent from public-sphere debates in colonial India, as Chatterjee has suggested.[36] These decades witnessed some of the same anxieties that were articulated in the late nineteenth century by social reformers who pointed out a need to build strong, healthy and masculine bodies in the face of the colonial onslaught.[37] With the emergence of strong nationalist sentiments in the 1920s, there was a renewed search for ways of empowering Indians and of overthrowing the burdens of imperialism. It was argued that for India to be free it had to be strong, robust and masculine.[38] Issues of sexuality and its associations with the physical well-being of individuals (and by extension of the social body) were becoming an acceptable subject of public debate among middle-class Indian men. A closer scrutiny of the public discussions on birth control in colonial India during the 1920s and 1930s illuminates how sexuality was related to the physical well-being of individuals and to that of a nation in the making. In the process, the public and the private spheres were braided more closely together.

Advocates of birth control such as Phadke and Pillay evaluated and promoted specific contraceptive technologies, but in doing so they also constructed what they believed to be 'ideal sexual behaviour'. Their discussions of the various contraceptive technologies reflected their understanding of sexuality. Abstinence as a method of contraception, Pillay argued, 'may be adopted by those who can practice it without physical or moral or mental decline'.[39] He added that, while prescribing this method to young couples, one had to bear in mind that sexual appetite, after hunger, was the most dominant influence in the life of human beings. Sex was constructed as a 'natural instinct'. Constructing the truth of sex as biological and timeless, Phadke wrote:

> Hunger and love are the two great mother impulses, the ultimate source of all other impulses. Why, we may go a step further and assert that . . . in the ultimate analysis of things the impulse of love, or what is vulgarly described as the impulse to reproduce, will be found to be more primary.[40]

The ambiguity about sex and its role within marriage is amply demonstrated in Phadke and Pillay's descriptions of various contraceptive technologies. Abstinence as a method of birth control was rejected out of hand since, according to Phadke, 'considering the common course of sexual desire and the control to which it can be ordinarily subjected, the sexual act has to be allowed at least once a week'.[41] Abstinence was regarded as self-denial, something that he went on to argue could not be asked of mortal men since it would be as 'ridiculous as asking the mountain tree tops not to wave when in a storm, or a lump of butter not to melt before a fire'.[42] Male sexual instincts were treated as a biological given, akin to hunger, thirst and sleep, and therefore preaching abstinence as a method of birth control was believed to be a denial of 'the natural rights of the married man'.[43] Even though sex was constructed as a 'natural' instinct, Phadke warned against 'sexual extravagance' within marriage:

> It should be deeply impressed on the minds of all that none but the married have the right to sexual intercourse and that illicit intercourse is a heinous guilt, bound to spell the ruin not only of the individual but also the family and the nation. Every married person must conscientiously believe that even in the married state sexual excess is a breach of duty, that is an unnamable sin to use marriage as a permit for sexual intemperance.[44]

The emerging discourse on sexuality was anxious to impose its own norms of morality, even while challenging utilitarian ideas of sex for procreation. Sexuality was located within the discourse of national destiny and, in order to safeguard national well-being, sexuality had to be placed under a strict regime of surveillance even within bourgeois households. The practices of the private domain were clearly understood as overflowing and impacting on the public life of the nation, and as such they could not be left unsupervised.

Pillay briefly described some male contraceptives methods such as coitus interruptus and the condom, largely because he considered these to be harmful and unreliable.[45] Coitus interruptus, he argued, could cause a harmful local effect on the male sexual organ and in the woman it could cause sacral pain and weakness, a sensation of pain and dragging in the pelvis, and general neurosis. Pillay argued that the absorption of seminal and prostatic fluids was highly beneficial to the whole system of the woman and this would be impossible in external ejaculation. He also rejected the condom as unreliable and, like coitus interruptus, as a device that did not permit the woman to absorb beneficial fluids. Moreover, male condoms were unacceptable for men who did not have a 'very strong sex capacity, since its constant use could reduce potency for consistent erection and proper ejaculation'.[46]

With male contraceptives discarded as unreliable, the focus during this period shifted to analysing female contraceptive devices. Advocating these created an uncomfortable disjuncture in the writings of birth-control advocates such as Pillay and Phadke. Both generally addressed men as their readers, since women's capacity to comprehend sexual information was considered inadequate if not completely lacking. Yet both these men promoted female contraceptives as more reliable than male contraceptives. Placing contraceptive responsibility on women created an interesting tension. It required women to be active participants in sexual acts at the same time that the dominant patriarchal understanding of sexuality constructed women as sexually innocent. The advocates sought to resolve this tension by imparting contraceptive information to women indirectly through their husbands. Therefore, even though the onus of contraceptive use fell on women, women were not entrusted with this sexual knowledge. Men alone were trusted with the important knowledge and task of determining family size and of ensuring the national health by exercising sexual control over their wives.[47]

Phadke discussed female contraceptives such as douching, pessaries and sponges. He recommended the cervical device known as the Dutch cap or Mensinga, introduced by Norman Haire, as opposed to the Pro-Race cap recommended by Stopes. Phadke referred to the disagreement between Haire and Stopes regarding the preferable method and added that his own inclination was towards the Dutch cap, since the 'possibility of sliding out of place is eliminated in its case and hence it looks like a surer weapon than the Pro-Race Cap'.[48] Without basing his statements on any clinical tests, Phadke stated that people feared the use of the Dutch cap might cause injury to a woman's womb, but added that they could rest assured since no one had complained about the product.

Birth-control advocates articulated a strict prescription on acceptable sexual behaviours. For instance, Pillay wrote extensively on the need for sex education, which could be incorporated into the school curriculum as 'character or moral training' and as 'sex education proper'.[49] He asserted that character or moral training should start at home, inculcating notions of 'regularity, obedience, conscience, personal cleanliness and reverence for the body, temperance, self control, proper sense of shame, and an initiation to helpful play'.[50] It was the responsibility of mothers to ensure that these 'qualities' were inculcated at home. 'Proper' sex instruction, which was to be the domain of the school, covered a very wide range of subjects: maternity, paternity, significance of marriage, fertilization and development, physiology and functions of sex organs, changes in adolescence, health rules, venereal diseases, hygiene of married life, prostitution, preparation for marriage, principles of heredity, preparation for parenthood, family life and 'Mother-craft'.[51]

Pillay's later work of 1944, *Ideal Sex*, reveals how birth-control advocates deployed the new 'scientific' discipline of sexology to articulate the need for promoting the spread of knowledge about birth control. These are important

texts for understanding the narratives on sexuality as they circulated among
the Indian middle classes during the early twentieth century. Pillay became
interested in the subject of birth control as an essential tool for promoting
'marital bliss' since, according to him, contraception made it possible to
divorce sex from reproduction. As a sexologist Pillay insisted that satisfactory
sex within marriage was one of the components of the utopia that he visualized, and he laid great emphasis on this. Although he defined sex as a biological function like hunger, he lamented that India, unlike Germany, did not
have organized marriage consultation centres where people could be 'educated'
and made 'sex conscious'.[52] The discourse on sexuality was thus internally
split, at once constructing sex as a natural bodily response while simultaneously
calling for its 'scientific' management. This fragmentation was even more
pronounced in the discussions on female sexuality and working-class sexual
practices.

According to Pillay in the same text, frigidity in women was a social myth
and not a reality. He argued that women would respond to sexual urges just
as they would to hunger. Pillay asserted that response to sexual stimulation in
women resembled the 'natural' response of sneezing when appropriate stimulation was applied to their nostrils or of eyes watering when chilly powder was
applied to them. In fact, he wrote that the only woman who would not
respond to sexual stimulation by a man was a woman 'who is a fool or a liar or
so ugly that no one wants to rouse her'. The danger with the 'deformed and
ugly' woman, according to Pillay, was that she would turn to homosexuality
from the lack of heterosexual stimulation. In the same text he claimed that
homosexual tendencies within women would cause frigidity in heterosexual
life. In seeking to represent homosexual woman as the 'other' and 'sexually
deviant', Pillay deployed the ultimate rhetorical manoeuvre of displacing her
sexuality onto the West. According to him, homosexuality among women was
not as common in India as it was in the West where, in large urban centres,
working girls were apparently establishing homosexual relationships.[53] Pillay,
as a sexologist, was anxious to define situations in which women might turn to
homosexual relationships, since for him these warranted social caution.

In *Ideal Sex* Pillay discussed many issues related to female sexuality. He
emphasized the need for married women to be sexually satisfied by their
husbands lest they take a lover. Sexually unsatisfied women, Pillay warned,
would 'in course of time become a bag of nerves, develop menstrual disorders
and may experiment with masturbation'.[54] While recognizing the need for
mutual sexual satisfaction within matrimony, Pillay advised that if there was
no sexual satisfaction for a woman in marriage she should learn to 'bear up
and cheer up' and 'take up social activity'.[55]

In constructing his image of a 'sexual utopia' Pillay emphasized the importance of mutual sexual attraction within marriage and thereby recognized that women were not merely passive objects of male desires within matrimony. But he was quick to add that, for a woman, raising a family was necessary for emotional satisfaction. A woman's emotional satisfaction would never be complete without having at least one child, he argued.[56] Women's sexuality in the ultimate analysis was tied to maternity. Thus, even when the more traditional ideals of female sexuality were questioned they were never completely discarded. Women were allowed sexual expressions exclusively within marriage, but even within marriage these were circumscribed by motherhood.

Even when Pillay sought to repudiate certain negative traditional associations of sex, he inadvertently ended up reinforcing them. This is particularly clear in his discussions on masturbation. In *Ideal Sex* he states in many places that masturbation was not a sexually harmful practice, adding that 'it does not produce insanity or any nervous disorder or sexual weakness, and it is not sinful or immoral, judged by the tenets of any religion'.[57] In other points in the same book masturbation is represented as a practice that would make boys self-centred and averse to marriage, and readers are warned that a masturbator 'is not likely to be ambitious as he would be content with whatever he could get without effort'.[58] When discussing masturbation in girls, Pillay argues that the practice would affect a girl's facial appearance and cause menstrual disorders, leucorrhoea and a dislike for society and companionship.[59] He advises that this practice should be avoided; if one was tempted, the best remedies were early dinner and a strict routine of exercises. Someone fighting the habit should also avoid reading 'sentimental four anna novels and thrillers', for these made a person think more frequently of sex than was good for them.[60] Pillay warns middle-class parents to protect their wards from the corrupting influences of servants who might initiate the children into the auto-erotic techniques of masturbation and other 'forbidden' sexual activities.[61] The final verdict was against masturbation.

Anxious middle-class projects of self-improvement allow us to better comprehend the internal contradictions and inconsistencies that marked the discourse of birth control and sexuality in twentieth-century colonial India. Just when sexual compatibility was constructed as an important component of conjugality, middle-class activists also encoded strict/oppressive sexual norms to ensure 'legitimate' sexual expressions. The writings of middle-class, upper-caste, male birth-control activists capture their understanding of the relationship between intimate private sexual practices and national progress. The activists in their surveillance of sexual practices linked the affairs of the home and personal health with the affairs and health of the emerging nation.

Conclusion

In trying to understand the trajectories of the birth-control movement in colonial India it is important to recognize the distinct political, social and cultural interests that determined the discourse on birth control. Most elite male proponents of birth control belonged to new categories of social experts such as demographers, sexologists and economists who, in the name of national welfare and scientific management, argued for strict surveillance of sexual behaviours. These advocate-experts linked the issue of birth control to what they argued was the problem of overpopulation and physical decline in Indians. The articulation of the issue of birth control as one intimately linked to demographic concerns served a variety of political interests and purposes. It gave the call for wider dissemination of contraceptive information a social and economic urgency that would have been hard to acquire and sustain had the issue been constructed solely as one of sexual reforms, divorcing marital sex from its utilitarian function of reproduction. The middle-class/upper-caste discourse of demographic crisis fed and fuelled, as much as it drew upon, the overall climate of social and political anxieties of the 1920s, 1930s and 1940s. It drew upon existing caste and community tensions and in turn provided these politics with statistical ammunition. The complaints about a decline in Hindu upper-caste numbers in comparison with Muslims and the lower castes deepened communal and caste tensions with seemingly objective evidence.

Middle-class Indian men during the 1920s and 1930s deployed the issue of population control as a new modality of power that safeguarded the privileges of class, caste, community and gender. Birth control provided Indian elites with a new technology to control the bodies of men and women belonging to the working class, lower castes and minority communities, as well as the aristocracy. The sexual practices of subaltern groups, the declining aristocracy and women were placed under strict surveillance as part of the goal of 'improving' national bodies. Despite the lip service paid to women's sexual desires, female sexual needs were not only seen as secondary to those of males but it was believed that they found their ultimate expression in maternity and 'mother-craft'. The emphasis on, and contests over, reproduction within the debates on birth control blurred distinctions between the private and public domains, demonstrating the difficulty in drawing lines between them and the importance of identifying flows between the two.

Acknowledgements

I would like to thank Barbara Ramusack, Sumita Chatterjee, Sanjay Joshi and Satadru Sen for reading and commenting on an earlier draft of this paper.

Bibliography

Ahluwalia, G, 1923, 'Indian Population Problem: Selective Lower Birth Rate, A Sure Remedy of Extreme Indian Poverty' in *Birth Control Review VII*, pp. 288–91.

Ahluwalia, S, 2000, 'Controlling Births, Policing Sexualities: A History of Birth Control in Colonial India, 1871–1946', PhD thesis, University of Cincinnati.

Alter, J, 2000, *Gandhi's Body: Sex, Diet and the Politics of Nationalism*, Philadelphia, University of Pennsylvania Press.

Chatterjee, P, 1986, *Nationalist Thought in a Colonial World: A Derivative Discourse?*, Delhi, Oxford University Press.

Engels, D, 1996, *Beyond Purdah? Women in Bengal, 1890–1939*, Delhi, Oxford University Press.

Fisher, K, 1998, 'Gender and the Conjugal Dynamics of Contraceptive Use: An Oral History Study of South Wales and Oxford Between the Wars', paper at the History of Twentieth Century Medicine Group, Wellcome Trust, London.

Forbes, G, 1996, *The New Cambridge History of India: Women in Modern India*, Cambridge, Cambridge University Press.

Gandhi, M K, 1997, *Hind Swaraj: Indian Home Rule*, Ahmedabad, Navajivan Publishing House (reprint).

Ghoshe, D N, 1938, 'Social Background to Pauperism in India', in *Population Problem in India*, in *Madras Law Journal*

Gordon, L, 1977, *Woman's Body, Woman's Right: A Social History of Birth Control in America*, New York, Penguin Books.

Gordon, L, 1990, *Woman's Body, Woman's Right: Birth Control in America*, New York, Penguin.

Gupta, C, 1999, 'Hindu Wombs, Muslim Progeny: The Numbers Game and Shifting Debates on Widow Remarriage, U. P. 1890–1930s', paper presented at the School of Oriental and African Studies, University of London.

Hansen, T, 1999, *The Saffron Wave: Democracy and Hindu Nationalism in Modern India*, Princeton, Princeton University Press.

Mathur, J, 1931, *The Pressure of Population: Its Effects on Rural Economy in Gorakhpur District, Lucknow.*

Mukherjee, R, 1938, 'Population Capacity and Control in India', in *Population Problem in India*, Mylapore, Madras Law Journal Office, pp. 7–17.

Parekh, B, 1997, *Gandhi*, Oxford, Oxford University Press.

Phadke, N S, 1925, 'Eugenics for India', *Birth Control Review*,IX.

Phadke, N S, 1927, *Sex Problem in India*, Bombay, D B Taraporevala.

Pillay, A P, 1931a, 'Eugenic Birth Control for India', *Birth Control Review*, IX.

Pillay, A P, 1931b, *Welfare Problems in Rural India*, Bombay, D B Taraporevala.

Pillay, A P, 1944, *Ideal Sex: A Doctor Answers Confidential Personal Questions*, Bombay, D B Taraporevala.

Pillay, A P, n.d., *Birth Control Simplified*, Bombay, D B Taraporevala.

Porter, R, and Hall, L, 1995, *The Facts of Life: The Creation of Sexual Knowledge in Britain, 1650–1950*, London, Yale University Press.

Prakash, G, 1999, *Another Reason: Science and the Imagination of Modern India*, Princeton, Princeton University Press.

Raina, B L, 1990, *Planning Family in India: Pre-vedic Times to Early 1950*, New Delhi, Commonwealth Publishers.

Ramusack, B, and Sievers, S, 1999, *Women in Asia*, Bloomington, Indiana University Press.

Sangari, K, and Vaid, S, 1989, *Recasting Women: Essays in Colonial History*, New Delhi, Kali for Women.

Sanjay, J, 2000, *Fractured Modernity: The Making of a Middle Class in Colonial North India*, Delhi, Oxford University Press.

Sarkar, S, 1983, *Modern India*, Madras, Macmillan India.

Sinha, M, 1995, *Colonial Masculinity: The 'Manly Englishman' and the 'Effeminate Bengali' in the Late Nineteenth Century*, Manchester, Manchester University Press.

Soloway, R, 1982, *Birth Control and the Population Question in England*, Chapel Hill, The University of North Carolina Press.

Tuteja, K, and Grewal, O, 1992, 'Emergence of Hindu Communal Ideology in Early Twentieth Century Punjab', *Social Scientist*, 20.

Urla, J, 1993, 'Cultural Politics in an Age of Statistics: Numbers, Nations, and the Making of Basque Identity', *American Ethnologist*, 20.

Wattal, P K, 1916 and 1934, *The Population Problem in India: A Census Study*, Benette, Coleman & Co.

Wattal, P K, 1934, 'Communities and Occupations', *The Population Problem in India*, p 99.

Notes

1. Chatterjee 1986; Prakash 1999.
2. Gandhi 1997; Parekh 1997; Chatterjee 1986.
3. Sarkar 1983, p. 243; Ramusack and Sievers 1999, p. 28.
4. Phadke 1927.
5. See Tuteja and Grewal 1992.
6. Sarkar 1983, pp. 216, 235.
7. Hansen 1999, p. 93.
8. Sarkar 1983, p. 167.
9. See Gupta 1999.
10. Soloway 1982; Gordon 1990.
11. Ahluwalia 1923,
12. Ibid., pp. 288–91.
13. Pillay 1931a.
14. Ibid., pp. 310–11.
15. Phadke 1925, pp. 316–17.
16. Phadke 1927, p. 8.
17. Mukherjee 1938, pp. 7–17.
18. Ghoshe 1938.
19. Ibid., pp. 141–52.
20. Engels 1996, pp. 203–14; Forbes 1996, pp. 167–71, 176–9.
21. Phadke 1925, p. 106.
22. Wattal 1938, p. 16.
23. Phadke 1927, p. 169.
24. Ibid., p. 295.
25. Ibid., p. 296.
26. See Raina 1990, p. 99.
27. Mukherjee 1938, p. 206.
28. Ibid., p. 139.
29. Urla 1993, p. 819.
30. Muhkerjee 1938, p. 139.
31. Pillay 1944, p. 221.
32. Wattal 1934, p. 99.
33. Ghoshe 1938, p. 152.
34. Mathur 1931.
35. Porter and Hall 1995, pp. 202–23.
36. See Sangari and Vaid 1989, pp. 233–54.
37. Ibid., pp. 27–88; see also Sinha 1995.
38. Alter 2000.

39. Pillay 1944.
40. Phadke 1925, p. 316.
41. Phadke 1927, p. 210.
42. Ibid., p. 211.
43. Ibid., p. 186.
44. Ibid., p. 262.
45. Pillay 1944.
46. Ibid., p. 226.
47. See Fisher 1998.
48. Phadke 1927, p. 236.
49. Pillay 1931b.
50. Ibid., p. 115.
51. Ibid., p. 117.
52. Pillay 1944, pp. 208–12.
53. Ibid., p. 226.
54. Ibid., p. 177.
55. Ibid., p. 200.
56. Ibid., p. 250.
57. Ibid., p. 73.
58. Ibid., p. 77.
59. Ibid., p. 50.
60. Ibid., p. 58.
61. Ibid., p. 137.

www.ingramcontent.com/pod-product-compliance
Lightning Source LLC
Chambersburg PA
CBHW061732270326
41928CB00011B/2207